THIS DATE IN NEW YORK YANKEE HATING

Going Negative on Baseball's Most Despised Team

THIS DATE IN NEW YORK YANKEE HATING

Going Negative on Baseball's Most Despised Team

Art McDonald

William D. Maharg Publishing
Greenville, S.C.

Published by William D. Maharg Publishing,
P.O. Box 25908, Greenville, S.C., 29616

Library of Congress Catalogue Card Number   98-092314
McDonald, Arthur S. (1953-   )

New York Yankees/ Arthur S. McDonald-1st. ed.

Includes bibliographical references and an index
1. New York Yankees 2. Baseball

ISBN 0-9669841-0-2

For additional copies contact:

William D. Maharg Publishing
P.O. Box 25908
Greenville, S.C., 29616
http://www.yankeehater.com

Cover design by Arthur S. McDonald, from an idea
by the late Dr. A.S. McDonald

Acknowledgements:

I will spare you a listing of the names of everyone who ever helped me by smiling at me. With these limits, I will acknowledge some special people. Jennie, Graham, and William McDonald provided understanding and patience, as their husband and father wrote this book. My friends Louis Valentine and Andy Telford were generous with their time and comments. Thanks also to numerous friends and colleagues, from my time in the corporate world, who resisted the urge to tell me I was a complete idiot for walking away from a good job to write this book. You know who you are.

The author:

Art McDonald, 45, is the author of *The 1988 Montreal Canadiens Haters Calendar*. Formerly a senior executive with a major company, Mr. McDonald lives in Greenville, S.C., with his wife and two sons.

This book is his revenge for the Yankees' scarring his early childhood. They overcame a three-games-to-one deficit to beat his beloved Milwaukee Braves in the 1958 World Series.

A note on the cartoons:

The author wrote the cartoons. As his artistic skills are worse than George Steinbrenner's interpersonal skills, he did not draw the cartoons.

A note on the cartoonist:

David Axe is a senior at Furman University in Greenville, S.C. He is a history major.

Foreword

This book is done on a day-by-day format. The author wishes to brighten any given day, whether it is today, the reader's birthday, or any day selected at random. This format permits the reader to open this book virtually anywhere and enjoy a less-than-wonderful moment in Yankee history.

For each day, there is an event, a note on someone who was born or died on that date, and a listing of supporting information pertinent to that date. While some events are more important, like Bill Mazeroski's home run to win the 1960 World Series, each contributes in its own way.

Throughout this book, I have done some things for convenience:

- I have used ERA, rather than Earned Run Average, for the number of runs a pitcher allows per nine innings pitched.
- Similarly, I have used RBI for Runs Batted In. RBI represents the number of runs a batter causes to score, normally with a hit. I have accepted that this abbreviation can be singular or plural; thus *he had the game-winning RBI; he led the league in RBI.*
- I have omitted half-games unless they are relevant. It is immaterial whether a team finishes sixteen or sixteen and one-half games out of first place. The former is easier on the reader.
- To avoid confusion, I have referred to New York's American League team as the "Yankees" throughout this book. I am aware they were officially the "Highlanders" until 1913. Similarly, I have called other teams by their more common names. For example, I have referred to the Braves, Indians, and Dodgers, who were at various times, the Bees, the Naps, and the Robins, by their modern names.
- I have tried to ensure the information in this edition is accurate, in all material respects, as of December 1998.

I welcome your comments and criticisms.

Finally, in the interest of full disclosure, I must declare my bias. As a boy, I was a big Milwaukee Braves fan. Like the *Happy Days* gang, I lived in Milwaukee in the 1950's and 1960's. I have remained loyal to the Braves, despite an O'Malley-style move of the team to Atlanta by the owners. (A friend once asked me how men could form a lifelong allegiance to a sports team at age seven, but could not commit to a woman.)

As cheering for the Braves in the 1990's is not difficult, there are those who accuse me of Yankee fan-like front-running. A pox on them.

Introduction:

"Hating the Yankees isn't part of my act; it is one of those exquisite times when life and art are in perfect conjunction."

Bill Veeck (1914-1986)

There was joy in St. Louis one September evening in 1922. The St. Louis Browns had beaten the New York Yankees to move into a virtual tie with New York for first place in the American League. Revelers fully expected the Browns to win the next day's game and go on to win their first pennant.

The Browns lost their crucial late-season game with the Yankees. So did the Indians in the 1950's, the White Sox in the 1960's, and the Red Sox in any decade beginning after the discovery of penicillin. One fears that, forty years from now, the Yankees will be beating the Jacksonville Burger Kings in a crucial September game at the WhopperDome.

Then there is the postseason. The Braves, while playing in two different cities, blew two-game leads in the World Series to the Yankees. Teams having that special season, like the 1927 Pirates, the 1951 Giants, and the 1998 Padres, saw the Yankees quickly make these seasons incomplete.

These Yankee victories might be merely intolerable if we could suffer in isolation. We cannot, as there are Yankee fans everywhere.

It is hard to believe, but there are people who are happy when the Yankees win. These people do have other interests. Like the Dallas Cowboys. Or their favorite group, the Beatles. Or politics, where they voted twice for Ronald Reagan and twice for Bill Clinton; votes they do not acknowledge during discussions of Iran-Contra or of Clinton's sex scandals.

Yankee fans might be native New Yorkers, whose behavior is understandable, as it was learned at an early age. But many of them are not.

They are front-runners. Desperately in need of something successful in their lives, they have hooked on to a winning team. Having lost that girl to someone with better looks, that scholarship to someone with superior brains, and that promotion to someone with more useful connections, they seek vicarious success.

They are not risk-takers. Cheering for a team like the Yankees, when a consequence of losing is seeing your team's lead drop to twelve games, hardly sets one up for disappointment. What's more, these Yankee fans have the perfect escape clause when the Yankees lose. They can honestly say something like "I am really just a casual fan," or "I like what Mike Hargrave (*sic*) has done with the Indians."

There is something wrong with these fans. Is there a child anywhere who was sad to see Goliath lose? Who rooted for the hare against the tortoise? How many people instinctively cheer against a comeback by the team that is losing?

Yankee fans do have their talents. They are best at disturbing games. They do this on many levels. The most basic is ruining your enjoyment of a game. Usually a simple statement like "Tino Martinez is the best first baseman in baseball" will do it.

Then there are the top-level disturbers, like the fan who ran onto the field, nullifying a game-ending out. Or the thousands of fans who made running the bases after Chris Chambliss's 1976 pennant-winning home run more dangerous than dating the fiancée of the first lineman picked in the NFL draft.

More recently, we have had Jeffrey Maier, the boy who skipped school to attend the first game of the 1996 American League Championship Series. He reached over into play to catch a ball, which the Oriole right fielder almost certainly would have caught. Maier thereby turned an out into a home run. In every ballpark, they announce that anyone attempting to interfere with a game in play will be ejected and possibly prosecuted. Does this happen to Maier? Does a talk show host advocate trying him as an adult? Is he forced to listen to his father's albums? No, no, and no. The Yankees treated him as a hero. He was on David Letterman's show and was a guest of honor at a World Series game.

Even if the win is stolen, Yankee fans will gloat. They see these wins as confirming their own wisdom and superior talents. These, after all, are why they chose the Yankees.

Worse, they believe there is a corollary to their choice of teams. Your being a Tiger or a Cardinal or a Dodger fan is evidence that you are a loser, ignorant of sports, and totally lacking in judgment.

Let us deal with this. No intelligent person would deny the Yankees are a great team with a rich history. They have won twenty-four championships, a remarkable achievement. Their all-time roster of players includes first-tier Hall of Famers like Babe Ruth, Lou Gehrig, Joe DiMaggio, and Mickey Mantle. It also includes merely great players like Bill Dickey and Whitey Ford. Others like Tony Lazzeri, Earl Combs, and Waite Hoyt are among those in the Hall of Fame who spent most of their careers with the Yankees. There is much to admire about these men.

Though these statements are true, they do not mean we have to like the Yankees. If being good were a requisite for being liked, the Soviet hockey teams of 1960-1984 would be on more than one person's list of all-time favorite teams.

We do not pick our teams because they are winners. Rather, we cheer for the Braves because we grew up in Boston, or Milwaukee, or Atlanta. We like the Cubs because they have not won in far too long. We hope for the Mariners because of Ken Griffey, Jr. and Alex Rodriguez. Invariably, inevitably, the Yankees beat these teams. This coupled with the aforementioned fans intensifies our hatred of the Yankees. And yes, we can hate them. It is easy.

We hate them for their management. We think of George Weiss exploiting the poorer teams and getting a Roger Maris or a Bobby Shantz for cash and some worn-out players. We see Casey Stengel with the cannot-be-wrong choice of having Elston Howard or Yogi Berra catch.

We hate their players. Two from the 1970's were especially difficult to endure. I can still see Mickey Rivers slowly walking to home plate. He is spinning his bat, no doubt exhausted from throwing a baseball like a child using his or her wrong hand. Then there was Reggie Jackson, a rare outfielder with more career errors than assists. His career strikeout total is one-third higher than the next worst whiffer's. Jackson established records for the most frequent use of the first person singular. Worse, he was on television more than any six evangelists or infomercial stars.

But most of all, we hate their owner, George Steinbrenner, whose name will appear frequently in this book. Recently, he has been demanding a new stadium. Owning a piece of history, where he can charge almost any price for tickets, is not good enough. There are Yankee fans who need luxury boxes in a stadium they can get to without traveling to the Bronx. Apparently they fear they will have the same sense of direction as Sherman McCoy had in *The Bonfire of the Vanities.*

Years ago, I wrote *The 1988 Montreal Canadiens Haters Calendar.* (Copies are available from William D. Maharg Publishing.) I received numerous letters from people, telling me of the depths of their hatred of this hockey team. Many wrote of the famous exhibition hockey game between the Canadiens and the Soviet Central Red Army team. This 1975 game matched the best teams from Canada and the Soviet Union. Like many sporting events during the Cold War, this game had implications beyond the sporting world. These correspondents told me they had hoped for the Soviets in the 3-3 tie.

I suspect there are Yankee haters who would root for the Saddam Hussein All-Stars if they played the Yankees. They might hope for a lot of injuries, but they would still cheer for the Iraqis.

To these, and milder Yankee haters, I say two things. Enjoy this book. Some day there will be another Stump Merrill.

Greenville, South Carolina
January, 1999

JANUARY 1, 1969

Former Yankee manager Casey Stengel was arrested for driving while intoxicated. Yankee haters like to note that Stengel's Brooklyn Dodgers, Boston Braves, and New York Mets compiled a 756-1,146 record.

Born January 1, 1911
Hank Greenberg

An intelligent man, Greenberg declined an offer of ten thousand dollars to sign with the Yankees. He became the star of four pennant-winning Tiger teams between 1934 and 1945.

Greenberg was the general manager of another pennant-winning team, the 1954 Indians. These teams were pleasant interruptions during a period otherwise dominated by the Yankees.

Yankee opponents whose teams won the most American League pennants:

- Eddie Collins won eight pennants with the Philadelphia A's and Chicago White Sox.
- Jack Barry was on six pennant-winners with the Philadelphia A's and Boston Red Sox.
- Eddie Plank was with the Philadelphia A's when they won six pennants.
- Several players have played with five pennant-winning teams.

JANUARY 2, 1995

The University of Southern California beat Texas Tech 55-14, in the Cotton Bowl. For the thirty-seventh consecutive year, Rice University failed to earn a trip to this Bowl. Rice once owned Yankee Stadium, having acquired it via a bequest. God punishes guilt by association.

Born January 2, 1963
Edgar Martinez

Martinez, the Mariners' designated hitter, hit .571 against the Yankees in the 1995 American League Division Series. He drove in the winning run in the eleventh inning of the final game. His Series-leading ten RBI included the game-winning grand slam home run in the fourth game.

Tino Martinez, Ken Griffey, Jr., and Jay Buhner also hit over .390 for the Mariners in this Series. Were they that good, or was Yankee pitching that bad?

Other notable single-game hitting performances against the Yankees in the postseason:

- Kansas City's George Brett hit three home runs, in the third game of the 1978 American League Championship Series.
- Cincinnati's Johnny Bench had two home runs and five RBI, in the final game of the 1976 World Series.
- Duke Snider, of the Brooklyn Dodgers, twice slugged two home runs in a single World Series game. He did it in the 1952, and in the 1955, World Series.
- Atlanta's Andruw Jones hit two home runs, in the first game of the 1996 World Series.

JANUARY 3, 1973

George Steinbrenner (who will be referred to as "Steinbrenner" in the rest of this book) became the principal owner of the Yankees. He said he would not be active in the day-to-day operations of the club, as he had enough problems with his shipping company. Like many Steinbrenner statements, this would prove to be untrue.

Serious problems experienced by Steinbrenner's shipping company:

- Steinbrenner used the company, and its employees, to make illegal political contributions. These resulted in Steinbrenner's criminal conviction.
- Steinbrenner was able to devote all his attention to his shipping company between 1990 and 1993 (During this period, he was serving a "lifetime" ban from baseball). Even with this attention, his shipping company filed for bankruptcy in 1993.

Born January 3, 1915
Sid Hudson

This Washington Senators' pitcher beat the Yankees 1-0, on "Babe Ruth Day" in 1947. No Yankee pitcher ever beat the Senators on "Sid Hudson Day."

JANUARY 4, 1974

Yankee fans were wondering who was going to manage the team. The Yankees had named Bill Virdon, an obvious second choice, as manager. Previously, they had hired Dick Williams, even though he was under contract to the A's. Oakland owner Charles Finley demanded compensation for releasing Williams from his contract. As Finley and the Yankees could not agree on this compensation, Virdon spent a forgettable nineteen months as Yankee manager.

Born January 4, 1930
Don McMahon

McMahon, the Braves' best relief pitcher, did not allow a run in three appearances against the Yankees in the 1957 World Series.

Yankee hating by the numbers, part one:

- **0.** Combined Gold Gloves, an award recognizing fielding excellence, that longtime Yankees Reggie Jackson, Tony Kubek, Clete Boyer, and Willie Randolph won.
- **1.** Horses, in a field of thirteen, that Eternal Prince beat in the 1985 Kentucky Derby. Steinbrenner co-owned this twelfth-place finisher.
- **2.** Games that Toronto pitcher Mike Willis had won in 1978 when he, and the last-place Blue Jays, beat the Yankees. Ron Guidry, who had a 22-2 record, was the losing pitcher.
- **3.** Batters that Yankee pitchers Tom Morgan (1954) and Harry Harper (1921) hit in a single inning.

WHO'S THE MANAGER? (January 4)

JANUARY 5, 1934

Two future Hall of Famers, pitcher Herb Pennock and shortstop Joe Sewell, became ex-Yankees, as the club released them.

Pennock, a left-hander, would appear in thirty games for the Red Sox in 1934. He would have a 3.05 ERA. Jimmie DeShong, a left-hander the Yankees kept, had a 4.10 ERA in thirty-one games for New York.

There is a French expression *Il met de l'eau dans son vin.* Literally translated, this phrase means "he puts some water in his wine." It refers to coming down a notch in importance. We will combine both meanings to describe keeping DeShong and releasing Pennock.

Born January 5, 1961
Henry Cotto

Cotto, a Yankee reserve, injured himself cleaning his ear with a Q-Tip.

Other bizarre injuries sustained by the Yankees:

- Tim Cumberland sprained an ankle. In 1970, this Yankee pitcher slipped on spilled pop around a soft drink machine.
- Ed Whitson injured his back. He hurt it, in 1985, pulling on a sock. New York was never meant for this pitcher.
- Gus Mauch broke a rib. A parking meter interrupted the Yankee trainer's walk.
- Bill Dickey hurt his head. Ecstatic over a win, this Yankee coach leapt up and hit his head on the roof of the dugout.
- Clark Griffith wound up with a sore mouth. Umpire Tim Hurst slugged this Yankee manager and part-time pitcher.
- Marshall Bridges sustained a gunshot wound. An incident in a bar, during spring training, led to this Yankee pitcher's injury.

JANUARY 6, 1968

Television viewers watched the last episode of *The Iron Horse*. This was a television series about a train, set in the American West. It was also a source of segues into tiresome stories about Lou Gehrig, the Yankees' "Iron Horse."

Born January 6, 1963
Bobby Davidson

Davidson, a pitcher, was one of a team-record forty-nine players used by the Yankees in 1989. New York used 206 players in the 1980's, thirty-one more than the league average of 175. Did you expect to see player stability on a team that had twelve managerial changes during this decade?

Players who made their only major-league appearances with the 1989 Yankees:

- Davidson pitched in one game and had an ERA of 18.00.
- Kevin Mmahat appeared in four games, with a 12.91 ERA.
- Marcus Lawton played in ten games. He hit .214.

JANUARY 7, 1958

New Yorkers saw the premiere of the official film of the 1957 World Series. This reminder of the Yankees' loss to the Braves brought back unpleasant memories to most of its audience.

Four decades ago, there was no instant replay or available-on-demand videos. For most fans, this film was the first replay of highlights like Eddie Mathews's game-winning home run.

Yankee fans did not have many chances to see their team's best pitcher, Whitey Ford, in the Series. This occurred because of managerial stupidity, rather than 1950's technology. Yankee manager Casey Stengel started his ace twice. A better-prepared Braves' manager, Fred Haney, arranged for his best pitcher, Warren Spahn, to start three times.

Died January 7, 1978
George Burns

Cleveland's first baseman won the Most Valuable Player award, in 1926, although he clearly did not deserve it. Babe Ruth had a higher batting average, hit forty-three more home runs, and had thirty-one more RBI. Still, there are injustices that are acceptable, and those that are not.

Speaking of unacceptable injustices, why the choice of the Yankees' Joe Gordon as Most Valuable Player in 1942 was wrong:

- Gordon did not finish in the top three in any offensive category.
- He had more errors than any other American League second baseman, while ranking only third in putouts and in assists.
- Ted Williams won the Triple Crown.

JANUARY 8, 1990

Steinbrenner paid forty thousand dollars to Howard Spira, a lowlife. This payment, for incriminating information on Yankee outfielder Dave Winfield, ultimately led to Steinbrenner's lifetime suspension from baseball.

Various explanations Steinbrenner gave for the payment to Spira:

- Steinbrenner wanted to prevent Spira from disclosing embarrassing information about former Yankee employees.
- Spira had threatened to go public with information about former Yankee manager Lou Pinella's gambling habits.
- Steinbrenner feared for his safety and that of his family.
- He did it out of the goodness of his heart. Years later, the two people who believed this explanation accepted President Clinton's denial of his affair with Monica Lewinsky.

Died January 8, 1994
Harvey Haddix

His obituaries emphasized the twelve perfect innings Haddix threw against the Milwaukee Braves in 1959. This feat dwarfed the Pirate pitcher's winning the fifth and seventh games of the 1960 World Series against the Yankees.

JANUARY 9, 1903

Bill Devery and Frank Farrell purchased the Yankees. While owned by these two, the Yankees finished last twice. This was two more times than they won the pennant.

If character counts, as we hear during political campaigns, then consider these owners. Farrell headed a syndicate that ran numerous betting establishments. Devery was a Tammany Hall politician and police official. His precinct, according to a report, was a "cesspool of vice and corruption."

Born January 9, 1936
Ralph Terry

Terry was the fifth Yankee pitcher in the seventh game of the 1960 World Series. He was also the last, as he allowed Bill Mazeroski's World Series-winning home run. This was Terry's second loss in the Series.

In the 1961 Series, Terry pitched as if he had inherited Farrell's betting establishments. He suffered the only Yankee loss. In his other start, Terry could not finish the third inning, despite having a 6-0 lead.

Other key players in the Pirates' 10-9 win in the seventh game of the 1960 World Series:

- Hal Smith hit a three-run home run, in the eighth inning, to give the Pirates a 9-7 lead.
- Bill Virdon's potential double play ball hit a pebble. All were safe, sustaining the Pirates' eighth-inning rally.
- Rocky Nelson hit a two-run homer to give the Pirates an early lead.

JANUARY 10, 1922

Washington acquired Roger Peckinpaugh. As their shortstop, Peckinpaugh led the Senators to the 1924 and 1925 pennants. Babe Ruth described him as the player who did the most damage to the second-place Yankees in 1924. Some might argue this distinction belonged to Yankee catcher Fred Hofmann, who hit .175 that season.

Most Valuable Player award winners, whose pennant-winning teams finished no more than five games ahead of the Yankees:

- Walter Johnson, 1924 Senators
- Hank Greenberg, 1935 and 1940 Tigers
- Lou Boudreau, 1948 Indians

Born January 10, 1938
Willie McCovey

McCovey spent most of his Hall of Fame career with the Giants. "Stretch" had more RBI, in fewer at bats, than his Yankee contemporary, Mickey Mantle, did.

JANUARY 11, 1964

As Yankee fans looked forward to the 1964 season, they realized the team's manager would be Yogi Berra. Formerly a Yankee catcher, this namesake of a cartoon character had never managed at any level.

Berra's Yankees did win the pennant. Yankee upper management believed this occurred in spite of Berra. They fired him after the 1964 season.

Other teams agreed the Yankees had made a boo-boo in hiring Yogi Berra. No team asked him to manage again until 1972.

Born January 11, 1815
Sir John A. Macdonald

Macdonald was the first Prime Minister of Canada. In an important late-season series in 1985, his country's Toronto Blue Jays won three games from the Yankees. This prompted Steinbrenner to say that the Yankees were being "out-played, out-front-officed, out-managed, and out-ownered."

Owners who have "out-owned" Steinbrenner while he has owned the Yankees:

- Jerry Reinsdorf's Chicago Bulls have won six NBA titles.
- Eddie DeBartolo's San Francisco 49ers have five Super Bowl wins.
- Dr. Jerry Buss's Los Angeles Lakers have taken five NBA titles.
- Peter Pocklington's Edmonton Oilers won five Stanley Cups.

JANUARY 12, 1984

Rich Gossage, the Yankees' best relief pitcher, signed as a free agent with the San Diego Padres. He was fed up with Steinbrenner. Gossage helped his new team win the National League pennant.

Born January 12, 1967
Mike Simms

Simms had four RBI, as his Texas Rangers beat the Yankees 16-5, in 1998.

Duke Sims and other lasts at old Yankee Stadium, which underwent substantial renovations following the 1973 season:

- Sims, that legendary Yankee, hit the last home run.
- John Hiller, the winning pitcher for Detroit, threw the last pitch, while Mike Hegan made the last out.
- Marvin Lane hit the last home run by a member of a visiting team. It was the first of his three major-league home runs.
- Lindy McDaniel was the losing pitcher.

JANUARY 13, 1954

Yankee legend Joe DiMaggio and Hollywood legend Marilyn Monroe were preparing for their wedding. Their tasks included arranging a room with a television for the wedding night.

Most wedding guides do not include arranging for a television as a critical planning detail. Then again, most marriages last longer than nine months. DiMaggio and Monroe separated 274 days after their January 14 wedding.

Died January 13, 1944
Kid Elberfeld

Elberfeld had a winning percentage of .276 as the manager of the 1908 Yankees. He had many problems, including a player named Kid Elberfeld, who hit .196.

Worst winning percentages by Yankee managers:

- .276, Elberfeld
- .329, Harry Wolverton, 1912
- .403, Frank Chance, 1913-1914
- .404, Bucky Dent, 1989-1990
- .436, Stump Merrill, 1990-1991

(Minimum of twenty games managed)

ELBERFELD AND LARY (January 13, 28)

JANUARY 14, 1976

Ted Turner was approved as the owner of the Atlanta Braves. Under his ownership, the Braves became one of the richer teams in baseball, successfully bidding against the Yankees for players.

Died January 14, 1959
John Ganzel

Ganzel, the Yankees' regular first baseman in 1903 and 1904, became the team's first serious holdout. He refused to play the entire 1905 and 1906 seasons.

Joe DiMaggio, the most famous Yankee holdout:

- DiMaggio wanted a salary of forty-five thousand dollars for the 1938 season.
- This was considerably more than the Yankees' offer of twenty-five thousand dollars, on a take-it-or-leave-it basis.
- General Manager Ed Barrow told DiMaggio that he was demanding more money than longtime Yankee star Lou Gehrig made. DiMaggio replied that Gehrig was a badly underpaid player.
- DiMaggio received no sympathy from the press or the public.
- He finally accepted the Yankees' terms in late April.

JANUARY 15, 1967

The Green Bay Packers completed a 14-2 season by winning the first Super Bowl. This was a dynasty in progress, a notable contrast to the Yankees, who were in serious decline. New York had finished last in 1966 and would finish next-to-last in 1967.

Some comparisons of Packer coach Vince Lombardi and Yankee manager Casey Stengel:

- Lombardi had a winning percentage of .728. Stengel's was .508.
- Lombardi won five championships in ten years. It took Stengel twenty-five years to win seven.
- Lombardi's postseason winning percentage is .900. Stengel's is .587.
- The Yankees fired Stengel. Lombardi left for a better job.
- Every Super Bowl winner gets the Vince Lombardi Trophy. There is not a single important trophy named for Stengel.
- Lombardi's best-known saying is "Winning isn't everything, it's the only thing." This shows a determination to succeed. Stengel's saying, "You can look it up," suggests a desire to direct librarians.

Born January 15, 1956
Rance Mulliniks

Toronto third baseman Mulliniks had two, of the record ten, home runs the Blue Jays hit in a 1987 game. This broke the previous mark of eight that the Yankees had co-held.

JANUARY 16, 1979

Montreal traded Darold Knowles to the St. Louis Cardinals. Someone asked this relief pitcher if one of his Oakland teammates was a hot dog. Knowles replied that there was not enough mustard in the world to cover Reggie Jackson.

Died January 16, 1965
Jimmy Williams

Williams, the Yankee second baseman, committed an error that gave the Red Sox two crucial runs, in the pennant-deciding game of the 1904 season. Boston beat the Yankees 3-2.

Other key figures in that 1904 pennant-deciding game:

- Yankee pitcher Jack Chesbro threw a ninth-inning wild pitch that allowed the winning run to score.
- Lou Criger singled and eventually scored on Chesbro's wild pitch.
- Bill Dineen was the winning pitcher for Boston. In the ninth inning, he bunted Criger into scoring position. Earlier in this season-ending series, Dineen was the winning pitcher, as Boston beat New York 13-2.
- Candy LaChance and Hobie Ferris each singled and scored on Williams's error.

JANUARY 17, 1970

What do Ron Hinckley, John Mercado, John Gaylord, Larry Knight, Robert Coultas, Jim Henley, Gary Leach, and Jim Hefflinger have in common?

They were the first eight picks by the Yankees in the amateur draft held on this date in 1970. None would ever appear in a major-league game.

Obviously, no one had told the Yankees that the term "amateur draft" referred to a draft of amateur players, not a draft by amateur selectors. This latter concept is called a "Rotisserie League."

Born January 17, 1915
Mayo Smith

Tiger manager Smith's teams finished a total of forty-eight games ahead of the Yankees during the 1966-1968 period.

Managers whose teams finished the most games ahead of the Yankees over a three-year period:

- Connie Mack's 1912-1914 Philadelphia A's finished 108 games ahead of the Yankees.
- In the more modern era, Earl Weaver's 1969-1971 Orioles beat the Yankees by an aggregate of sixty-four games.
- More recently, Cito Gaston's 1990-1992 Blue Jays were fifty-nine games ahead of the Yankees.

JANUARY 18, 1938

Grover Cleveland Alexander became the fourteenth player elected to baseball's Hall of Fame. Of the fourteen, only Babe Ruth had ever played for the Yankees.

Born January 18, 1948
Webster Hubbell

Hubbell, one of Hillary Rodham Clinton's former law partners, was convicted of fraud. His illegal acts included billing personal expenses to his law firm. Hubbell should have a future as a Yankee scout, given Steinbrenner's comment that all scouts do, after the player draft, is pad their expense accounts.

Yankee hating by the numbers, part two:

- **4.** Times that Yankees Joe Collins and Mickey Mantle struck out against Brooklyn's Carl Erskine, in a single World Series game.
- **5.** Home runs that Texas's Juan Gonzales hit against the Yankees in the 1996 Division Series. Gonzales had nine RBI and a .438 batting average.
- **6.** The most triples hit in an American League game. Two teams have hit this many against the Yankees.
- **7.** Gold Gloves that Yankee castoff Vic Power won, while playing with the Indians, the Twins, and the Angels. Power, a first baseman, hit .300 or better three times.

JANUARY 19, 1980's and 1990's

Some people spent part of a housebound winter evening watching a rerun of a certain episode of the television series, *Cheers*. A highlight of this episode was Carla's physically attacking an especially obnoxious Yankee fan.

Two Ty Cobb stories for a winter day:

- Cobb stole second base in a 1907 game between his Tigers and the Yankees. Before the Yankee infielder returned the ball to the pitcher, Cobb had gone to third base. In each of the next two games, Cobb scored from first base on a bunt. He took advantage of mental lapses by Yankee first baseman Hal Chase and third baseman George Moriarty.
- Cobb said that Yankee pitcher Carl Mays should be banned from baseball if Mays had deliberately tried to hit Ray Chapman. (Mays's pitch had killed the Cleveland shortstop.) The New York media quoted Cobb, but deleted the qualifying phrase. This led to Cobb receiving death threats, from some of the Yankee fans who knew how to write. Cobb got his revenge by getting four hits and six RBI, as the Tigers beat the Yankees.

Born January 19, 1938
Phil Everly

Don and Phil Everly sang of their native Kentucky. Brooklyn fans felt another Kentucky native, Dodger shortstop Pee Wee Reese, was a better player than his Yankee counterpart, Phil Rizzuto. They were right. Reese was elected to the Hall of Fame ten years before Rizzuto.

JANUARY 20, 1960

Mickey Mantle reacted angrily to the Yankees' offer of a 20 percent pay cut for the 1960 season. He threatened to cut his uniform number by an identical percentage. Mantle, who obviously was not mathematically gifted, said he would wear number 6.5, rather than his usual number seven.

Born January 20, 1965
Kevin Maas

In 1990, Yankee first baseman Maas set a dubious record. He had the fewest RBI, forty-one, by a player with more than twenty home runs. He had help in setting this record. As a team, the Yankees made sure no one was on base when Maas batted.

New York had the worst batting average in the American League. Not surprisingly, the Yankees were last in walks. No pitcher was stupid enough to pitch around players like Bob Geren or Alvaro Espinoza. Both these regulars hit less than .225.

The IRS refers to citizens as "taxpayers." This term includes those who evade their obligations. Just as the IRS calls a tax cheat like Pete Rose a "taxpayer," baseball refers to batters like Geren and Espinoza as "hitters."

Fewest RBI by an American League player with twenty or more home runs, in the last fifty years:

- Chris Hoiles broke Maas's record. He drove in forty runs, in 1995.
- Maas had forty-one RBI, in 1990.
- Carlton Fisk drove in forty-three runs, in 1984.
- In 1987, Fred McGriff had forty-three RBI.

JANUARY 21, 1953

It was a bad day for the Yankees, as the results of the Hall of Fame balloting were announced. Former Yankees Bill Dickey, Joe DiMaggio, Lefty Gomez, Tony Lazzeri, Waite Hoyt, and Red Ruffing failed to get enough votes for election. All but Dickey would fail again the following year.

Born January 21, 1960
Andy Hawkins

Hawkins had a 5-12 record for the Yankees in 1990. This hardly justified the rich contract he signed with them as a free agent. He was particularly awful at Fenway Park that season. In three starts there, Hawkins pitched a total of one inning. He allowed eighteen runs, thirteen hits, and six walks. For those who love statistics, Hawkins had a 162.00 ERA in Boston.

Hawkins was even worse in 1991. He had an 0-2 record, with a 9.95 ERA, when the Yankees unloaded him.

Hawkins had signed with the Yankees following the 1988 season. In 1987, he had a 3-10 record and a 5.05 ERA. Think of Hawkins as the Yankees' wait-until-the-last-moment-before-you-call-someone New Year's Eve date. In 1988, forty-five-year-old Tommy John had started thirty-two games for the Yankees. Such a team obviously was in desperate need of a pitcher, any pitcher.

Moments from Hawkins's July 1990:

- July 1: Hawkins pitched a no-hitter, yet lost 4-0. (See July 14.)
- July 6: Despite pitching eleven shutout innings, Hawkins eventually lost.
- July 12: Hawkins was the losing pitcher, as Chicago's Melido Perez threw a no-hitter.
- July 19: Bo Jackson hit three home runs off Hawkins.
- July 27: Although the Yankees scored ten runs for him, Hawkins failed to get the win.

JANUARY 22, 1976

Phil Rizzuto failed to get enough votes for election to the Hall of Fame. This was his final year of eligibility for selection by the Baseball Writers Association of America. Years of campaigning to influence the Veterans Committee followed. No doubt worn down, the Committee finally selected the Yankee shortstop in 1994.

Born January 22, 1949
Mike Caldwell

Pitching for the Milwaukee Brewers, Caldwell compiled a career record of 13-7 against the Yankees. Three of these wins were shutouts in 1978. Caldwell's thirteenth win, a 12-0 shutout, was his tenth victory at Yankee Stadium.

Some Hall of Famers, who played against the Yankees in Milwaukee, for teams other than the Brewers:

- Hank Aaron, Eddie Mathews, Warren Spahn, and Red Schoendeinst played for the Milwaukee Braves in the 1957 and 1958 World Series.
- Luis Aparicio and the Chicago White Sox played a limited schedule of home games in Milwaukee in the late 1960's.

JANUARY 23, 1944

The New York Rangers suffered their worst-ever defeat, 15-0 to the Detroit Red Wings. This made numerous Yankee fans unhappy. Many of these fans had discovered hockey when the Rangers won the Stanley Cup, in 1940.

Born January 23, 1916
Johnny Sturm

In over five hundred at bats as the Yankee first baseman in 1941, Sturm had thirty-six RBI. He hit .239. He achieved another distinction by becoming the first married major-leaguer to be drafted during World War II. Given Sturm's 1941 season, it is unlikely the Yankees bothered to ask Sturm's draft board to reverse its decision.

Fewest RBI, by an American League first baseman, since the dead ball era ended in 1920:

- Sturm had thirty-six RBI in 1941.
- Lou Finney had forty-one RBI in 1936 for Philadelphia.
- Rod Carew drove in forty-four runs for the Angels in 1982.
- Detroit's Lu Blue had forty-five RBI in 1922. Blue, Finney, and Carew, unlike Sturm, hit better than .300.

(Minimum of five hundred at bats)

JANUARY 24, 1956

Damn Yankees was playing on Broadway. Based on the book, *The Year the Yankees Lost the Pennant,* the play tells the story of a Senators' fan. Frustrated by the play of his team, he makes a deal with the Devil. Satanic powers transfer the fan into a baseball star named Joe Hardy, who leads the Senators to the pennant over the Yankees.

Died January 24, 1960
Russ Ford

Ford, a pitcher, was the most prominent Yankee to jump to the Federal League. This was a third major league that tried to compete with the National and American Leagues in 1914 and 1915.

Most players would not have made such a decision. Ford traded living in New York for living in Buffalo. He gave up playing for a solvent franchise in an established league. His new team had players named Everett Booe and Rubber Krapp. (I am not making this up.)

For Ford, Buffalo had two attractions. It was close to his native Canada. More importantly, it provided an escape from the Yankees. In 1913, Ford's Yankee team had lost thirty-seven more games than it had won.

Yankees who jumped to the Federal League:

- Ford won twenty games for the Buffalo Blues.
- Al Schulz was a twenty-one-game winner for the Blues. In 1913, Schulz had an 8-14 record with the Yankees. ESPN's Chris Berman might refer to this pitcher as "I Throw Nothing."
- Bill McKechnie, a utility player for the Yankees, discovered his real calling, managing, in the Federal League.
- Rollie Zeider hit .274 for the Chicago Whales.

JANUARY 25, 1966

Tony Kubek retired because of a back injury. Although inevitable, it was always good to see members of the Yankees' championship teams retire. That the Yankees had nobody who could adequately replace these players was not inevitable, but more enjoyable.

Some Yankee double play combinations that followed Kubek and Bobby Richardson:

- Ruben Amaro and Horace Clarke, 1967
- Tom Tresh and Clarke, 1968
- Gene Michael and Clarke, 1969-1973
- Jim Mason and Sandy Alomar, Sr., 1974
- Fred Stanley and Alomar, 1975

Died January 25, 1991
Hoot Evers

In a 1950 game with the second-place Yankees, the first-place Tigers hit four home runs in a single inning. Evers had one of these record-tying home runs. Evers's second four-bagger, a two-run, inside-the-park home run, in the bottom of the ninth, won the game.

Detroit had a reasonable chance of winning the American League pennant in 1950. Evers, Vic Wertz, and George Kell all drove in more than one hundred runs. Only Cleveland had a better team ERA. Unfortunately, the Tigers could not overcome having a former Yankee, Red Rolfe, as their manager.

Detroit fired Rolfe in 1952. He had the Tigers bound for 104 losses and a last-place finish.

JANUARY 26, 1969-date

It is sports banquet season. A frequently told story involves Mickey Mantle. The storyteller points out that Mantle struck out 1,710 times and walked 1,734 times during his career. Assuming five hundred at bats per season, Mantle played seven seasons, without hitting the ball.

Reggie Jackson made Mantle look like a contact hitter. He had almost four thousand at bats (2,597 strikeouts and 1,375 walks) without hitting a fair ball.

How Mantle's non-hitting record compares with other top home run hitters:

- Hank Aaron had 2,785 at bats, without hitting the ball (1,402 walks, 1,383 strikeouts).
- Willie Mays had 2,989 (1,463 walks, 1,526 strikeouts).
- Frank Robinson had 2,952 (1,420 walks, 1,532 strikeouts).

Born January 26, 1961
Wayne Gretzky

No Yankee has ever dominated baseball the way Gretzky has dominated hockey. Gretzky won nine Most Valuable Player awards, three times the number any Yankee has won.

JANUARY 27, 1954

Yankee manager Casey Stengel held a press conference. He showed his ability to judge talent by predicting the Red Sox would be the Yankees' strongest competition for the pennant. Boston would finish forty-two games behind the pennant-winning Cleveland Indians in 1954.

Born January 27, 1969
Phil Plantier

In a late-season game in 1991, pinch hitter Plantier hit a three-run home run. This hit gave the Red Sox a victory over the Yankees.

That season, Plantier, a Red Sox reserve, hit over .300, with more than ten home runs. No Yankee achieved this in 1990, 1991, or 1992.

Yankee batters might have been inspired by the hitting prowess of their three managers during this period. Only Bucky Dent played in the major leagues. His career average is .247.

Highest percentage of total votes received in being elected to baseball's Hall of Fame:

- 98.8%, Tom Seaver, 1992
- 98.8%, Nolan Ryan, 1999
- 98.2%, Ty Cobb, 1936
- 98.2%, George Brett, 1999
- 97.8%, Hank Aaron, 1982

(None of these players spent a minute in a Yankee uniform. You might question how someone could fail to vote for players like Cobb or Aaron and still be considered qualified to vote in future elections. Please direct your inquiries to the Baseball Writers Association of America.)

JANUARY 28, 1948

At a press conference, the Red Sox introduced their new manager, former Yankee skipper Joe McCarthy. Under McCarthy, the Red Sox would finish ahead of the Yankees in 1948.

If a 1990's media corps had been in attendance, the questions would have been less friendly. McCarthy would have had to explain about quitting the Yankees for "health reasons." Someone would have asked if McCarthy would win a close pennant race for the first time in his career. (He would not. Boston would lose the pennant on the last day of each of McCarthy's two full seasons as Red Sox manager.)

Born January 28, 1906
Lyn Lary

Lary's base-running gaffe limited Lou Gehrig to a share of the 1931 home run title. Thinking a Gehrig home run to be an out, Lary went to the dugout. Gehrig continued to run the bases and was called out for passing Lary.

Yankee hating by the numbers, part three:

- **8.** Home runs New York's Roger Maris hit in 1965, fifty-three fewer than his total in 1961.
- **9.** The Yankees' longest World Series winless streak. This streak comprised the final three games of the 1921 Series, four losses and a tie in 1922, and the first game of the 1923 Series.
- **10.** Games, out of sixteen, that the Yankees lost in 1985 before manager Yogi Berra was fired. Steinbrenner had promised Berra the chance to manage for the entire season.
- **11.** Games relief pitcher Lee Guetterman won in 1990. He led all Yankee pitchers in wins.

JANUARY 29, 1948

Commissioner Happy Chandler fined the Yankees five hundred dollars. Our favorite team was signing players who were still in high school. This was in violation of a rule designed to protect younger players.

Many of them were not as smart as Hank Greenberg was. Hoping to sign the eighteen-year-old Greenberg, Yankee scout Paul Krichell invited him to Yankee Stadium in 1929. Pointing to Lou Gehrig, Krichell said the first baseman's career would be over in a few years. By then, Greenberg would be the Yankee first baseman. The future Hall of Famer did not believe Krichell and eventually signed with Detroit.

Perhaps Krichell meant to point to left fielder Bob Meusel and predict, correctly, that Meusel's career would be over in a few hours. Perhaps he honestly underestimated Gehrig's career by seven or eight seasons. Perhaps wives will accept President Clinton's definition of extramarital sex from their straying husbands.

Teenagers who starred for Yankee opponents:

- Ty Cobb hit .316 for the 1906 Tigers.
- In 1938, Cleveland pitcher Bob Feller led the American League in strikeouts.
- Al Kaline played in 147 games for the 1954 Tigers, hitting .276.
- Tony Conigliaro slugged twenty-four home runs for the 1964 Red Sox.
- Robin Yount hit .267, in 147 games, for the 1975 Brewers.

Died January 29, 1820
King George III

The Declaration of Independence describes this English king as having "a History of repeated Injuries and Usurpations, all having in direct Object the Establishment of an absolute Tyranny." No wonder writer Red Smith dubbed Steinbrenner, "George III."

JANUARY 30, 1930

Former St. Louis Browns' star Ken Williams, a lifetime .319 hitter, joined the Yankees. Although he had batted .345 in 1929, Williams did not make the team. Instead of Williams, the Yankees used outfielders like Dusty Cooke and Sammy Byrd. Decisions like this ensured that Bob Shawkey lasted only one season as Yankee manager.

Teams with the most members of the thirty-home run, thirty-stolen base club, of which Williams was the only member for thirty-four years:

- New York/San Francisco Giants have seven (Barry Bonds three times, Bobby Bonds and Willie Mays twice).
- Milwaukee/Atlanta Braves have four (Ron Gant twice, Hank Aaron, and Dale Murphy).
- New York Mets have four (Howard Johnson, three times, Darryl Strawberry).
- Colorado Rockies have three (Ellis Burks, Dante Bichette, and Larry Walker).
- Three teams, one of which is not the Yankees, have two.

Born January 30, 1923
Walt Dropo

Dropo, the White Sox first baseman, was involved in a brutal fight with the Yankees' Enos Slaughter, in 1957.

In a sense, Slaughter won the fight. Dropo's ejection was more costly to the White Sox than Slaughter's was to the Yankees. In 1957, Dropo was the more dangerous hitter.

In the 1956 World Series, Yankee second baseman Billy Martin commented on Slaughter's fielding ability. He told manager Casey Stengel "If you play the National League bobo out there (in left field) tomorrow, we're going to lose."

JANUARY 31, 1944

In an effort to increase the sales of War Bonds, the War Finance Committee of New York offered an incentive. Purchasers had the opportunity to vote for their favorite athlete ever. Ward Cuff, of the NFL's New York Giants, was in second place. He had 50 percent more votes than Babe Ruth.

Born January 31, 1929
Duke Maas

Yankee pitcher Maas had an ERA of 81.00 in the 1958 World Series. By 1961 he had improved. His ERA that season was only 54.00.

Yankee pitchers who had infinite ERA's for a season:

- Bob McGraw appeared in one game in 1918. He walked all four batters he faced. Later that season, McGraw joined the military. We still managed to win World War I.
- Doc Medich did this in 1972.
- In 1979, Bob Kammeyer gave up seven hits in achieving this dubious distinction. He never pitched again in the major leagues.

(A pitcher has an infinite ERA if he allows an earned run while failing to retire any batters.)

FEBRUARY 1, any year

While studying the Civil War, history students learned about the Battle of Bull Run. Some were happy, as they considered the result a Yankee loss in a key contest.

Born February 1, 1944
Paul Blair

Although Blair did time with the Yankees, we will forgive him because of one memorable moment.

Yankee manager Billy Martin sent Blair into the game. He was to replace Reggie Jackson, who had been loafing. As Blair reached right field, he had the best view as Mount St. Reggie began to anger. An eruption occurred when Jackson reached the dugout and "insulted Martin's mother." Only the intervention of the Yankee coaches prevented a nationally televised fistfight.

Yankee hating from A to Z, part one:

- **A.** Steve Adkins. In his major-league debut, this Yankee pitcher walked eight batters in one and two-thirds innings.
- **B.** Carl Bernstein. He and fellow journalist Bob Woodward were instrumental in ensuring the Watergate scandal was properly investigated, and wrongdoers charged. One G. Steinbrenner, Yankee owner, was among those who were ultimately convicted.
- **C.** Charity work. Steinbrenner ordered pitcher Jim Abbott to cease this "extracurricular activity."
- **D.** Steve Dunning. This Cleveland pitcher scored the winning run against the Yankees in consecutive games in 1971.

FEBRUARY 2, 1955

Allie Reynolds stunned the Yankees by retiring. Reynolds had averaged sixteen wins a year for the Yankees in the 1950's.

Reynolds left the Yankees by choice. Another veteran Yankee pitcher, Eddie Lopat, did not. Having seen enough of Lopat and his 4-8 record, the Yankees practically gave him away in July. Relieved to be rid of Lopat, the Yankees relaxed on the day they traded him. A bad Kansas City team beat them 12-2.

Born February 2, 1968
Scott Erickson

Erickson was the winning pitcher, as Baltimore handed the Yankees their sixth consecutive defeat. This slump, late in the 1997 season, left New York nine games behind the Orioles. It eliminated any realistic chance the Yankees had of winning the American League East.

Some observations on George Halas, born on this date in 1895:

- Halas was a co-founder of the National Football League. Some people feel he was the most important sports figure born during the first week of February 1895. They believe this, knowing that Babe Ruth was born during that week.
- Halas had the good sense to leave the Yankees to play professional football. So did Deion Sanders. Unfortunately for the Yankees, Jake Gibbs, an outstanding college football player, but a mediocre major-league catcher, chose to remain with the team.

FEBRUARY 3, 1938

Lou Gehrig finished filming *Rawhide*. This movie is no worse than *Headin' Home* or *The Babe Comes Home*, the two movies Babe Ruth made during his career as a Yankee player.

Brief summaries of the Ruth and Gehrig movies:

- Gehrig played a good guy in *Rawhide*, a musical Western. In one scene, he throws billiard balls at the bad guys.
- In his autobiography, Ruth stated there never was a movie quite like *The Babe Comes Home*. He added "Thank God."
- In *Headin' Home*, Ruth's character discovers, as an adult, that he has a talent for hitting baseballs. (These things happen all the time in real life.) He uses this talent to attain fame.

Born February 3, 1945
Bob Griese

Steinbrenner was an assistant coach with the Purdue football team in the mid-1950's. Purdue has not won the Big Ten title since. Not even Griese, the Heisman Trophy runner-up in 1966, could help the Boiler-makers recover from Steinbrenner's coaching.

FEBRUARY 4, 1969

Bowie Kuhn became commissioner of baseball. Will we overlook transgressions, like his role in the 1981 split season, just because he suspended Steinbrenner for two years? No, but had it been a lifetime ban...

Born February 4, 1875
Lefty Davis

In 1903, Davis made the first out in Yankee history. Given his .237 batting average that season, he made numerous other outs as well. Davis is the first of many less-than-productive left-handed outfielders for the Yankees.

Baseball has always sought corporate revenue. More recently, the owners seem to be strip-mining the game. They have sold stadium names and have leased advertising space on the top of dugouts.

One day, the owners might sell the chance to sponsor a Lefty Davis Award. This could go to the most useless Yankee. Such an award would be particularly attractive for a Southern-based company.

There could be a Veterans' Committee. This group would recognize the ineptitude of past Yankee players like Frank Crosetti, Bill Robinson, Walt Williams, and Tim Leary.

Notable firsts from the first Yankee game:

- Washington's Rabbit Robinson was the first batter.
- Al Orth, who was the first winning pitcher, threw the first pitch against the Yankees.
- Jack Chesbro was the first losing pitcher, as Washington won 3-1.
- Scoops Carey scored the first run by a Yankee opponent.
- Gene DeMontreville had the first extra-base hit, as well as the first RBI, against the Yankees.

FEBRUARY 5, 1942

The Yankees traded Tommy Holmes to the Braves for Buddy Hassett and Gene Moore. Holmes played eleven seasons following the trade. He had a career batting average of .302. In 1945, Holmes led the National League in hits, doubles, and home runs, while striking out only nine times.

Only Hassett played for the Yankees, and for only one season.

Born February 5, 1934
Hank Aaron

Aaron, the Braves' Hall of Famer, broke many of Babe Ruth's records, most notably for career home runs.

Some of Babe Ruth's records that Aaron surpassed:

- most career home runs: Aaron, 755 (Ruth had 714.)
- most RBI: Aaron, 2,297 (Ruth drove in 2,211.)
- most home runs with one club: Aaron, Braves, 733 (Ruth hit 659 as a member of the Yankees.)
- most seasons with twenty or more home runs: Aaron, twenty (Ruth had sixteen.)
- most seasons with thirty or more home runs: Aaron, fifteen (Ruth did it thirteen times.)
- most successful recording career by a namesake of a famous home run hitter: Aaron, M.C. Hammer (Babe Ruth, a 1970's group, went from relative obscurity to total obscurity.)

FEBRUARY 6, 1996

Some observed Babe Ruth's birthday by renting *The Babe*, a movie starring John Goodman. They concluded it was the third-best movie with this title. It ranked behind *Babe,* the story of a pig, and *Babe,* a 1970's television movie about the legendary female athlete, Babe Didrikson.

Born February 6, 1911
Ronald Reagan

In the 1952 movie, *The Winning Team*, the future president played Yankee-killer Grover Cleveland Alexander.

The longest presidential administrations without a World Series win by the Yankees:

* Reagan's, 1981-1989, and Woodrow Wilson's, 1913-1921
* Theodore Roosevelt's, 1901-1909
* Richard Nixon's, 1969-1974
* Lyndon Johnson's, 1963-1969

(Excluding administrations that ended before the first World Series in 1903)

FEBRUARY 7, 1941

Baseball players and coaches competed in the quarterfinals of their annual golf tournament. All the Yankees who entered had been eliminated before this round.

Golf would be a tricky game for the Yankees. They could not buy a putting touch from a cash-starved owner. They would be subject to rules that are uniform and absolute. Steinbrenner could not blame his "golf people" for his bad shots.

Born February 7, 1936
Frank Leja

Leja was a prominent Yankee prospect who hit .043 in twenty-six major-league games. Expected to be the next Lou Gehrig, he was not even the first Lou Klimchock (Klimchock hit .232 for five major-league teams).

Some other hyped Yankee rookies who never made it:

- Brien Taylor, the first pick in the 1991 amateur draft, received a precedent-setting bonus. He has yet to pitch an inning in the major leagues.
- Rich Berry received a large signing bonus in 1958. He never played in the majors.
- Tommy Carroll had thirty major-league at bats.
- Jim Brideweser received a forty-thousand-dollar bonus. This represents about eight hundred dollars for every at bat he had with the Yankees.

FEBRUARY 8, 1983

Commissioner Kuhn informed Mickey Mantle that the former Yankee was no longer welcome in baseball. Mantle had accepted a job with an Atlantic City casino.

Died February 8, 1956
Connie Mack

Owner-manager Mack led the Philadelphia A's to eight American League pennants, including three in a row, from 1929 to 1931.

Arguments why the 1929 Philadelphia A's were better than the 1927 New York Yankees. (Many believe the 1927 Yankees are baseball's greatest team.):

- The 1929 A's finished eighteen games ahead of the 1929 Yankees. There were no major differences between the Yankee teams of 1929 and 1927, with one notable exception. By 1929, Bill Dickey, a Hall of Fame catcher, had replaced Pat Collins, a mediocre receiver.
- Lefty Grove was the ace of the A's staff. He won election to the Hall of Fame twenty-two years before the Yankees' best pitcher, Waite Hoyt, did.
- Philadelphia had six starters who hit better than .300. New York had five.

FEBRUARY 9, 1969-1982

Earl Weaver was already prepared for the coming season. He believed teams won games by acquiring players in the off-season. During Weaver's fifteen full seasons as manager, the Orioles finished first or second eleven times. As New York was in the Orioles' division, this reduced the Yankees' chances of doing well.

Born February 9, 1914
Bill Veeck

Veeck owned the 1948 Indians and the 1959 White Sox. These teams, along with the 1954 Indians, whom Veeck helped develop, interrupted the Yankees' 1947-1964 string of American League pennants.

Some of Bill Veeck's paybacks to the Yankees for mistreating him early in his career:

- His teams won three American League pennants.
- Veeck sided with Joe DiMaggio, in one of his holdouts with the Yankees.
- Veeck proposed an unrestricted draft and a pooling of television revenue. Baseball eventually implemented both ideas, making it harder for any team to become a dynasty.
- As owner of the White Sox in the 1970's, Veeck upset Yankee manager Billy Martin. He told Martin of Steinbrenner's offer to trade Martin for White Sox manager Bob Lemon.

FEBRUARY 10, 1916

Newark, of the Federal League, sold Germany Schaefer to the Yankees. It was not the best use of the Yankees' money. Schaefer appeared in one game for New York and did nothing. He did not bat, score a run, steal a base, or make a play in the field.

Born February 10, 1955
Greg Norman

Norman, the two-time British Open champion, uses golf balls in a more conventional way than Yankee fans and Roger Maris did. They threw them at each other at Yankee Stadium, in 1962.

Other golfing tie-ins:

- Yankee outfielder Sammy Byrd, an excellent golfer, did not succeed on the PGA tour.
- Ty Cobb devoted a chapter of his autobiography to describing his win over Babe Ruth in a series of golf matches.

FEBRUARY 11, 1936

Associated Press published a survey of players' salaries. It showed how the Yankees treated their players. For example, Lou Gehrig saw his annual salary decline by two thousand dollars between 1931 and 1935. In this period, he had averaged thirty-eight home runs and 112 RBI per season.

Born February 11, 1905
Ed Walsh

In 1933, this son of a Hall of Fame pitcher stopped Joe DiMaggio's sixty-one-game hitting streak in the Pacific Coast League. DiMaggio thus fell six games short of the record for Organized Baseball.

Yankee hating by the numbers, part four:

- **12.** Hits Mickey Mantle would have needed to be a career .300 hitter. At least Mantle came close. Reggie Jackson missed by 375 hits.
- **13.** Excess of Reggie Jackson's career strikeouts over his career hits
- **14.** Upper estimate, per Steinbrenner, of the number of games Yankee manager Lou Pinella lost through mismanaging in the 1986 season.
- **15.** Complete games that Chicago's Jack McDowell pitched in 1991. All Yankee pitchers, combined, had three.

FEBRUARY 12, 1981

Spring training opened. New Yankee manager Gene Michael made people roll their eyes by saying he did not expect to have any problems with Steinbrenner. Meanwhile, the Yankee owner had taken a financial hit. An arbitrator had granted catcher Rick Cerone a salary that was one-third higher than the Yankees had offered.

Born February 12, 1892
Tom Rogers

In the 1921 World Series, Rogers and fellow Yankee pitchers Jack Quinn and Rip Collins allowed eight consecutive hits. This set a World Series record, while leading to eight New York Giant runs.

Rogers should not have been in the same neighborhood as a World Series game. He had pitched only eleven innings in the regular season, walking nine and compiling a 7.36 ERA.

Highest ERA's in a single World Series by a Yankee pitcher:

* 81.00, Duke Maas, 1958
* 54.00, Collins, 1921
* 40.50, Johnny Allen, 1932
* 33.75, Bump Hadley, 1937
* 27.00, Zack Monroe, 1958

FEBRUARY 13, 1955

Yankee players Mickey Mantle, Bob Cerv, and Johnny Sain remained unsigned. Many hoped these players would copy Hall of Fame out-fielder Edd Roush and hold out for most of the season. (Before the mid-1970's, baseball players had two choices. They could play for the team that held their rights or not play at all.)

Born February 13, 1883
Hal Chase

Chase caused numerous problems during his time with the Yankees, from 1905 to 1913. He is generally acknowledged as one of the more corrupt players in baseball history.

This would not disqualify him from playing for the Yankees. New York's owners, Frank Farrell and Bill Devery, had unsavory backgrounds. (See January 9.)

Actions by Hal Chase:

- It is virtually certain that Chase threw games while with the Yankees.
- He led American League first basemen in errors a record five times.
- Chase set the American League record for career errors by a first baseman, with 285.
- He tormented Frank Chance, his manager.
- Playing organizational politics, Chase got Yankee manager George Stallings fired, despite his winning record. Stallings later managed the "Miracle Braves" to victory in the 1914 World Series.

FIXER CHASE PLAYS FOR GAMBLER FARRELL
(January 9, February 13)

FEBRUARY 14, 1962

As spring training opened, Yankee catcher Yogi Berra was concerned about winning a golf tournament. He had practice round scores of eighty-six, eighty-seven, eighty-eight, and eighty-nine. Neither the scores, nor the trend, were encouraging.

Berra would play in eighty-six games in 1962. He almost eighty-sixed his career, hitting .224.

Died February 14, 1966
Bill Stumpf

In 1912, Stumpf set the Yankee club record for the most at bats in a season, 129, without at least one extra-base hit.

To show how inept a feat this was, consider Mario Mendoza, for whom the Mendoza Line is named. The Mendoza Line divides those hitting below .200 from talented major-leaguers. For example, Walt Williams's .113 average for the 1974 Yankees was well below the Mendoza Line.

In his last full major-league season, Mendoza had seven more extra-base hits than Stumpf had in 1912.

In honor of Valentine's Day, Yankee romances that did not last:

- Joe DiMaggio and Marilyn Monroe
- Derek Jeter and Mariah Carey
- Dave Winfield and Ruth Roper
- Billy Martin and his first three wives

FEBRUARY 15, 1939

The Yankees announced that pitcher Spud Chandler was going to miss at least the first two months of the season. Chandler, who had a 14-5 record in 1938, had fractured a bone in his leg while working out. This injury would limit him to eleven games in 1939.

Born February 15, 1945
Ross Moschitto

Moschitto appeared in ninety-six games for the Yankees in 1965, batting twenty-seven times. He had a .185 batting average, struck out nearly half the time, and did not steal any bases. It seems his only talent was working out in the off-season without hurting himself.

Some other useless Yankee substitutes:

- Ruben Amaro hit .156, in sixty-one games, in 1966 and 1968.
- Joe DeMaestri had a .184 batting average, in seventy-one games, in 1960 and 1961.
- Harry Williams, a first baseman in 1913 and 1914, hit .192 in eighty-six games.
- Frank Baker proved that having a famous name does not always help. (Frank "Home Run" Baker is in baseball's Hall of Fame.) He hit .194, in seventy-one games, in 1970 and 1971.

FEBRUARY 16, 1953

Babe Herman, who earned a reputation as one of the "Daffy Dodgers," had become a Yankee scout. After a thorough search for players, he signed one of his first prospects, a first baseman named Don Herman. Babe said he thought his son had a future in baseball. Perhaps, but it was not as a player.

Two incidents that made Babe Herman's reputation:

- He tripled into a double play. Trying to stretch a certain double into a triple, Herman arrived at third base. Unfortunately, two slower, and more prudent, Dodger base runners were already there. Herman and Chick Fewster were tagged out.
- Herman was not a great fielder, once being hit on the head with a fly ball. He denied it, but allowed that the ball might have hit him on the shoulder.

Died February 16, 1960
Stuffy McInnis

McInnis was a member of Philadelphia's famous "$100,000 infield." He had a double and a triple, as the A's beat the Yankees 7-0, in 1912. This loss gave the Yankees a 1-7 record to start the season.

Yankee scores from the first week of the 1912 season were of minimal interest. Stories of the sinking of the *Titanic* dominated the news. Unlike the Yankees, the *Titanic* had hit something.

FEBRUARY 17, 1987

Don Mattingly, the Yankees' best player, won a record $1.975 million salary at arbitration. Steinbrenner was neither happy nor gracious.

Steinbrenner said, "The monkey is clearly on his back. He has to deliver a championship for the Yankees like Reggie Jackson did when he was the highest-paid Yankee. . . . He can't play like little Jack Armstrong of Evansville, Indiana. He goes into the category of modern-player-with-agent looking for the bucks."

Mattingly did not deliver a championship in 1987. With an owner who belonged to the category of modern-owner-with-staff looking for more revenue, the Yankees finished fourth.

Born February 17, 1930
Roger Craig

Craig won the fifth game of the 1955 World Series. Pitching for the Cardinals nine years later, he relieved starter Ray Sadecki. Craig and Ron Taylor held the Yankees scoreless from the second inning on, as the Cardinals won to tie the Series, at two games each.

Besides Craig, some other former "Amazin' Mets" (1962-1967) who hurt the Yankees:

- In 1974, Tommy Davis hit .289 and drove in eighty-four runs, helping the Orioles win the American League East over the Yankees.
- Charley Smith was the career .239 hitter the Yankees received in a trade for Roger Maris.
- Dallas Green had a 56-65 record as Yankee manager.

FEBRUARY 18, 1943

Joe DiMaggio entered the army, where he remained until the end of the war. Twenty-six Yankees, who had major-league experience, spent at least one season in the service during World War II.

Born February 18, 1954
John Travolta

Travolta is the star of the movie, *Saturday Night Fever*. A song from this movie, "Night Fever," was *Billboard* magazine's number one song of 1978. Meat Loaf's "Paradise by the Dashboard Light" could have been but was not, peaking at number thirty-eight one week. What was the difference? Former Yankee Phil Rizzuto did vocals for "Paradise by the Dashboard Light." No Yankee had anything to do with "Night Fever."

How the Yankees did before they learned to recover from Saturday nights:

- They lost the first Sunday game in New York, to St. Louis, in 1917.
- Detroit beat New York 16-3, in 1907. This was the first Sunday game in Detroit in five years.
- New York lost the first Sunday game in Cleveland 14-3, in 1911.

(New York City banned Sunday baseball in the early part of this century. This ban caused the Yankees to play a game in Newark, in 1904. By winning, they ruined this Sunday for almost seven thousand fans. As a result, the Yankees have not been invited back to Newark.)

FEBRUARY 19, 1962

There was excitement, as the New York Mets began their first spring training. New Yorkers no longer lived in a city where the Yankees were the only major-league baseball team.

Born February 19, 1962
Alvaro Espinoza

Espinoza had twenty RBI in 1990. This set a major-league record for the fewest RBI by a player who appeared in more than 150 games.

Players like Espinoza remain in the major leagues because they are "good glove, no hit." This would be true of Espinoza, if only he had been a better fielder. In 1989 and in 1990, only one American League shortstop had more errors than Espinoza did.

Most at bats in a season with no home runs by a Yankee:

- 597, Hal Chase, 1906
- 543, Roger Peckinpaugh, 1917
- 515, Willie Keeler, 1903
- 505, Charlie Hemphill, 1908
- 503, Espinoza, 1989

FEBRUARY 20, 1975

Catfish Hunter was preparing for the 1975 season. Hunter had become a Yankee by signing the first lucrative free-agent contract. He spent much of his time denying the contract would affect his pitching. Perhaps he was right, but he started the season with an 0-4 record, a 7.47 ERA, and a new nickname, "Fatcatfish."

Born February 20, 1896
Bob O'Farrell

O'Farrell, the Cardinal catcher, threw out Babe Ruth, who was trying to steal second base. This play ended the 1926 World Series.

Comments on Ruth's Series-ending play:

- "The only stupid play of his life."(Yankee General Manager Ed Barrow)
- "The Yankees came to our rescue. They decided to let Ruth run." (Cardinal second baseman-manager Rogers Hornsby)
- "My thought in going down was to pull the unexpected." (Ruth)
- "Maybe it was good thinking, and maybe it wasn't." (O'Farrell)

FEBRUARY 21, 1969

Ted Williams was named manager of the Washington Senators. Under Williams, the 1969 Senators won twenty-one more games than they had won in 1968. This improvement enabled them to finish five games ahead of the Yankees.

Born February 21, 1948
Bill Slayback

Slayback had a brief career, winning six games. One of these was his debut with the Tigers. Slayback took a no-hitter into the eighth inning, eventually beating the Yankees 9-3.

Yankee hating by the numbers, part five:

- **16.** Consecutive games the Yankees played, in 1944, without hitting a home run.
- **17.** Home runs by which the 1996 Orioles exceeded the Yankees' record for home runs hit by a team in a season.
- **18.** Consecutive seasons without a Yankee pennant, 1903-1920.
- **19.** Managerial changes Steinbrenner made, in eighteen years, before Buck Showalter lasted four years as Yankee manager. Steinbrenner did not exactly work his way up in talent. He began with Ralph Houk, whose teams had won two World Series. Steinbrenner tried managers like Gene Michael and Clyde King. Eventually he hired Bucky Dent. This is a progression somewhat like Elizabeth Taylor's in husbands. At one point, the actress was married to a superb actor, Richard Burton. Her most recent husband, Larry Fortensky, is best-known as someone she met in rehab.

FEBRUARY 22, 1952

The Eastern Dog Club held its annual show. Bob Wiesler, who had a 13.50 ERA for the 1951 Yankees, was in the military and could not be entered.

Born February 22, 1934
Sparky Anderson

Anderson led two teams, in different leagues, to dominating performances over the Yankees. His 1976 Reds swept the Yankees in the World Series. Anderson's 1984 Tigers led the American League from the beginning to the end of the season, an unbeatable accomplishment.

Two reasons to like A's owner Charles O. Finley, born on this date in 1918:

- Finley ended the virtual farm team relationship the Kansas City A's had with the Yankees. Under their previous owner, the A's would send the Yankees promising stars, like Roger Maris. As token compensation, they would receive fading veterans, like Hank Bauer.
- Finley prevented the Yankees from hiring Dick Williams as their manager. New York wound up with Bill Virdon, rather than the manager whose teams had won the previous two World Series.

FEBRUARY 23, 1966

Ken Harrelson, of the Kansas City A's, beat former Yankee Ralph Terry to win the National Baseball Players Golf Tournament. Terry lost by fifteen strokes.

Born February 23, 1929
Elston Howard

The most certain indication the Yankee dynasty was over came in August 1967. New York sent Howard to a contending team, the Red Sox.

Howard had played in over fifteen hundred games for the Yankees. He still was one of the better catchers in the American League.

New York received two marginal players for Howard. For years it had been the reverse. Good players like Enos Slaughter, Sal Maglie, or Johnny Mize would go to the Yankees, usually for little in return.

Events that took the Yankees from first place in 1964 to last place in 1966:

- They had reduced their spending on player development, in anticipation of the sale of the club.
- Roger Maris and Mickey Mantle became less effective.
- Injuries occurred, notably to shortstop Tony Kubek and pitcher Whitey Ford.
- "Can't miss" prospects like Jake Gibbs and Roger Repoz missed.
- There is a God.

FEBRUARY 24, 1937

Lou Gehrig and Joe DiMaggio were dissatisfied with the contracts the Yankees had offered. General Manager Ed Barrow went public with the club's position: Gehrig and DiMaggio could accept the club's offer or not play. Many hoped the players would call Barrow's bluff and learn he was not bluffing.

Born February 24, 1874
Honus Wagner

Wagner got as many Hall of Fame votes as Babe Ruth did in the inaugural election. This should not be surprising given the views of people like Ed Barrow, Ruth's manager in Boston and general manager in New York. Barrow considered the Pittsburgh shortstop the better player. Remember this the next time some Yankee fan shows you a listing of baseball's greatest players.

Players who got more votes than notable Yankee players did in Hall of Fame elections:

- Ty Cobb received 222 votes to Babe Ruth's 215, in 1936.
- In 1954, Rabbit Maranville got 209 votes. Bill Dickey had 202.
- George Sisler obtained 235 votes to Willie Keeler's 207, in 1939.
- Sandy Koufax beat out Yogi Berra, 344 votes to 339, in 1972.
- In 1987, Billy Williams got 354 votes, while Catfish Hunter received 315.

FEBRUARY 25, 1994

Tonya Harding finished eighth in the figure skating competition at the Winter Olympics. She subsequently pleaded guilty to hindering the investigation into an attack on Nancy Kerrigan, a rival skater. Harding's husband and some of his associates had planned and carried out this assault.

There was no word on whether Steinbrenner, who usually blamed his "baseball people" for the Yankees' problems, would fire his "figure skating people." Steinbrenner had provided Harding with financial support.

Born February 25, 1944
Stump Merrill

Merrill managed the Yankees to a record of 120-155, a .436 percentage. Merrill's teams finished an aggregate of forty-one games out of first place. Even a bad attorney could argue persuasively that Merrill was the worst manager in baseball in 1990 and 1991.

Yankee managers, during the Steinbrenner era, who have not managed since being fired:

- Merrill
- Bucky Dent
- Clyde King
- Bob Lemon
- Yogi Berra

THE BABE IS RIGHTSIZED (February 26)

FEBRUARY 26, 1935

At a press conference, the Yankees announced the release of Babe Ruth to the Boston Braves. As the Yankees wanted to get rid of Ruth, they sought no compensation. Ruth never returned to the Yankees in any capacity, especially not as manager, the one job he coveted.

Born February 26, 1887
Grover Cleveland Alexander

Alexander was dominant against the Yankees in the 1926 World Series. After winning the second and sixth games, the Cardinal pitcher recorded the most famous save in World Series history, in the seventh game.

One more time, the details of Alexander's save:

- Having celebrated the night before, a hungover Alexander was called in to face Tony Lazzeri (114 RBI that season). It was the seventh inning. There were two outs and the bases were loaded.
- On a one-ball, one-strike count, Lazzeri hit a long foul. He then struck out.
- Alexander did not allow a run in the eighth or ninth innings.

FEBRUARY 27, 1985

Dave Winfield made his first appearance in the Yankee clubhouse since leaving hurriedly after the last game of the 1984 season. In that game, Don Mattingly, Winfield's teammate, had won the batting title by outhitting Winfield. Many believed the hasty exit occurred because Winfield's anger exceeded his sportsmanship.

Born February 27, 1877
Art Goodwin

This Yankee pitcher had an ERA of 81.00 for his career. In his only major-league appearance, Goodwin gave up three runs in one-third of an inning. Even the Yankees could tell he was not a major-league pitcher.

Eighty-four years later, it took them longer to reach the same obvious conclusion on Kevin Mmahat. In 1989, Mmahat allowed twenty-one base runners in eight innings, compiling an ERA of 12.91.

In 1989, the Yankee manager was Dallas Green. As a major-league pitcher, he had won only twenty games. With this background, he probably needed a push to get rid of Mmahat. It likely came from the Yankee public relations department. It was tired of being accused of typographical errors in spelling Mmahat's name.

Other Arthurs who have caused problems for the Yankees:

- Art Nehf, the New York Giant pitcher, beat the Yankees in the final games of the 1921 and the 1922 World Series.
- Art Passerella called a clearly safe Yankee runner out in the tenth inning of a game in the 1952 World Series. Brooklyn won the game 6-5, and took a 3-2 lead in the Series.
- Yankee pitcher Art Ditmar lost twice, with a 21.60 ERA, in the 1960 World Series. Years later, a commercial showed people watching the seventh game of this Series. In this commercial, Ditmar, not Ralph Terry, gave up Bill Mazeroski's Series-winning home run. Given Ditmar's performance in the Series, this was an honest error.
- Arthur Miller married Marilyn Monroe after she divorced Joe DiMaggio.

FEBRUARY 28, 1955

Mickey Mantle's twin brothers, Roy and Ray, were designated for reassignment within the Yankee organization. Neither of the twins was good enough to beat out Dick Tettlebach. In 1955, Tettlebach was a twenty-four-year-old prospect. Soon, he would be a former major-leaguer, with a .150 career average.

Neither Roy nor Ray would ever play for the Yankees. Signing them in the first place could be explained by nepotism, too much faith in genetics, or stupidity. Or, as Humphrey Bogart said in *Casablanca*, "It was a combination of all three."

Died February 28, 1972
Dizzy Trout

This Detroit pitcher had a 6-0 record against the Yankees in 1944.

Dizzy's son also tormented the Yankees. Steve Trout had eighty-eight wins in the majors, but none, in four decisions, as a Yankee. Steve cost the Yankees three players. One was Bob Tewksbury, who would win over one hundred major-league games.

Some other father-son combinations who pitched effectively against the Yankees:

- Jim Bagby, Sr. won thirty-one games, as Cleveland won the 1920 pennant over the Yankees. Jim, Jr. helped stop Joe DiMaggio's fifty-six-game hitting streak.
- Joe Coleman and Joe Coleman won a combined 192 American League games.
- Clyde Wright won one hundred American League games. His son, Jaret, beat the Yankees in the second and fifth games of the 1997 American League Division Series.

FEBRUARY 29, 1944

The Yankees released two lists, their 1944 training camp roster and the list of Yankees in military service. It was clear the latter list, which included Joe DiMaggio, Tommy Henrich, Phil Rizzuto, and Red Ruffing, had better players on it.

Born February 29, 1904
Pepper Martin

A leader of the Cardinals' "Gas House Gang," Martin had a career World Series batting average of .418. This average is forty-five points higher than the Yankees' best.

Martin had one of the great nicknames in sports, "the Wild Hoss of the Osage." This nickname is infinitely better than Yankee nicknames like "Twinkletoes" (George Selkirk) or "Bootnose" (Fred Hofmann).

Players who have won professional sports titles in more years than any Yankee:

- Henri Richard (born February 29, 1936) won eleven Stanley Cups with the Montreal Canadiens.
- Bill Russell led the Celtics to eleven NBA titles.
- Jack Nicklaus won major championships in golf in thirteen different years. (He won eighteen major titles in all.)
- Margaret Smith Court was the Australian Open tennis champion in eleven different years.

MARCH 1, 1969

Mickey Mantle retired. Maybe this was not good news. Mantle had a .237 batting average in 1968.

Why the New York media should not have suggested that Bobby Murcer was the next Mickey Mantle:

- In an equivalent number of minor-league at bats, Mantle's batting average was fifty-five points higher than Murcer's. In these games, Mantle hit eleven more home runs and drove in sixty-eight more runs than his successor as the Yankees' best player did.
- Mantle was, by many accounts, the fastest player in the American League. Murcer was not even the fastest player on the Yankees.
- Mantle was the superior fielder. In his first major-league season, Mantle accepted more chances per game and had a better fielding average than Murcer did in his first season.

Born March 1, 1917
Harry Caray

In 1964, while broadcasting for the Cardinals, Caray interviewed Leo Durocher, a Dodger coach. Durocher indicated he could be interested in managing the Cardinals, which led to his being offered this job for the 1965 season. St. Louis manager Johnny Keane learned of the deal and talked with the Yankees. Keane eventually became their manager. He was the wrong manager, at the wrong time, for the wrong team.

MARCH 2, 1949

Joe DiMaggio entered the hospital. He had a heel injury that would prevent him from playing until late June.

Died March 2, 1956
Fred Merkle

Merkle hit seven home runs in 1914. This puts the twelve the Yankees hit as a team into perspective. Like Merkle's Giants, the Yankees played their home games at the Polo Grounds.

Before you can hit a home run, you must learn how to hit the ball. With a league-low batting average of .229, the 1914 Yankees did not have this fundamental skill.

Highest percentage of Yankee home runs hit by an individual opponent:

- 133 percent. Home Run Baker hit twelve, to the Yankees' nine, in 1913.
- 75 percent. Baker had nine, while the Yankees had twelve, in 1914.
- 72 percent. Buck Freeman slugged thirteen, to the Yankees' eighteen, in 1903.
- 71 percent. Harry Davis hit twelve, and the Yankees hit seventeen, in 1906.
- 64 percent. Boston's Babe Ruth had twenty-nine, while the Yankees had forty-five, in 1919.

(Harmon Killebrew hit forty-nine home runs in 1969. This was 52 percent of the Yankees' total, the highest percentage in more recent years.)

MARCH 3, 1954

Yankee second baseman, and future manager, Billy Martin was drafted by the army. He missed all of the 1954, and most of the 1955, seasons. No, he was not fired five times as a platoon leader.

Other Yankees who lost seasons to military service in the 1950's:

- Bobby Brown, 1952-1954
- Tommy Carroll, 1958
- Jerry Coleman, 1952-1953
- Whitey Ford, 1951-1952
- Tom Morgan, 1952-1953
- Bob Wiesler, 1951-1952

Born March 3, 1960
Neil Heaton

Despite having an artificial hip, Bo Jackson hit a home run, in 1993, against Yankee pitcher Heaton.

Heaton was finished as a major-leaguer after the 1993 season. Yankee management eventually realized that most batters had healthy hips.

MARCH 4, 1943

It was a bad night at the Academy Awards for Yankee fans. *Pride of the Yankees*, nominated as Best Picture, lost. So did this movie's star, Gary Cooper. He had been nominated as Best Actor for his portrayal of Yankee star Lou Gehrig.

Born March 4, 1897
Lefty O'Doul

O'Doul failed as a Yankee pitcher and left the club. He became one of the greatest hitters in baseball history, with a lifetime batting average of .349.

Other players who became stars after the Yankees sold, traded, or released them, 1901-1950:

- Hippo Vaughn won twenty or more games five times. He led the National League in wins, ERA, strikeouts, and shutouts in 1918.
- Dazzy Vance won 197 games, primarily for the Dodgers, and earned induction into the Hall of Fame.
- Playing mostly with the Dodgers, Dixie Walker was a career .306 hitter. Walker won the 1944 National League batting title.
- Jack Fournier hit .313 during his major-league career, which he spent mostly with the Cardinals and Dodgers.

MARCH 5, 1973

Yankee pitchers Fritz Peterson and Mike Kekich announced they had exchanged families. Peterson insisted it was not a "sex thing." Kekich emphasized that this unusual baseball trade was a "life swap," rather than a "wife swap."

Reactions to the Peterson-Kekich swap:

- Baseball Commissioner Bowie Kuhn said, "I deplore what happened and am appalled at its effect on young people. It is a most regrettable situation that does no good for sports in general."
- Marilyn Peterson left Kekich shortly after the swap.
- Early in the 1973 season, the Yankees traded Kekich to Cleveland. They received Lowell Palmer, who never appeared in a game for the Yankees during his 5-18 major-league career.
- Yankee General Manager Lee MacPhail said, "We might have to call off Family Day."

Born March 5, 1921
Elmer Valo

His single drove in the tying and winning runs, as the A's scored seven times in the last inning to beat the Yankees 7-6. In the first game of this 1949 doubleheader, Philadelphia rallied from a 7-3 deficit to win 8-7.

A few years later, Valo ruined Casey Stengel's sixty-fifth birthday. He had three doubles and a home run, as the A's beat the Yankees 12-2.

FRITZ AND SUSANNE AND MIKE AND MARILYN
(March 5)

MARCH 6, 1969

Washington scored five runs on only one hit, as Yankee pitchers issued eleven walks. Had Tommy Byrne, the control-challenged Yankee pitcher of the 1940's and 1950's, been working as a pitching coach?

Yankee pitchers who led the American League in walks:

- George Mogridge, 1918
- Joe Bush, 1924
- Hank Johnson, 1928
- Tommy Byrne, 1949, 1950, 1951
- Bob Turley, 1955, 1958
- Al Downing, 1964
- Dave Righetti, 1982
- Phil Niekro, 1985

Born March 6, 1900
Lefty Grove

In one inning in a game in 1928, Grove struck out Yankee sluggers Babe Ruth, Lou Gehrig, and Bob Meusel on nine consecutive pitches. Grove's seventy-nine wins, from 1929 to 1931, helped Philadelphia win the American League pennant in each of these seasons.

MARCH 7, 1954

Beginning their first spring training, the Baltimore Orioles won their second consecutive exhibition game. As the St. Louis Browns (1902-1953), the Orioles had been a low-budget, non-competitive franchise. In Baltimore, they became a contender by 1960, eliminating a dozen or more easy wins for the Yankees each season.

Born March 7, 1963
Kim Ung-Yang

According to the fifteenth edition of the *Guinness Book of World Records,* Ung-Yang has an IQ of 210, the highest ever measured. Reggie Jackson claimed to have an IQ of 160. Out of what, asked teammate Mickey Rivers, one thousand?

We know Reggie did not have a high batting average, but how does his best single-season RBI total, 118, compare with those of some true superstars of the post-World War II era?:

- Hank Aaron exceeded this total seven times and equaled it twice.
- Stan Musial had more RBI three times.
- Willie Mays bettered Jackson's total three times.
- Ken Griffey, Jr. has already exceeded it three times.

MARCH 8, 1914

Investors announced the formation of the Federal League. This league provided jobs to scores of players. Many were has-beens like Three-Finger Brown. Once a great pitcher, Brown, by 1914, was a thirty-seven-year-old coming off an 11-13 season.

Other Federal Leaguers were "never wases" like Larry Schlafly. This second baseman had last played, briefly and poorly, for the Senators seven years earlier.

Even with these low standards for players, the Federal League had no room for Ezra Midkiff. In 1913, Midkiff, the Yankee third baseman, had hit .197 and driven in fourteen runs. He had been baseball's sixteenth-best third baseman. In 1914, no team wanted to give Midkiff the chance to be the twenty-fourth best.

A complete listing of the major-league teams, of the twenty-four, who won fewer games than the Yankees did in 1914 and 1915 combined:

- Cleveland Indians
- St. Louis Browns
- Cincinnati Reds
- Pittsburgh Pirates
- Baltimore Terrapins (Federal League)

Born March 8, 1922
Al Gionfriddo

Brooklyn led the Yankees 8-5, in the sixth game of the 1947 World Series. New York had two runners on base with two outs. Joe DiMaggio hit what looked like an extra-base hit. Gionfriddo went to deep left-center field and made one of the best catches in World Series history. His catch saved at least two runs. Brooklyn eventually won 8-6.

MARCH 9, 1940

Hank Greenberg was learning how to play left field, after giving his first baseman's job to Rudy York. This change of positions won the 1940 pennant for the Tigers. York and Greenberg combined for seventy-four home runs and 280 RBI.

Born March 9, 1963
Terry Mulholland

In 1991,Tim Leary had an ERA of 6.49. This was the worst-ever by a Yankee who pitched at least one hundred innings. Three years later, Mulholland equaled this dubious record.

Canada has a national lottery called the 6/49. Players select six numbers between one and forty-nine. If these six numbers are drawn, the player wins several million dollars. The odds of winning this prize are one in fourteen million.

These should be the odds of an intelligent team retaining a pitcher like Leary or Mulholland. Not being intelligent, the Yankees tried to defy these odds. They gave Leary another chance in 1992. Leary had a 5.57 ERA, before the Yankees paid Seattle to take him. (Officially, the Yankees received Sean Twitty. He has yet to appear in a major-league game. Country singer Conway Twitty, who has been dead for several years, probably has a brighter future in baseball.)

Worst single-season ERA's by Yankee pitchers:

- 6.49, Mulholland, 1994
- 6.49, Leary, 1991
- 6.27, Wade Taylor, 1991
- 5.95, Jeff Johnson, 1991
- 5.77, Jack Quinn, 1912

(Minimum of one hundred innings pitched)

MARCH 10, 1960

A transcript of former Yankee shortstop Phil Rizzuto criticizing Mickey Mantle, for holding out, became available. (Years later, Rizzuto called Mantle one of the three best Yankee outfielders ever, along with Joe DiMaggio and Charlie Keller. In fairness, Rizzuto had never seen Babe Ruth play.)

Whitey Ford, New York's top pitcher, was a close friend of Mantle. Ford defended Mantle and criticized Rizzuto, saying his former team-mate was a "fine guy to talk like that. Rizzuto always did all right for himself when he was playing; and when in his last two years he spent most of his time sitting in the bullpen, he was well paid for that too."

Years later, Rizzuto insulted Eddie Stanky, the White Sox manager. Stanky responded, "I've heard from former Yankees time and again that Phil Rizzuto was an alibi player, so a guy like him ripping me isn't going to disturb me."

Born March 10, 1958
Steve Howe

This relief pitcher's career with the Yankees, though brief, was, to be kind, colorful.

Some highlights from Steve Howe's career with the Yankees:

- He was suspended from baseball for life, following his seventh drug incident.
- He had an ERA of 18.00 in the 1995 Division Series.
- On an appeal play, he threw the ball into the stands, allowing a run to score.

MARCH 11, 1954

In a preseason win over the Yankees, the Milwaukee Braves scored eleven runs. This was one of sixteen losses, in twenty-four exhibition games, for New York that spring.

Born March 11, 1945
Dock Ellis

Ellis, a Yankee pitcher and no fan of Steinbrenner, said, "Maybe we should make a lot of trouble so he'll keep (flying). Sooner or later, his plane's gonna crash." This remark has also been attributed to Graig Nettles, who did say that as a boy he wanted either to play baseball or join the circus. As a Yankee, Nettles continued, he was doing both.

Some other comments by Graig Nettles:

- "He's gone from Cy Young to sayonara." (on the decline in team-mate Sparky Lyle's pitching)
- "They have nine votes, and George has ten." (on the true power of Steinbrenner's "baseball people")
- "(Yankee President Al) Rosen is just someone to blame when George (Steinbrenner) does something wrong."

MARCH 12, 1963

The Yankees had only one hit in losing a preseason game to the Milwaukee Braves. New York did not face great pitchers. If they ever build a Hall of Mediocre, the Braves' pitchers that day— Frank Funk, Claude Raymond, and Larry Maxie— will be in it.

Born March 12, 1930
Vernon Law

Law won his first two starts for the Pirates, over the Yankees, in the 1960 World Series. Pitching on two-days' rest, Law made his third start in the seventh game of the Series. He limited the Yankees to one run before tiring in the sixth. Pittsburgh ultimately won the game on Bill Mazeroski's ninth-inning home run.

Comments on Vernon Law's performance in the 1960 World Series:

- New York scored seven runs against Law in eighteen innings. They had forty-eight, in forty-four innings, against the rest of the Pirate staff.
- Pittsburgh won all three games Law started. They lost three of the other four by scores of 16-3, 12-0, and 10-0.
- Law had two hits in six at bats, with a double and a RBI.

MARCH 13, 1975

Walt Williams, who was normally an outfielder, was trying to learn a new position, second base. It was encouraging to see the Yankees looking for a position for a player who had hit .113 the previous season.

Born March 13, 1922
Cliff Mapes

Although he was an average player, Mapes wore Babe Ruth's number three.

Mapes was an inquisitive man. After a close play had cost the Yankees an important game, Mapes asked if the umpire had bet on the game. His curiosity cost Mapes a two-hundred-dollar fine.

Other Yankees who wore Babe Ruth's number three, and their best seasons wearing this number:

- George Selkirk (who wore the number from 1936 to 1942) had several productive seasons for the Yankees.
- Bud Methany (1943-1946) had a .261 average in 1943. He hit nine home runs and had thirty-six RBI.
- Roy Weatherly, Eddie Bockman, and Frank Colman (all 1946) had a combined .207 batting average for the Yankees.
- Joe Medwick and Hal Peck were with the Yankees briefly in 1947, but never played.
- Allie Clark (1947) had sixty-seven at bats as a Yankee.

MARCH 14, 1956

Boston beat the Yankees 2-0, limiting them to four hits. Earlier that week, the Yankees had two hits in a loss to the Cardinals. This lack of offense was a pleasant reminder of the Yankees' most recent meaningful game, a 2-0 loss in the seventh game of the 1955 World Series.

Born March 14, 1944
John Miller

Miller was the first Yankee to hit a home run in his first major-league at bat. He should have retired as soon as he crossed the plate. Miller would have nine more hits in his thirty-two-game major-league career.

Inept players who helped the Yankees finish last in 1966:

- Miller hit .087.
- Ray Barker had a .187 batting average.
- Mike Ferraro was an infielder who could not field (a .925 fielding average) or hit (a .179 batting average).
- Switch-hitter Dick Schofield proved he could not hit from either side of the plate by batting .155.

MARCH 15, 1995

According to a National Labor Relations Board ruling, Steinbrenner and the other owners were "failing and refusing to bargain collectively in good faith." Their transgressions included using replacements for striking players. Yankee captain Don Mattingly called these replacements "a stain on Yankee Tradition."

Like many good hitters, Mattingly has excellent eyesight. He was able to spot this stain, despite the far larger one made by Steinbrenner's ownership.

Born March 15, 1960
Mike Pagliarulo

By saying, "The only 'Boss' I know is Bruce Springsteen," the Yankee third baseman put self-styled "Boss" Steinbrenner in his place.

Songs of note for this book:

- "Big Shot," with its reference to cocaine use, was played in stadiums to torment Yankee pitcher and drug user Steve Howe.
- "The Addams Family Theme" reminded Yankee Wade Boggs of his affair with Margo Adams. This extramarital relationship involved, among other things, a palimony suit, the FBI, and jokes by late-night comics.
- Steely Dan chose the Alabama Crimson Tide, not the Yankees, as a "winner in this world" in "Deacon Blue."
- Six songs finished ahead of "Mrs. Robinson" (with its line about Joe DiMaggio) on *Billboard's* listing of the top songs of 1968.

MARCH 16, 1995

Despite the prior day's ruling (see March 15), the Yankees continued using replacement players in exhibition games. Those searching for a silver lining realized that this could be the worst Yankee team ever.

Perhaps the replacement Yankees could have beaten the 1986 Yankees, who had a lineup that included:

- catcher Joel Skinner (.236 average),
- second baseman Bryan Little (.195 in fourteen games),
- shortstop Wayne Tolleson (See November 22.),
- third baseman Leo Hernandez (.227 in seven games),
- outfielder Henry Cotto (.212 in thirty-five games),
- designated hitter Ron Kittle (.218 average), and
- pitcher Mike Armstrong (9.35 ERA in seven games).

Born March 16, 1906
Lloyd Waner

Waner hit .400 against the Yankees in the 1927 World Series. He and his brother, Paul, combined for 5,611 hits. This is 758 more than the three DiMaggio brothers had.

Lloyd and Paul Waner were called "Little Poison" and "Big Poison." "Poison" was a play on "person," and on what the Waners did to opponents.

Yankee pitcher Jim Coates could have had this nickname, for different reasons. He poisoned Yankee World Series hopes in 1960 and 1962. New York lost all five games in which Coates pitched.

Then there was Coates's appearance. Teammates would ask him if he was endorsing iodine. They had seen his likeness on the side of the bottle.

MARCH 17, 1981

Reggie Jackson sought a confrontation with Steinbrenner. He was up-set because Steinbrenner— and who could better recognize this— had said that Jackson talked out of both sides of his mouth.

Died March 17, 1959
Howard Ehmke

In 1920, Ehmke beat New York in the fastest 1-0 game in American League history. Three years later, only a controversial hit by the Yankee leadoff batter deprived Ehmke of a perfect game.

Yankee hating by the numbers, part six:

- **20.** Wins, out of twenty-one games, by the Red Sox against the Yankees at Fenway Park, 1972-1974
- **21.** Games George Mogridge started in 1916, when he set the Yankee record for consecutive losses, with eleven.
- **22.** Times the Yankees played a dreadful (61-93) Red Sox team in 1922. New York lost thirteen of these games to keep that season's pennant race close.
- **23.** Errors Yankee catcher Thurman Munson made in 1975. This was the highest total by a catcher since Houston's John Bateman had made that many in 1963.

MARCH 18, 1985

Joe Pepitone was arrested. Police charged him with possession of drugs for the purpose of trafficking and possession of a weapon. He was later convicted. At the time of his arrest, Pepitone identified himself as "Joe Pepitone, formerly of the Yankees."

Some Joe Pepitone stunts:

- He committed a crucial error in the final game of the 1963 World Series.
- Through drinking and womanizing, he was frequently out of shape. He often failed to hustle.
- He incurred huge debts. One of his managers, Leo Durocher, described these as being at a level that the combined resources of the Bank of England and the Bank of America could not satisfy.
- Citing "personal problems," he went AWOL during the 1969 season.

Born March 18, 1837
Grover Cleveland

A well-known candy bar was named for Cleveland's daughter, Ruth, who was born during his presidency. Its name, Baby Ruth, has nothing to do with the Yankee slugger.

PEPITONE HITS BOTTOM (March 18)

MARCH 19, 1965

Although they were using their best players, the Yankees lost a pre-season game to the Twins. Pitchers Mel Nelson, Dave Boswell, and Jerry Fosnow limited the Yankees to two hits. These three pitchers had appeared in a combined forty-nine major-league games.

Born March 19, 1871
Iron Man McGinnity

This pitcher left the Orioles (the Yankees' predecessors), in 1902, with fellow future Hall of Famers John McGraw and Roger Bresnahan. McGinnity won an average of twenty-seven games in his first five seasons with his new team, the New York Giants.

Events leading to the Orioles' releasing these players:

- McGraw, who was the Orioles' manager, did not like the American League's restraints on arguing with umpires. He hated his indefinite suspension by the League and loathed its president, Ban Johnson.
- McGraw demanded his release by the Orioles, in lieu of repayment of his loan to the team.
- McGraw was involved in arranging the purchases of the Orioles and the New York Giants. There were conditions to these acquisitions. These included the release of McGraw, McGinnity, and Bresnahan. In return, the National League agreed not to fight the American League's entry into New York the following season. In 1903, the Orioles took advantage of this provision, and became the Yankees.

MARCH 20, 1942

Mel Harder, who had been released by the Indians, re-signed with the club. Joe DiMaggio believed Harder was the hardest pitcher for him to hit. Harder pitched for the Indians for six more seasons.

Died March 20, 1984
Stan Coveleski

Coveleski earned a reputation as a Yankee killer during his Hall of Fame career. He helped lead two teams, the 1920 Indians and the 1925 Senators, to pennants over the Yankees.

Pitchers with the most victories against the Yankees:

- Walter Johnson, sixty
- Eddie Cicotte, thirty-five
- Lefty Grove, thirty-five
- Hal Newhouser, thirty-three
- Early Wynn, thirty-three
- Coveleski, thirty-two
- Red Faber, thirty-two

MARCH 21, 1986

Britt Burns learned he would not be able to pitch during the coming season. He had a hip injury that would end his major-league career. Burns, whom the Yankees acquired in a trade, had won eighteen games for the White Sox the previous season.

The previous paragraph was brought to you, *Sesame Street* style, by the term "due diligence." Using this business practice, an acquirer investigates a proposed purchase. He or she makes sure there are no undisclosed problems. This practice prevents the business equivalent of acquiring Britt Burns. New York gave up Joe Cowley, a twelve-game winner, and Ron Hassey, a catcher who had hit .296. In Burns, the Yankees received a pitcher who would never throw another pitch in the major leagues.

Born March 21, 1939
Tommy Davis

Davis hit .400, as the Dodgers swept the Yankees in the 1963 World Series.

Key hits by the Dodgers in the 1963 World Series:

- John Roseboro hit a three-run home run, in the first game, which the Dodgers won 5-2.
- Willie Davis had a two-run double in the second game; the Dodgers won 4-1.
- Tommy Davis's single drove in the only run of the third game.
- Willie Davis drove in the winning run, in the fourth game, with a sacrifice fly.

MARCH 22, 1962

Rogers Hornsby took a verbal shot at Roger Maris. The Yankee star had refused to pose for a picture with Hornsby, a member of baseball's Hall of Fame. Hornsby asked, "What do you think of that bush leaguer, that swelled-up _____, that_____? He refused to pose with me. He couldn't carry my bat. He didn't hit in two years what I hit in one."

Some Yankees who did not hit .424 (Hornsby's best season average) in two seasons:

- Frank Crosetti hit .194 in 1940 and .223 in 1941, a .417 total.
- Tom Tresh's .219 batting average in 1967 and .195 average in 1968 comprised a .414 total.
- By hitting .240 in 1968 and .171 in 1969, Bill Robinson had a combined .411 average.
- Frank Fernandez followed his .170 average in 1968 with a .223 average in 1969, resulting in a .393 total.

Born March 22, 1931
William Shatner

Like Michael J. Fox, Celine Dion, Shania Twain, and numerous others, this actor is a Canadian-born entertainer.

In 1985, Yankee fans offended Shatner's compatriots. They booed the Canadian national anthem twice during a big series with the Toronto Blue Jays. To make amends, the Yankee Stadium announcer reminded the crowd of Canada's help to the U.S. during the Iranian hostage crisis. He asked them to listen politely while "O Canada" was sung. Was an international incident avoided? It might have been had the singer not forgotten the words.

MARCH 23, 1936

It became apparent that Joe DiMaggio's unusual injury was serious. DiMaggio had left his foot in a diathermy machine for too long and had suffered burns. Having more important things to do than pay attention to a future Hall of Famer, the Yankee trainer had left DiMaggio unattended.

Some lesser players given numbers eventually retired by the Yankees (after the player, for whom the number was retired, wore it):

- Nick Etten wore number five, while DiMaggio was in the military.
- Dick Simpson had number nine after Roger Maris wore it.
- Celerino Sanchez was given Phil Rizzuto's number ten.
- Numerous players wore Babe Ruth's number three. (See March 13.)

(Etten was a decent player; Simpson and Sanchez dreamed of being good enough to be a utility infielder.)

Born March 23, 1886
Cy Slapnicka

Slapnicka was a scout for the Cleveland Indians. His most important signing was future Hall of Famer and Yankee rival Bob Feller.

MARCH 24, various years

Millions of basketball fans watched the NCAA tournament. No team from the now-defunct Yankee Conference ever won this event. As noted previously (January 2), God punishes guilt by association.

Born March 24, 1893
George Sisler

Sisler hit .420, as the St. Louis Browns challenged the Yankees for the 1922 pennant. In *The Old Man and the Sea*, Ernest Hemingway mentions Sisler's son, Dick, as prominently as he mentions Joe DiMaggio.

Greatest dominance by the American League batting champion versus the Yankees' best:

- One hundred and thirty-six points. In 1912, Ty Cobb hit .410; Bert Daniels hit .274.
- One hundred and eighteen points. Cobb hit .390 in 1913, while Birdie Cree hit .272.
- One hundred and seventeen points. Tris Speaker had a .386 average in 1916; Home Run Baker's was .269.
- Ninety-four points. In 1909, Cobb hit .377; Hal Chase had a .283 average.
- Ninety-one points. Sisler hit .420 in 1922, while Wally Pipp hit .329.

MARCH 25, 1983

Steinbrenner was fined fifty thousand dollars. He had accused National League umpires of favoring National League teams in interleague exhibition games.

Assume there are two outs in the ninth inning. Philadelphia leads the Yankees 3-2, in a preseason game. It is seventy-four degrees. There are no clouds. Beaches, golf courses, and other diversions await. On a close play, the National League umpire ends the game by calling a Yankee out. He does this because (choose one of the following reasons):

(a) the runner was out,
(b) nobody wants to work any longer than necessary on a day like this,
(c) as a National League umpire, he has to favor his league's teams.

To date, Steinbrenner is the only person who would choose (c).

Some other fines levied against Steinbrenner included:

- three hundred thousand dollars for his post-Pine Tar Game comments (See December 23.),
- twenty-five thousand dollars, plus two hundred thousand dollars in damages, for tampering in the Dave Winfield trade,
- twenty-five thousand dollars for criticizing the umpires' competence, in the 1998 American League Championship Series, and
- numerous five-thousand-dollar fines for offenses like tampering with unsigned players, questioning the integrity of an umpire, and calling the co-owners of the White Sox "Abbott and Costello."

Born March 25, 1969
Travis Fryman

Fryman executed a sacrifice bunt in the twelfth inning of the second game of the 1998 American League Championship Series. Tino Martinez, the Yankee first baseman, hit Fryman with the ball, trying to retire him. Leaving the ball on the ground, the Yankees argued Fryman had run illegally in fair territory. While they argued, Enrique Wilson, who had been on first base, scored. Cleveland won the game 4-1.

MARCH 26, 1920

Buck Weaver, baseball's best third baseman, learned that the White Sox would not trade him to the Yankees.

Home Run Baker's wife had died. Baker chose to care for his children, rather than play for the Yankees in 1920. This left the Yankees desperate for a third baseman. Unable to get Weaver, the Yankees had to use Aaron Ward. This virtual rookie led the American League in strikeouts.

As the Yankees finished three games behind Cleveland, the inability to obtain Weaver was critical.

Weaver hit .331 in 1920.

Born March 26, 1976
The Toronto Blue Jays

Spotting the Yankees seventy-six seasons of player development, the Blue Jays finished ahead of the Yankees in every season, but one, between 1984 and 1993.

Yankee hating from A to Z, part two:

- **E.** Ox Eckhardt. He beat Joe DiMaggio for the 1935 Pacific Coast League batting title. Eckhardt hit .399, DiMaggio .398.
- **F.** Bill Freehan. Detroit's All-Star catcher and his teammate, Willie Horton, hit ninth-inning home runs on successive nights. These gave the Tigers two wins against the Yankees, in 1970.
- **G.** Bob Garibaldi. In 1962, New York offered this pitcher a then-incredible $125,000 signing bonus. The Yankees did not suffer the costs of this poor judgment, as Garibaldi signed with the Giants. He did not win a game during his major-league career.
- **H.** Burt Hooton. Pitching for the Dodgers, Hooton won games in three different World Series against the Yankees.

104

MARCH 27, 1972

Hank Aaron reminisced before a Braves-Yankees exhibition game. He said the Yankees were one of the teams with whom he had considered signing. Aaron chose the Braves because they offered him more money than the others did. Whew!

Died March 27, 1949
Frank Gleich

Gleich's nickname was "Inch." We will assume this name referred to the average distance of this Yankee outfielder's hits.

Gleich had a career slugging average of .133. He was not with the Yankees for defensive reasons. His career fielding average was an abysmal .826.

It is virtually impossible for a major-league player, with more than forty at bats, to have an aggregate slugging and fielding average of less than .960. There might be another such player. And someday O.J. Simpson might find the real killers.

Worst career slugging averages by a Yankee:

- .025, Skeeter Shelton
- .127, Angel Aragon
- .133, Gleich
- .143, Art Lopez

(Minimum of forty at bats)

MARCH 28, 1986

The Yankees traded Don Baylor to the Red Sox. Baylor's leadership, as well as his thirty-one home runs and ninety-three RBI, helped Boston win the 1986 American League pennant.

Teams Baylor played with, and their best seasons:

- Baltimore Orioles (1970-1975) won the 1970 World Series. That year, Baylor was a late-season call-up. He played a more meaningful role on the Orioles' 1973 and 1974 American League East champions.
- Oakland A's (1976, 1988) took the 1988 American League pennant.
- California Angels (1977-1982) captured the 1979 and 1982 American League West championships.
- Boston Red Sox (1986-1987) won the 1986 American League pennant.
- Minnesota Twins (1987) were the 1987 World Series champions.
- In Baylor's three seasons with the Yankees (1983-1985), the team could do no better than second place in its division. Not even a winner like Baylor could help these teams.

Died March 28, 1990
Johnny Neun

Neun was the third Yankee manager in 1946, following Joe McCarthy and Bill Dickey. This is the type of progression Yankee haters like to see.

MARCH 29, 1970

Derek Sanderson, of hockey's Boston Bruins, had become the special target of New York Ranger fans. They booed him, waved rubber chickens at him, and called him clever names like "hairy fairy." Sanderson, in turn, called New York fans "sick animals."

The full name of the Yankees' current star is Derek Sanderson Jeter.

Died March 29, 1959
Johnny Allen

In his second season with the Indians, former Yankee Allen had a 15-1 record. This set a major-league record for winning percentage. Allen's mark stood for twenty-two years. In 1959, Pittsburgh's Elroy Face broke Allen's record, by winning eighteen, of nineteen, decisions.

That season Face proved he could dominate the National League. He faced players like Hank Aaron, Willie Mays, and Stan Musial. After such a performance, earning three saves in the 1960 World Series against the Yankees was not even a challenge.

Yankee hating by the numbers, part seven:

- **24.** Games the Yankees lost during July 1908, their worst month ever.
- **25.** This was the Yankees' worst year of the Ruth-Gehrig-DiMaggio era. New York finished seventh, twenty-eight games behind the Senators.
- **26.** Days after Ruth's penultimate home run that he hit his last home run as a Yankee.
- **27.** Shutouts the Yankees suffered in 1914, once every five and one-half games.

MARCH 30, 1870

Congress declared the Fifteenth Amendment to the Constitution ratified. This Amendment provides that the right to vote shall not be denied on account of race or color.

A mere eighty-five years later, the Yankees became one of the last major-league teams to integrate.

Achievements by African-American players before the Yankees integrated, in 1955:

- Willie Mays was the Most Valuable Player in the National League in 1954.
- Jackie Robinson won the same award in 1949.
- Roy Campanella won two National League Most Valuable Player awards. He would win a third in 1955.
- Larry Doby led the American League in home runs and RBI in 1954.

Born March 30, 1921
Dick Fowler

Fowler and Joe Coleman pitched shutouts, for Philadelphia, in a 1947 doubleheader against the Yankees.

Philadelphia owner-manager Connie Mack had success with Canadian-born pitchers. Fowler won forty-two games between 1947 and 1949. Phil Marchildon won sixty-eight games for the A's.

New York missed out on these pitchers. Later, they missed Canadians like Hall of Famer Ferguson Jenkins and Most Valuable Player award-winner Larry Walker.

Canadian-born Russ Ford played for the Yankees, early in the twentieth century. In a two-year period, he lost twenty-one games and jumped to the Federal League. Another Canadian, Dave Pagan, had a 1-3 record for New York in 1975. These experiences must have convinced the Yankees that Canadian athletes were better off playing hockey.

MARCH 31, 1979

Children were looking up the word "portent" in the dictionary. Newspapers were using this word, as they described the Yankees' preseason record of 5-17.

Some low moments from the 1979 preseason:

- New York lost its first seven games against major-league teams.
- Yankee relievers allowed the Cardinals to score six runs in the ninth inning.
- Ron Guidry gave up ten runs, to the White Sox, in three and one-third innings.
- After the Yankees lost to the Mets, Steinbrenner promised to get tough. He noted he had seen players out after curfew. ("I saw you peeking," said one seven-year-old to the other.)

Born March 31, 1928
Gordie Howe

Even today, almost two decades after he retired, Howe is known as "Mr. Hockey." During his era, hockey players scored as many goals as hitters had home runs. A forty-goal scorer was an all-star, and a thirty-goal scorer could expect a raise.

Howe drew considerable attention when he scored his 715th goal. This surpassed the number of home runs Babe Ruth had hit in his career.

APRIL 1, 1997 and 1998

Playing like April Fools, the Yankees suffered their earliest losses. They lost to the Mariners, in 1997, and to the Angels, in 1998.

Memorable season openings:

- In 1982, the Yankees lost both games of a doubleheader to the White Sox.
- There were far more empty seats than fans at the Yankees' 1974 opener, at Shea Stadium.
- Mickey Vernon hit a home run in extra innings to beat the Yankees in 1954.
- Boston's Babe Ruth threw a three-hitter, as the Yankees lost 10-3, in 1917.
- Rain and snow postponed the Yankees' first two games of the 1990 season. Unfortunately for the Yankees, the weather improved. New York lost ninety-five games in 1990.

Died April 1, 1914
Rube Waddell

In his first major-league start, the A's pitcher struck out thirteen Orioles. Waddell, a future Hall of Famer, gave up only two hits to the Yankees' predecessors. (In 1903, a terrible Oriole team moved to New York. They became a mediocre Yankee team.)

APRIL 2, 1998

Playing sleepy, dopey, goofy baseball, the Yankees lost 10-2 to the Disney-owned Angels.

Born April 2, 1937
Dick Radatz

In a 1963 game, Radatz relieved Red Sox starter Earl Wilson, with nobody out in the ninth inning. New York trailed by a run, but had the bases loaded. Mickey Mantle, Roger Maris, and Elston Howard were coming to bat. Ten pitches later, Mantle, Maris, and Howard were strikeout victims.

Notable performances by a relief pitcher against the Yankees in the World Series:

- Jesse Barnes pitched sixteen innings in relief, winning twice, for the Giants in 1921.
- Elroy Face had three saves for the Pirates in 1960.
- Brooklyn's Hugh Casey earned two wins and a save in 1947.
- Grover Cleveland Alexander had the most famous save in World Series history. (See February 26.)

APRIL 3, 1938

A minor-league team, the New Orleans Pelicans, scored thirteen runs and beat the Yankees. Lefty Gomez, the Yankees' ace pitcher, allowed most of the runs. Losing to a team with a name like the "Raiders" is one thing; it is quite another to lose to a team called the "Pelicans."

Born April 3, 1856
Guy Hecker

He, not Babe Ruth, was the best-hitting pitcher ever. Hecker, who had a lifetime record of 175-148, won the 1886 American Association batting title. Hecker, the pitcher, won twenty-six games that season.

Questionable managerial decisions leading to the Yankees' losing the 1960 World Series:

- Yankee manager Casey Stengel did not start Whitey Ford until the third game, meaning his best pitcher could pitch only twice. Worse, Art Ditmar (born on this date in 1929) started the first game. He was gone in the first inning.
- Stengel let pitcher Bobby Shantz bat in the eighth inning of the seventh game. Elston Howard and Bob Cerv, who hit .462 and .357, respectively, in the Series, could have pinch hit.
- When Shantz tired in the bottom of the eighth, Stengel brought in Jim Coates. Three batters later, Hal Smith hit a three-run homer to give the Pirates a 9-7 lead.
- Stengel chose Ralph Terry, who was primarily a starter, to pitch the ninth inning. Ryne Duren, a relief pitcher who had pitched effectively during the Series, was available. Terry had a short afternoon's work. Bill Mazeroski, the first hitter he faced, broke the 9-9 tie with his World Series-winning home run.

APRIL 4, 1994

Jacobs Field opened. This stadium, where almost every game has been a sellout, has generated enormous revenue. With it, the Indians have become competitive with the Yankees, despite playing in a considerably smaller market.

Stadiums where Cleveland has beaten the Yankees:

- Jacobs Field
- Cleveland Stadium
- League Park
- Neil Park in Columbus, Ohio. Cleveland won a game played here in 1903 (It was illegal to play on a Sunday in Cleveland). Eighty-two years later, the Yankees proved they had no more business playing in the home of the Ohio State Buckeyes than Purdue did. They lost 14-5 to their farm team.

Born April 4, 1888
Tris Speaker

Joe DiMaggio was a superb center fielder for the Yankees. He is revered, in part because of the mystique the New York media helped create. Speaker was better. His lifetime batting average, .344, is higher than DiMaggio's .325. He accepted as many chances per game as DiMaggio did (Chances accepted is a measure of the ability to get to a ball). Speaker had three times as many assists.

DiMaggio is not even the finest center fielder mentioned in a song. In 1965, Bobby Goldsboro recorded "Broomstick Cowboy." This song tells of a small boy dreaming of many things, including Giants' center fielder Willie Mays.

APRIL 5, 1984

Kansas City scored fourteen runs in the first three innings against the Yankees. They coasted to a 15-4 win. LaMarr Hoyt, who won the 1983 Cy Young Award, might have helped. Fortunately, the Yankees had traded him to the White Sox, on this date in 1977.

There were many knocks against Yogi Berra when he managed the Yankees in 1964. One was that he could not handle a pitching staff. Given the 15-4 score, Berra had not learned much in the previous twenty years.

Born April 5, 1877
Wid Conroy

Yankee left fielder Conroy had the second-worst batting average among American League outfielders in 1907. He hardly compensated by having the seventh-worst fielding average.

Yankee hating by the numbers, part eight:

- **28.** Total division or league titles that other New York-based baseball teams have won.
- **29.** Games Jose Rijo started for Cincinnati in the 1990 regular season. This one-time Yankee was the Most Valuable Player of the 1990 World Series. That year, Rijo's former team got as close to making the World Series as Iraqi leader Saddam Hussein did to winning the Nobel Peace Prize. They finished last.
- **30.** Games by which the Indians won the 1995 Central Division. The Yankees have never had such a dominance.
- **31.** Excess of hits the Yankees had over the Pirates, who still won the 1960 World Series.

APRIL 6, 1963

Pedro Gonzalez was named the Yankees' outstanding rookie of spring training. He would have five hits in twenty-six at bats during the regular season. A groundskeeper must have been the second-best rookie.

Born April 6, 1903
Mickey Cochrane

Perhaps baseball's greatest catcher, Cochrane played on five American League pennant-winners between 1929 and 1935. During this period, the Yankees won only one pennant.

The top players in the voting for the American League's Most Valuable Player Award for 1934:

- Cochrane, Detroit
- Charlie Gehringer, Detroit
- Lefty Gomez, Yankees (We will allow the voters one mistake.)
- Schoolboy Rowe, Detroit

(Lou Gehrig, who finished fifth, won the Triple Crown that season. In the opinion of the voters, the Yankee captain was the second-best player whose surname started with "Gehri.")

APRIL 7, 1973

New owner Steinbrenner watched, as the Yankees got off to a poor start. They gave up twenty-five runs in losing two games to Boston. Meanwhile, Steinbrenner was under investigation for making an illegal contribution to Richard Nixon's re-election campaign. In 1973, the Yankees would have a season that was only slightly better than Nixon's.

(Some readers might not know what Nixon's 1973 was like. Let me try and make it perfectly clear. By November of that year, Nixon was saying "I am not a crook.")

Born April 7, 1873
John McGraw

Manager McGraw's New York Giants won two World Series over the Yankees. These wins were due, in part, to McGraw's ability to outthink Yankee manager Miller Huggins.

In fairness to Huggins, it is hard to manage well when the heart of your lineup— Babe Ruth, Bob Meusel, and Wally Pipp— hits a combined .223 in the two Series.

Most World Series games won by a manager against the Yankees:

- McGraw's New York Giants won eleven.
- Walter Alston's Brooklyn and Los Angeles Dodgers won eleven.
- Tom Lasorda's Los Angeles Dodgers had eight wins.
- Fred Haney's Milwaukee Braves beat the Yankees seven times.

APRIL 8, 1974

Hank Aaron hit his 715th home run, to break Babe Ruth's record for career home runs.

Some things Aaron did better than Ruth did:

- Aaron stole 240 bases; Ruth stole 123.
- Ruth's postseason batting average was thirty-six points less than Aaron's.
- Aaron had a higher fielding average, made fewer errors, and accepted more chances per game than Ruth did.
- Aaron won two batting titles, while Ruth won one.
- Ruth struck out nearly sixteen times per one hundred at bats, almost 40 percent more frequently than Aaron did.

Died April 8, 1997
Bob Cain

Cain won his first major-league start, as the White Sox defeated the Yankees 15-0, in a 1950 game. New York could have used Eddie Gaedel. Cain would walk this midget on four pitches in 1951.

APRIL 9, 1925

Babe Ruth collapsed in Asheville, North Carolina. A few days later, he entered St. Vincent's hospital, in New York City. He remained there until May 29 with the "bellyache heard 'round the world." His illness was a major reason for the Yankees' seventh-place finish in 1925.

Explanations of Ruth's illness:

- Ruth claimed he had not watched his diet. Out of an obligation to the fans, he had played in exhibition games, instead of resting.
- Claire Ruth, Babe's wife, said he suffered a groin injury sliding into a base.
- Ruth's physician reported that Ruth had the flu and intestinal problems.
- According to the popular version, Ruth ate too many hot dogs.
- There was a rumor that Ruth had contracted a sexually transmitted disease.

Born April 9, 1879
Doc White

Pitchers White, Nick Altrock, Ed Walsh, and Frank Owen led the White Sox to the 1906 pennant. New York finished second to the team nicknamed the "Hitless Wonders."

Two years earlier, White had helped deprive the Yankees of the pennant. He beat New York twice in three days, late in the season.

APRIL 10, 1985

The Yankees were starting the season with three consecutive losses, in which they gave up twenty-nine runs. Although the team rallied to lose only seven of its next thirteen games, manager Yogi Berra still lost his job.

Born April 10, 1930
Frank Lary

Detroit pitcher Lary was nicknamed "the Yankee Killer."

How Frank Lary earned his nickname:

- Lary beat the Yankees seven times in 1958. He had only nine wins against the other six American League teams.
- In his career, Lary won twenty-eight games against the Yankees, losing only thirteen.
- A loss to Lary, in May 1959, dropped the Yankees into last place.
- In July 1961, the first-place Yankees played the second-place Tigers. Lary drove in the winning run.

APRIL 11, 1977

There was comedy in Kansas City. Dressed like Steinbrenner, a fan made fun of the Yankee owner's profligate ways by passing out fake money. Steinbrenner's team worked overtime in losing to the Royals in thirteen innings.

Born April 11, 1964
Bret Saberhagen

Saberhagen had a 20-6 record for Kansas City in 1985. Cy Young Award voters found this more impressive than Yankee Ron Guidry's 22-6 record.

Yankees who had more impressive statistics, yet lost major awards:

- Triple Crown winner Lou Gehrig did not receive the Most Valuable Player award in 1934.
- In 1927 and 1928, Babe Ruth hit 114 home runs. He won zero Most Valuable Player awards.
- Joe DiMaggio hit forty-six home runs and had 167 RBI in 1937. Detroit's Charlie Gehringer, who had fourteen home runs and ninety-six RBI, was named Most Valuable Player.
- Andy Pettite, who had a 21-8 record, lost the 1996 Cy Young Award to Pat Hentgen, who was 20-10 for Toronto.

APRIL 12, 1965

Baseball season opened. This was the first of eight consecutive seasons when the Yankees were never in first place after April 30.

During this period, eight other American League teams spent time in first place. Let us express this in television terms. (CBS, the Yankees' owner during this period, had trouble understanding baseball.) It is the equivalent of eight networks, but not CBS, having a top-rated show, at some point during an eight-year period.

Lengthy periods when Yankees were not in first place after April 30:

- April 1965 to the end of the 1972 season
- June 1910 to the end of the 1914 season
- May 1989 to the end of the 1992 season
- July 1983 to the end of the 1985 season

Died April 12, 1945
Franklin Roosevelt

Pitcher Bobo Newsom used the thirty-second President as an inspiration, in a win over the Yankees. Early in the 1936 opener in Washington, Newsom suffered a broken jaw. He stayed in the game, saying Roosevelt, who was at this game, had "come out to see him."

APRIL 13, 1998

A beam fell at Yankee Stadium, canceling the game. This occurred on the twentieth anniversary of hundreds of Reggie! Bars falling on their namesake, Reggie Jackson.

Comments about the candy bar that the fans threw at Jackson:

- "Open it and it tells you how good it is." (Catfish Hunter)
- "It tastes like cowflop." (Ken Holtzman, who played with Jackson and Hunter in Oakland and New York)
- "When a streak hitter can get a candy bar named after him, you conclude the word 'superstar' has been devalued. Or even the word 'candy bar.' " (Bob Uecker in *Catcher in the Wry*. New York: G.P. Putnam's Sons, 1982, 120.)
- Columnist Dave Anderson called it the only candy bar in the world that tastes like a hot dog.

Born April 13, 1891
Charlie Meara

His .286 slugging average in 1914 was closest to the Yankees' worst-ever as a team. New York slugged .287 that season. Such a slugging average is not easy to achieve. It means you have a team of Bob Ueckers. Uecker, whose career is justifiably a source of his humor, had a career slugging average of .287.

SECOND PRIZE, TWO REGGIE BARS (April 13)

APRIL 14, 1920

Babe Ruth played his first game with the Yankees. He dropped a fly ball, in the eighth inning, allowing two runs to score. Philadelphia won 3-1.

Born April 14, 1941
Pete Rose

In the 1976 World Series, the Reds' third baseman intimidated Yankee leadoff hitter Mickey Rivers. By playing halfway between third base and home plate, Rose took away the bunt. Without this part of his game, Rivers hit .167 in the Series.

Some of Mickey Rivers's antics while with the Yankees:

- His irate wife chased him around a parking lot. They were driving separate cars.
- Continually in need of money, Rivers would refuse to play if he did not get a salary advance. This occurred, most notably, before the final game of the 1977 American League Championship Series.
- Rivers missed a parade celebrating a Yankee World Series victory. He refused to attend because the team would not pay his way there.
- He spent considerable time at racetracks. Given his need for money, we can assume he picked winners as often as he hit Cincinnati's pitching in the 1976 Series.

APRIL 15, 1976

Remodeled Yankee Stadium opened. Rudy May walked the first Minnesota batter on four pitches. Dan Ford hit May's next pitch for a home run. There was cause for hope.

Born April 15, 1947
Integrated baseball in the twentieth century

Jackie Robinson played for the Dodgers against the Braves. Later that season, Larry Doby joined the Indians. He helped them become the team that won the 1948 American League pennant.

Yankees who had trouble with their taxes:

- Billy Martin constantly had tax liens attached to his salary.
- Darryl Strawberry was convicted of tax evasion. He remains indebted to the IRS.
- Many players, who earned huge salaries, protested President Clinton's tax reform package. This package cost a player making a million dollars a year the proceeds from one autograph show. This presumes that the player, unlike Strawberry, included these proceeds in his income for tax purposes.

APRIL 16, 1978

Several Yankee players appeared selfish when they skipped a charity luncheon. When they fined the players for not attending, the Yankees themselves looked heavy-handed.

Born April 16, 1892
Dutch Leonard

Boston sold this pitcher to the Yankees. Showing good judgment, Leonard refused to report. He wound up in Detroit.

A later Dutch Leonard, no relation, beat the Yankees on Lou Gehrig Day. That day, he must have felt like "the second luckiest man, on the face of the earth."

Some Yankees who have been banned from baseball for life:

- The first Dutch Leonard admitted throwing a game.
- Ray Fisher (with the Yankees 1910-1917) agreed to become a college baseball coach, while under contract to the Reds.
- Hal Chase (1905-1913) was banned for the reasons noted earlier. (See February 13.)
- Benny Kauff (1912) was kicked out after being charged with auto theft.
- Joe Gedeon (1916-1917), Lee Magee (1916-1917), and Cozy Dolan (1911-1912) were involved in trying to fix games.
- Steinbrenner (1973- when will it end?) received a lifetime ban for paying an unsavory character for information on Yankee star Dave Winfield. Unfortunately, he was reinstated.

APRIL 17, 1935

Babe Ruth played his first game with the Boston Braves. He hit a home run against baseball's best pitcher, Carl Hubbell. His former team, the Yankees, who thought Ruth could not help them anymore, lost.

Some Yankees who made history's lousiest teams worse:

- Ruth had almost twice as many strikeouts as hits for the 1935 Braves. Boston had the worst winning percentage, .248, in National League history.
- Marv Throneberry was the symbol of the 1962 Mets, losers of 120 games.
- Charlie Hemphill helped the 1899 Cleveland Spiders compile baseball's worst-ever record, 20-134. He had the worst fielding average in the league.
- Jimmy Walsh played for the worst American League team ever, the 36-117 A's of 1916. The good news is that his batting average improved by forty-two points over what he hit for the Yankees in 1914. The bad news is that he hit .233 in 1916. This was the worst of any American League outfielder.

Born April 17, 1913
The Yankee era at the Polo Grounds

This era began in an appropriate way. Washington beat the New York Giants' new tenants 9-3.

APRIL 18, 1977

Toronto beat the Yankees 5-1. This win was one of only fifty-four for the Blue Jays in their initial season. Despite having the biggest payroll in baseball, the Yankees were beginning the season with eight losses in ten games.

Some contributors to the Blue Jays' 1984-1993 streak, when they finished ahead of the Yankees nine times in ten years:

- Dave Stieb was Toronto's ace pitcher. His best game might have been in 1989. He retired the first twenty-six Yankees and wound up with a two-hitter.
- Tom Henke had twenty or more saves seven times.
- Jimmy Key won ten or more games in seven consecutive seasons.
- George Bell hit 202 home runs.
- Cito Gaston was Toronto's batting instructor and, later, its manager.

Born April 18, 1959
Dennis Rasmussen

Toronto manager Bobby Cox called this Yankee pitcher "she." Rasmussen had not become Denise Rasmussen; he had displeased Cox by throwing at Toronto batters.

APRIL 19, 1979

Relief pitcher Goose Gossage broke his thumb in a fight with reserve catcher Cliff Johnson. Gossage, perhaps the Yankees' most indispensable player, would miss several weeks of the season.

Relief pitching problems arising soon after this fight:

- Seattle beat the Yankees by hitting three home runs off relief pitcher Dick Tidrow.
- In another game against Seattle, relievers Paul Mirabella and Ron Davis were ineffective. Enter Tidrow. Exit ball game, as Tidrow gave up the game-winning hit.
- Selflessly, Ron Guidry, the best pitcher in baseball, offered to go to the bullpen. Stupidly, the Yankees accepted. Guidry would miss two starts.

Born April 19, 1918
Whitey Kurowski

Kurowski's two-run home run gave St. Louis a 4-2 win in the final game of the 1942 World Series. His hit came in the top of the ninth inning off Yankee pitcher Red Ruffing.

In this Series, Ruffing allowed six runs in two different ninth innings. His ERA in this most important inning was 32.40.

APRIL 20, 1912

Boston beat the Yankees in the first major-league game ever played at Fenway Park. Two Red Sox hits, an error, and a passed ball led to the winning run.

Fenway Park is famous for its left field wall. Thirty-seven feet high, the "Green Monster" is barely three hundred feet from home plate. For most of the period from 1939 to 1996, Ted Williams, Carl Yastrzemski, Jim Rice, and Mike Greenwell played in front of this wall. (Greenwell, the worst of the four, has a .303 lifetime batting average.)

When he was heavyweight champion, Joe Louis fought frequently. Often his opponents were fighters with considerably less talent than Louis had. Writers called this practice the Bum of the Month Tour. Which brings us to the Yankee left fielders since 1939.

Born April 20, 1961
Don Mattingly

Mattingly played in 1,785 games for the Yankees. This is the most for any Yankee without appearing in the World Series or the League Championship Series.

Most at bats by a Yankee in a season without a triple:

- 640, Mattingly, 1992
- 599, Mattingly, 1988
- 595, Tino Martinez, 1996
- 590, Horace Clarke, 1973
- 588, Clarke, 1967
- 587, Mattingly, 1991

APRIL 21, 1981

Steinbrenner ordered fifty thousand copies of the Yankees' yearbook to be pulled from sale. He did not like his picture. Did he really think there could be an attractive picture of himself?

Born April 21, 1966
Chris Donnels

Donnels was the fourth consecutive pinch hitter to hit safely in a 1995 game against the Yankees. This hit permitted Boston's Donnels, Scott Hatteberg, Lee Tinsley, and Carlos Rodriguez to establish a major-league record.

Yankee hating by the numbers, part nine:

- **32.** Consecutive innings the Yankees went without scoring in May 1991.
- **33.** Average IQ of the five characters who have Y-A-N-K-S written on their chests in a 1998 adidas commercial. Let us consider these characters. Five of them pile into the backseat of a taxi. They have left their shirts at home. They are rooting for the Yankees. What could possibly make one think they are less than bright?
- **34.** Seasons since a Yankee pitcher led the American League in strikeouts.
- **35.** Lou Gehrig's salary, in thousands of dollars, for 1939, his final season as a Yankee. This was a four-thousand-dollar cut from the prior year. Thanks for the seventeen-year career, Lou.

STEINBRENNER'S PRIORITIES (April 21)

APRIL 22, 1903

In their first game, the Yankees lost 3-1 to the Senators. Washington would win only eighty more games over the next *two* seasons.

The five-thousandth Yankee loss:

- This loss occurred in August 1978.
- California won 6-3, leaving the Yankees seven games behind the Red Sox.
- Don Aase was the winning pitcher, Ed Figueroa the loser.
- California's Don Baylor had a home run and two RBI.
- No member of the 1903 Yankees or the 1903 Senators was still alive in 1978. Washington's Lew Drill, the last survivor of the Yankees' first game, had died in 1969. Drill would have played in, seen, or heard about more than four thousand Yankee losses.

Born April 22, 1881
Neal Ball

Ball had one of the worst seasons ever by a shortstop. He committed eighty errors and had a fielding average of .898 for the 1908 Yankees. With an average shortstop, the Yankees might have lost only ninety-seven or ninety-eight games that season.

APRIL 23, 1919

Boston beat the Yankees 10-0. While this was embarrassing, consider the Red Sox 13-0 win in 1941. Joe DiMaggio made three errors in that Memorial Day classic.

Born April 23, 1921
Warren Spahn

Spahn won more games than any other left-handed pitcher. His 363 wins are more than the combined victories by Yankee left-handers Lefty Gomez and Ron Guidry. Referring to his stints with the Boston Braves in 1942, and with the New York Mets in 1965, Spahn said, "I played for (longtime Yankee manager) Casey Stengel before and after he was a genius."

Warren Spahn and other National League pitchers against the 1961 Yankees in that year's All-Star games:

- There were two games in 1961. No Yankee had an extra-base hit in either game.
- Mickey Mantle, Roger Maris, Tony Kubek, and Elston Howard combined for one hit in seventeen at bats.
- In the first of the two games, Spahn struck out Mantle and Maris. He got Kubek and Whitey Ford to ground out.

APRIL 24, 1960

Baltimore's Albie Pearson and Billy Klaus hit grand slam home runs against the Yankees. These were the only home runs either player hit that season. In their major-league careers, Pearson and Klaus, who weighed a combined 305 pounds, hit sixty-eight home runs between them.

Yankee designated hitter Steve Balboni almost met the combined Pearson-Klaus weight total. He had only forty-one home runs in five seasons in New York. His nickname was "Bye-Bye," which was what the Yankees told him, twice.

Born April 24, 1967
Omar Vizquel

Cleveland shortstop Vizquel hit .500, as the Indians beat the Yankees in the 1997 Division Series.

Highlights of the 1997 Division Series:

- Manny Ramirez doubled to drive in two runs in the fifth game. This hit and a superb defensive play by Jim Thome won the game, and the Series, for the Indians.
- Cleveland rallied to win the fourth game. They tied the score, in the eighth inning, on Sandy Alomar, Jr.'s home run. Vizquel's ninth-inning single won the game for the Indians.
- Matt Williams hit a two-run home run. This provided the winning margin in the second game.
- Jaret Wright won two games.

135

APRIL 25, 1912

Philadelphia beat the Yankees 5-4. This was the Yankees' eighth loss in nine games. New York continued to play poorly, allowing the winning run on two singles, a wild pitch, and a throwing error.

Fewest road wins by the Yankees in a full season:

- nineteen in 1912
- twenty-one in 1908
- twenty-three in 1918
- twenty-seven in 1925
- twenty-nine in 1967

(New York's 1908 and 1912 teams did not do much better at home. Unfortunately for these teams, the American League did not schedule games at neutral sites.)

Died April 25, 1970
Gene Steinbrenner

He is the only likeable Steinbrenner to be involved in baseball. Gene's career comprised three games for the 1912 Phillies. In the hereafter, he is likely nicknamed "No Relation."

APRIL 26, 1964

By winning their sixth straight NBA title, the Boston Celtics broke the record for consecutive championships. This record had belonged to the Yankees and the Montreal Canadiens. Boston eventually won eight championships in a row, and eleven in thirteen years. These feats are unmatched in North American team sports.

Teams that have equaled or exceeded the Yankees' five consecutive championships in North American team sports:

- Boston Celtics had eight straight NBA championships, 1959-1966.
- UCLA Bruins took seven NCAA basketball championships in a row, 1967-1973.
- Edmonton Eskimos won Canadian Football League titles in five consecutive years, 1978-1982.
- Montreal Canadiens earned five straight Stanley Cups, 1956-1960.

(Alumni will chastise me for ignoring Obscure State's ten consecutive championships in a sport like archery. I apologize for overlooking this, and similar achievements, which matter to about five people.)

Born April 26, 1917
Virgil Trucks

Tiger pitcher Trucks won five games in 1952. One of these wins was a no-hitter against the Yankees.

Early in the game, the official scorer had awarded the Yankees a hit, on a play Johnny Pesky mishandled. A few innings later, after checking with Pesky, the scorer changed this play to an error.

This would not happen today. If it did, a Yankee player would have his agent threaten to sue the scorer. Such a change might cost the player a bonus for having at least fifty hits in a season.

APRIL 27, 1982

Reggie Jackson returned to Yankee Stadium with his new team, the California Angels. He hit a home run off Ron Guidry, in a 3-1 Angel win. Angry with the Yankee owner for losing Jackson, the crowd chanted "Steinbrenner sucks!"

Reactions to the Yankee Stadium chant:

- "It was about the only fun I had all night." (Guidry)
- "Some people have a way of saying the right thing at the right time." (Jackson)

Born April 27, 1894
Bob Williams

Williams hit .164 in forty-six games with the Yankees. He was out of baseball before he turned twenty. He did not even make the Federal League.

Williams might have been the inspiration for something former Yankee manager Casey Stengel said. Stengel's Mets had a twenty-year-old catcher, Greg Goossen. Ever one to encourage his players, Stengel pointed out that in ten years, Goossen had an excellent chance to be thirty.

APRIL 28, 1966

There were many questions in New York's lunchrooms. Did you hear the Yankees lost last night? Why can't the Yankees beat the Senators, a 2-9 team? Do you realize the Yankees are in last place? Why was Roger Maris benched in favor of Lu Clinton? Did you hear there were more ushers than fans at Yankee Stadium last night? Are the Yankees really 2-10? How do you get to Shea Stadium?

Died April 28, 1986
Pat Seerey

Seerey had three home runs and a triple, as Cleveland beat the Yankees 16-4, in 1945.

Seerey hit .224 in his career. He had 20 percent more strikeouts than hits. True, Seerey is one of a limited number of players to hit four home runs in a game. And Dan Quayle is one of a limited number of politicians to become vice president.

Some Yankees who have served time in prison:

- Pedro Ramos (born on this date in 1935) violated probation on drug charges.
- Pascual Perez was convicted on drug charges.
- Luis Polonia had sex with a minor.
- Joe Pepitone committed drug and weapons offenses.
- Ken Clay was convicted of grand larceny.

APRIL 29, 1929

Philadelphia beat the Yankees 10-1, in an early-season meeting between the previous season's best teams. This win was no fluke. Philadelphia would finish eighteen games ahead of the Yankees in 1929.

Born April 29, 1934
Luis Aparicio

Aparicio scored the winning run, as the White Sox took over first place in 1960. This ruined Casey Stengel's seventieth birthday.

Things got worse for the Yankee manager. Within three months of his birthday, Stengel's team scored fifty-five runs, but lost the World Series. A few days after this defeat, the Yankees fired Stengel.

Yankee hating by the numbers, part ten:

- **36.** Total wins for the Yankees by all members of the three-hundred-win club. As Yankees, Phil Niekro won thirty-two games, Gaylord Perry won four.
- **37.** Strikeouts by Yankee hitters in the four-game 1963 World Series
- **38.** Points by which Yankee third baseman Home Run Baker, who sat out the 1920 season for personal reasons, outhit his replacement the following year. Baker hit .294 in 1921. Aaron Ward had hit .256 in 1920.
- **39.** Home runs St. Louis's Ken Williams hit, as he beat Babe Ruth for the 1922 home run title. Williams also won the American League RBI title that year. He drove in fifty-six more runs than Ruth did.

APRIL 30, 1946

Cleveland's Bob Feller pitched a no-hitter at Yankee Stadium. Feller struck out eleven Yankees. It must have been an especially happy day for Feller, who once said, "I would rather beat the New York Yankees regularly than pitch a no-hit game."

Other no-hitters against the Yankees:

- Cy Young, Boston, June 30, 1908
- George Foster, Boston, June 21, 1916
- Ray Caldwell, Cleveland, September 10, 1919
- Virgil Trucks, Detroit, August 25, 1952
- Hoyt Wilhelm, Baltimore, September 2, 1958

Died April 30, 1977
Elam Vangilder

Vangilder, of the St. Louis Browns, pitched 203 innings in 1927. This was the most that season, by an American League pitcher (other than Yankee pitchers), without giving up a home run to Babe Ruth.

St. Louis no longer had Ruth's nemesis, Hub Pruett, on its pitching staff. In Pruett's place, they had pitchers like Milt Gaston. Hardly a great pitcher, Gaston allowed four of Ruth's record-setting sixty home runs in 1927.

Gaston was twice as good as Ruth was in an important skill, longevity. He lived to be one hundred years old; Ruth died at fifty-three.

141

MAY 1, 1975

Hank Aaron broke Babe Ruth's record for RBI in a career. Earlier that week, the Brewers' designated hitter had tied the record at Yankee Stadium. Aaron finished his career with eighty-five more RBI than Ruth had.

Some less than well-known American Leaguers who drove in more than 100 runs in a season between 1962 and 1974. (Only one Yankee achieved this during that period.):

- Dick Stuart, Red Sox
- Norm Sieburn, Athletics
- Floyd Robinson, White Sox
- Ken Harrelson, Red Sox

Died May 1, 1992
Celerino Sanchez

Sanchez represents the descent of the Yankee infield from the team's glory years. In 1966, the Yankees had Clete Boyer, an All-Star, playing third base. After they traded Boyer, the Yankees tried Charley Smith, Bobby Cox, Jerry Kenney, and Rich McKinney. They reached bottom when they gave the position to Sanchez. In 1972, Sanchez played in seventy-one games. He hit .248, with no home runs and twenty-two RBI.

This decline is like President Clinton's diminishing standards in women. In the 1970's, he married an accomplished woman, Hillary Rodham. At one time, Clinton was rumored to have had a liaison with a former Miss Arkansas. More recently, his only requirements seem to be that his partners be female and breathing.

MAY 2, 1923

Yankee shortstop Everett Scott played his one-thousandth consecutive game. Perhaps he was tired. New York lost 3-0 to the Senators.

What some prominent Yankees achieved before becoming bad guys:

- Scott played for the Red Sox during most of his consecutive-games-played streak.
- As a Red Sox pitcher, Babe Ruth had a record of 17-5 against the Yankees.
- Casey Stengel hit two game-winning home runs against the Yankees in the 1923 World Series.
- Waite Hoyt retired thirty-four consecutive Yankee hitters, during an extra-inning game in 1919.
- Ed Barrow managed the Red Sox when they won the 1918 World Series.

Born May 2, 1941
Clay Carroll

Frequently, achievements by Yankee players are overpublicized, while superior feats by non-Yankees are ignored.

Consider Yankee reliever Sparky Lyle. In 1972, he made the cover of *Sports Illustrated.* This was part of the significant publicity he received for his thirty-five saves with a fourth-place team. Meanwhile Carroll saved thirty-seven games for Cincinnati, who won the National League pennant. This earned Carroll mention in the agate-typed sections of some sports publications.

MAY 3, 1952

In one of their worst deals, the Yankees traded Jackie Jensen for Irv Noren. In 1958, Jensen would be named the Most Valuable Player in the American League. Noren would have finished third if there had been an award for the best American League outfielder of the 1950's, whose last name began with *N*.

This would not have been a great achievement. Bob Nelson would have finished fourth. He hit .205 in seventy-nine major-league games. (Bob Nieman and Ron Northey were the best of this limited group.)

Born May 3, 1945
Davey Lopes

Lopes had two home runs and five RBI in the first game of the 1978 World Series. His Dodgers beat the Yankees 11-5.

Great moments in fielding by a Yankee:

- On this date in 1990, the aptly-named Mike Blowers committed four errors, while playing third base.
- In a 1990 game, outfielders Jim Leyritz and Jesse Barfield misplayed fly balls, allowing four runs to score. New York's Andy Hawkins, who did not allow a hit, was the losing pitcher.
- Third baseman Rich McKinney had four errors in a 1972 game.
- Tommy John, a pitcher, committed three errors on one play, in 1987.
- Norm Sieburn lost two fly balls in the sun during the 1958 World Series.

MAY 4, 1912

Aided by ten runs in an inning, the Yankees scored fifteen in the game. They still needed a field goal, as Philadelphia won 18-15.

Died May 4, 1963
Dickie Kerr

White Sox pitcher Kerr had a 14-4 record against the Yankees. From another perspective, the Yankees lost fourteen times to a pitcher who won fifty-three major-league games.

As a minor-league manager, Kerr made a hitter out of a sore-armed pitcher named Stan Musial. "Stan the Man" broke many of Babe Ruth's records. (See November 21.)

The best career won-lost percentages against the Yankees:

- .777, Kerr (14-4 record)
- .773, Babe Ruth (17-5)
- .765, Ted Higuera (13-4)
- .706, Bill Lee (12-5)
- .696, Bernie Boland (16-7)
- .683, Frank Lary (28-13)

(Minimum of ten victories)

MAY 5, 1904

After losing their first thirteen games of the season, the Washington Senators finally found a team they could beat. They defeated the Yankees 9-4. Washington would lose 113 games in 1904.

What this loss meant:

- New York lost the 1904 pennant by a one and one-half games.
- When a team loses the pennant by that slim a margin, it has to think of games it should have won. This clearly would have been one of them.

Born May 5, 1884
Chief Bender

The Yankees have had trouble with doctors*, lawyers,** and Indian chiefs. Bender, a Chippewa, won 212 games, many of them for five pennant-winning Philadelphia teams.

* Mike Marshall, Ph.D., won ten games and had thirty-two saves for the 1979 Twins. Hub Pruett, the pitcher who dominated Babe Ruth, later became a physician.
** Tony LaRussa, an attorney, was the manager of the 1989 Oakland A's. That year, the A's won all twelve of their games with the Yankees.

MAY 6, 1966

After losing to the California Angels, the Yankees had a 4-16 record. They fired manager Johnny Keane.

Ralph Houk became the manager of this last-place team. For six months, Houk worked his managerial magic. When the season ended, the Yankees were still in last place.

It had become obvious that the team had been allowed to decline. One of those responsible was the team's general manager, a fellow named Ralph Houk.

Born May 6, 1931
Willie Mays

Mays's presence in New York, with the Giants and the Mets, took attention and fans away from the Yankees. Mays outperformed Mickey Mantle, the Yankees' top player of Mays's era. Mays had a higher career batting average. He hit more home runs, stole more bases, and won twelve Gold Gloves.

American League outfielders who won more Gold Gloves than Mickey Mantle did, 1957-1966:

- Al Kaline, of the Detroit Tigers, won nine.
- Chicago's Jim Landis earned five.
- Chicago's Minnie Minoso, Boston's Carl Yastrzemski, and Cleveland's Jimmy Piersall won two.

(1957-1966 is the period beginning when Gold Gloves were first awarded, and ending when Mantle became a first baseman. Mantle won one Gold Glove during this period.)

MAYS AND MANTLE (May 6)

MAY 7, 1979

The Seattle Mariners, who would lose ninety-five games in 1979, won 12-4 at Yankee Stadium.

The Yankees' first trip to Seattle to play the Mariners:

- New York lost both these 1977 games. This proved the Yankees could lose indoors, as well as outdoors.
- Yankee pitcher Catfish Hunter gave up seven runs in two and one-third innings.
- Bill Laxton (3-10 lifetime) and the almost-as-immortal Tommy Moore (2-4 lifetime) were the winning pitchers for Seattle.

Born May 7, 1943
Steve Whitaker

Whitaker made a major contribution to the Yankees' team-record 1,043 strikeouts in 1967. He struck out eighty-nine times in 441 at bats.

Whitaker did not improve in 1968. He hit .117. Two years later, he had a .111 batting average for the San Francisco Giants. As Whitaker had proved he could not hit on either coast, his major-league career was over.

MAY 8, 1981

Seattle beat the Yankees on Tom Paciorek's solo home run in the ninth inning. Paciorek hit a more dramatic ninth-inning home run the next night. It came with two men on base and gave the Mariners a 6-5 win.

Born May 8, 1937
Mike Cuellar

Cuellar led Oriole pitchers in wins in 1969 and 1970. Baltimore won 217 games in those years, breaking the Yankees' record for most wins in consecutive seasons.

Yankee hating from A to Z, part three:

- **I.** Iraq. Comedian Jay Leno called Saddam Hussein the "Steinbrenner of Iraq."
- **J.** Doc Johnston. Cleveland's first baseman went five-for-five and stole home in September 1920 game. His performance helped the Indians finish three games ahead of the Yankees.
- **K.** Billy Knickerbocker. He had the worst fielding average by an American League second baseman in 1942. New York's Joe Gordon, who was named Most Valuable Player (!), had the second-worst.
- **L.** Herman Long. This shortstop had the first multiple-error game in Yankee history. In his twenty-two games with the Yankees, Herman Long fielded like Herman Munster. Unfortunately, he could not hit like the television character. Long had a .188 average for the 1903 Yankees.
- **M.** Dan Meyer. His three-run home run helped Seattle sweep the Yankees in their first-ever series at the Kingdome.

MAY 9, 1998

Minnesota's Matt Lawton hit a grand slam, as the Twins won 8-1. This ended a ridiculously long Yankee winning streak.

Lawton's brother, Marcus, also hurt the Yankees. Marcus played for New York in 1989. He thought he was an outfielder. After Lawton mishandled two of eleven chances, the Yankees thought he would have a better future as a designated hitter. After he hit .214, they realized baseball would have a better future without Marcus Lawton.

Born May 9, 1960
Tony Gwynn

In 1998, Bernie Williams became only the ninth Yankee to lead the American League in batting. Gwynn, the San Diego outfielder, has led the National League eight times.

Former Yankee Reggie Jackson's performance in the 1983 American League batting race:

- He hit .194, a mere 167 points behind the leader, Boston's Wade Boggs.
- Only Oakland's Dan Meyer and Minnesota's Tim Laudner had lower averages.
- Jackson had almost twice as many strikeouts as hits.
- He did hit fourteen home runs. Only forty-six American Leaguers hit more.

151

MAY 10, 1946

Boston won its fifteenth in a row, 5-4 over the Yankees. This streak effectively ended the American League pennant race.

Died May 10, 1992
Tom Seats

Seats won only two games in his American League career, but these wins were important. They came in 1940, when Seats's Tigers won the pennant by two games over the Yankees.

Yankee hating by the numbers, part eleven:

- **40.** Home runs New York's Ralph Terry allowed in 1962. No Yankee pitcher has allowed more.
- **41.** Jersey number of Tom Seaver, who symbolized the Mets, as they became New York's most popular baseball team.
- **42.** Games the Philadelphia A's had won, with one game remaining in the 1915 season. Win number forty-three, against 109 losses, came in the major-league debut of Elmer Myers. He shut out the Yankees, striking out twelve.
- **43.** Hits Tommy Thompson allowed in thirty-two career innings. He was one-half of the most useless set of brothers to play for the Yankees. His brother, Homer, never batted, but played long enough to make an error. Both were with the last-place 1912 Yankees.

MAY 11, 1940

After their eighth consecutive loss, 9-8 to the Red Sox, the Yankees were in last place. They would remain there until May 26. Yankee haters must have enjoyed reading the standings to Yankee fans. ("Let me see now, are the Yankees in first place? No. How about second place? No....")

The Yankees' worst-ever seasons:

- 50-102; 1912
- 51-103; 1908
- 57- 94; 1913
- 67- 95; 1990
- 71- 91; 1991
- 1973. Some years can not be judged by win-loss records alone. The year started with Steinbrenner's acquisition of the team. Spring training began with the Peterson-Kekich family-swapping scandal. (See March 5.) New York opened the season with two blowout losses in Boston. (See April 7.) They finished the 1973 season by dropping from a first-place tie to seventeen games back, over a nine-week period. Immediately after the Yankees' final game, their manager resigned, Yankee Stadium was closed for renovations, and New York City belonged to the playoff-bound Mets.

Born May 11, 1903
Charlie Gehringer

Detroit's second basemen played against the Yankees, at a Hall of Fame level, for nineteen seasons.

MAY 12, 1967

In the most humiliating home game in their history, the Yankees lost 14-0 to Baltimore. Jim Palmer pitched a one-hitter, allowing only one Yankee to reach base.

Born May 12, 1916
Hank Borowy

Having no need for a pitcher with a 10-5 record, the Yankees sold Borowy to the Cubs, in July 1945. Borowy won eleven games for his new team, leading them into the World Series. Chicago played the Tigers, the Yankees having finished fourth.

In honor of his birthday, some things Yogi Berra said that are more stupid than funny:

- "Steve McQueen must have made this movie before he died."
- "I don't know. They were wearing bags over their heads." (Berra had been asked if the streakers he saw were male or female.)
- "I usually take a two-hour nap from 1:00 to 4:00."
- "Only in America." (Berra had been told that a Jew had been elected Mayor of Dublin.)
- "You mean now?" (Berra had been asked for the time.)

MAY 13, 1969

The Yankees lost to the Seattle Pilots. At least the Pilots did not score seven runs in the first inning, as they had the previous day. Seattle, a first-year team, had won two of its last two games. New York, a sixty-ninth-year team, had won two of its last seventeen.

Born May 13, 1950
Juan Beniquez

Oriole outfielder Beniquez hit six home runs in 1986. Half of these came in one game against the Yankees.

The Yankees were one of eight different American League teams for whom Beniquez played during his career. This number of teams makes it easier for him to forget his term in New York. He likely does not want to remember that injuries and a .254 average limited him to sixty-four games as a Yankee.

Fewest home runs in a season, with three of them coming in a game against the Yankees:

- six, Beniquez, 1986
- eleven, Lee Lacy, 1986
- twelve, Pat Mullin, 1949
- fourteen, Pat Seerey, 1945

MAY 14, 1941

With nine losses in thirteen games, the Yankees were in a slump. Things got worse the next day, when Chicago won 13-1 at Yankee Stadium.

Allowing the 1941 White Sox to score thirteen runs was not easy. Chicago was far from being an offensive machine. The White Sox were last in the American League in runs scored and in batting average. Their leading home run hitter, Joe Kuhel, would hit twelve that season.

This game was not a total loss for the Yankees. Joe DiMaggio extended his hitting streak to one game.

Born May 14, 1881
Ed Walsh

Chicago's Hall of Fame-bound pitcher beat the Yankees nine times in 1908. He was almost as dominant in 1911, beating New York seven times.

Most wins in a season against the Yankees:

- Walsh won nine in 1908.
- Three pitchers— Walsh in 1911, Eddie Cicotte in 1916, and Frank Lary in 1958— won seven.
- Several pitchers, including Tiger teammates Dizzy Trout and Hal Newhouser, have beaten the Yankees six times in a season.
- Numerous pitchers have five wins in a season. Johnny Babich did it in 1940. These wins cost the Yankees the pennant, as New York finished two games out of first place. Babich's team, the Philadelphia A's, won only fifty-four games that season.

MAY 15, 1912

Ty Cobb attacked a particularly obnoxious Yankee fan during a game at New York's Hilltop Park. League President Ban Johnson suspended Cobb, as American League rules protected even Yankee fans. Feeling this special protection and the suspension to be unfair, Cobb's Detroit teammates staged the first strike in major-league history.

Born May 15, 1952
Rick Waits

Pitching for Cleveland, Waits beat the Yankees in the final game of the 1978 regular season. This loss meant the Yankees had to play the Red Sox in a one-game playoff for the division title.

Consequences of the May 15, 1957 brawl at the Copacabana nightclub:

- Yankee players Billy Martin, Hank Bauer, Mickey Mantle, Whitey Ford, Yogi Berra, and Johnny Kucks were fined. They had allegedly attacked a group of hecklers.
- A grand jury was convened to look into the matter.
- Although a judge ultimately threw the case out of court, one of the hecklers sued Bauer for $250,000.
- Having an excuse to get rid of a player he could not stand, Yankee General Manager George Weiss traded Martin to Kansas City.

COBB BEATS UP YANKEE FAN (May 15)

MAY 16, 1976

George Allen, the outstanding NFL coach, emphasized the present. He was willing to trade promising players for useful veterans. Forgetting about the adjective, *useful*, the Yankees traded pitcher Larry Gura for veteran catcher Fran Healy. Gura would win 111 games for his new team, the Royals. He would have an 11-6 career record against the Yankees. Healy would have 188 at bats for the Yankees, before becoming a broadcaster. In this role, he was better than, maybe, Jerry Coleman.

Some stupid things Yankee second baseman-turned-broadcaster Jerry Coleman said:

- "Winfield goes back to the wall. He hits his head on the wall and it rolls off. It's rolling all the way to second base. This is a terrible thing for the Padres."
- "There's a hard shot to LeMaster–and he throws Madlock into the dugout."
- "The first pitch to Tucker Ashford is grounded into left field. No, wait a minute. It's ball one, low and outside."
- "Rich Folkers is throwing up in the bullpen."

Died May 16, 1985
Johnny Broaca

Broaca struck out five consecutive times in a 1934 game. A few years later, he quit the Yankees. Apparently believing that doing nothing was better than being a Yankee, Broaca sat out the 1938 season. Eventually, Cleveland acquired this pitcher for a nominal amount of cash.

MAY 17, 1961

A first-year expansion team, the Washington Senators, won its second consecutive game at Yankee Stadium. Washington would finish last in 1961, forty-seven games out of first place.

Born May 17, 1948
Carlos May

May, a designated hitter for the Yankees, was "Mr. May" by reason of birth; Dave Winfield earned the name. Steinbrenner gave his star player this nickname in a cruel comparison with "Mr. October," Reggie Jackson.

Dave Winfield and postseason play, or why "Mr. May" is reasonably accurate:

- In his twenty-three-year career, Winfield played in the postseason twice.
- In twenty-six postseason games, Winfield hit .208, with two home runs and nine RBI.
- Winfield had one hit, in twenty-two at bats, in the 1981 World Series.

MAY 18, 1959

With no game scheduled, the Yankees had time to read the newspaper. They were able to check the standings and see themselves in seventh place. Then they could read about the previous day's 10-0 loss to the Kansas City A's.

Died May 18, 1995
Jack Kramer

This Red Sox pitcher beat the Yankees twice during the last two weeks of the 1948 season. His second win eliminated New York from contention. Four years earlier, Kramer pitched for the American League champions, the St. Louis Browns. His victory, on the second-last day of the season, eliminated the Yankees from that season's pennant race.

Some comments on Brooks Robinson (born on this date in 1937) and the Baltimore Orioles:

- Robinson's Orioles finished ahead of the Yankees every season between 1965 and 1975.
- During this period, Baltimore finished an average of thirteen games ahead of the Yankees.
- Comparing these two teams is like comparing the acting talents of Katharine Hepburn with those of Pia Zadora. You do not need to make detailed arguments.
- Robinson, a third baseman, won eleven Gold Gloves during this eleven-year period. All Yankee players combined won nine.

MAY 19, 1991

Steve Sax, who had been playing second base, became the Yankees' third baseman.

Sax's former teammate, and fellow poor fielder, Pedro Guerrero said he prayed a lot. Guerrero first prayed that the other team would not hit the ball to him. He then prayed they would not hit it to Steve Sax.

The Yankees' worst single-season fielding averages, by position:

- catcher, Ed Sweeney, .955; 1912
- first base, Hal Chase, .973; 1907
- second base, Harry Niles, .928; 1908
- third base, Harold Paddock, .894; 1912
- shortstop, Neal Ball, .898; 1908
- outfield, Patsy Dougherty, .898; 1905
- outfield, Guy Zinn, .893; 1912
- outfield, Lefty Davis, .906; 1903

Born May 19, 1954
Rick Cerone

As a Yankee, this catcher (a) hit into a triple play, (b) twice pitched in blowout losses and, most importantly, (c) told Steinbrenner to go screw himself.

MAY 20, 1922

Babe Ruth returned from his six-week suspension. (See October 16 for details.) Yankee fans booed Ruth, as he struck out twice, popped out, and grounded out.

The umpires were not popular either. They overruled the final out, nullifying a Yankee victory. Given a second chance, St. Louis scored six runs to win the game.

Born May 20, 1921
Hal Newhouser

Newhouser is one of several pitchers to defeat the Yankees six times in a season. He did this while winning consecutive Most Valuable Player awards, in 1944 and 1945.

Some Yankee opponents who were exempt from military service in World War II:

- Newhouser suffered from a heart problem.
- Detroit slugger Rudy York had a knee injury.
- Tiger pitcher Dizzy Trout's poor eyesight kept him out of the military. He could see well enough to beat the Yankees six times in one season.
- Cleveland shortstop Lou Boudreau was exempt because of an arthritic ankle.
- Philadelphia third baseman George Kell had bad knees.
- Unlike Boudreau, Newhouser, and Kell, Pete Gray will never make the Hall of Fame. Gray, who had one arm, played for the Browns in 1945. He had his moments, such as a doubleheader against the Yankees. Gray drove in two runs in the first game and scored the winning run in the second game.

MAY 21, 1971

Gomer Hodge's single in the bottom of the ninth inning beat the Yankees. Cleveland's pinch hitter had a brilliant few weeks in early 1971, but still had only nine RBI in his major-league career. In other words, he was slightly more productive than Gomer Pyle.

As a team, the Yankees were pitching like Barney Fife and hitting like Aunt Bee. The Mayberry All-Stars, I mean the New York Yankees, had lost nine of their previous eleven games.

Born May 21, 1936
Barry Latman

Latman pitched 177 innings in 1961. This was the most by a Yankee opponent without giving up a home run to Mickey Mantle or Roger Maris. These Yankee teammates hit a combined 115 home runs that season.

Safe at Home:

- This is the title of a forgettable movie featuring Mantle and Maris. Classic film festivals invariably forget to feature this movie.
- Detroit's Earl Torgeson stole home to defeat the Yankees, in a 1955 game.
- Zeke Bonura stole home in the fifteenth inning, as his White Sox beat the Yankees, in 1935.

MAY 22, 1913

In a game between the league's two worst teams, the Yankees lost to the Browns. Despite having fifteen base runners, the Yankees were unable to score a run.

In 1913, the Yankees were seventh, in the eight-team American League, in hitting. They were seventh in pitching, seventh in fielding, and seventh in the standings. Like a politician who is frequently wrong, the 1913 Yankees could take comfort in being consistent.

Died May 22, 1956
Harry Howell

Howell lost twenty-one games, in 1901, for the Yankees' predecessors, the Baltimore Orioles. (In 1903, Howell and the Orioles became the New York Yankees.)

Pitchers who lost twenty or more games in a season for the Yankees:

- Al Orth lost twenty-one, in 1907.
- Joe Lake had twenty-two losses, in 1908. His teammate, Jack Chesbro, lost twenty.
- In 1912, Russ Ford suffered twenty-one losses.
- Sam Jones dropped twenty-one games for the 1925 Yankees. Jones had a 4.63 ERA. He followed this with an even-higher ERA in 1926. This convinced the Yankees the thirty-four-year-old Jones was through. They traded him for Joe Giard and Cedric Montgomery Durst. Giard played one season for the Yankees, compiling an ERA of 8.00. Durst's name suggested he was a member of the British aristocracy; his play, as a Yankee, virtually confirmed it.
- Mel Stottlemyre had twenty losses, in 1966.

MAY 23, 1977

Sport magazine hit the newsstands. In this month's issue, Reggie Jackson took several verbal shots at Thurman Munson, the Yankee captain. Maybe Reggie had a point; Munson was picked off base in the eighth inning, as the Yankees lost.

Some things Reggie Jackson told *Sport* magazine:

- Jackson called himself the "straw that stirs the drink."
- Munson, according to Jackson, could only "stir the drink" badly.
- Jackson saw himself as a "tremendous intellect," while Munson was "jealous and nervous and resentful." (Someone suggested to Munson that Jackson might have been quoted out of context. Munson replied, "for four pages?")

Born May 23, 1948
Reggie Cleveland

Dave Winfield complained of his troubles being accepted by the Yankees, saying, "The only chance you have around here is to be dead, retired, or Reggie." Cleveland, who pitched for thirteen seasons, but never for the Yankees, meets two of these requirements.

MAY 24, 1946

Yankee manager Joe McCarthy resigned, citing health reasons. Actually, he was sick of the team's new part-owner, Larry MacPhail. The wording of McCarthy's letter of resignation was telling. McCarthy said, "My doctor advises that my health would be seriously jeopardized if I continued. This is the sole reason for my decision which, as you know, is entirely voluntary on my part."

Bill Dickey, who had been a Hall of Fame catcher for the Yankees, replaced McCarthy. Later that season, Dickey would resign. His replacement was Johnny Neun, who had been, well, Johnny Neun.

What happened to the other Yankee managers who are in the Hall of Fame:

- Casey Stengel was fired.
- Miller Huggins died.
- Clark Griffith resigned.
- Bob Lemon and Yogi Berra, who made the Hall of Fame as players, were each fired twice.

Born May 24, 1941
Bob Dylan

In 1990, *Spy* magazine called Dylan, Henry Kissinger, Mel Brooks, and the New York Yankees "coasters; high profile, low productivity."

Brooks's wife, actress Anne Bancroft, played Mrs. Robinson in *The Graduate*. In a song from this movie, Paul Simon expressed a nation's longing for heroes like Joe DiMaggio. By 1990, the Yankees were so bad that their fans had a longing for players like Joe DeMaestri. (DeMaestri was a utility infielder for the Yankees in 1960 and 1961.)

MAY 25, 1982

Following Steinbrenner's failure to make his promised contributions, the David M. Winfield Foundation sued the Yankee owner.

Other moments in Steinbrenner's relationship with his star player:

- Steinbrenner paid Howard Spira forty thousand dollars. He wanted incriminating information on Winfield and his charitable foundation. While under investigation for these payments, Steinbrenner suggested the investigators should see if Winfield bet on baseball.
- In what was not an oversight, the Yankees failed to submit Winfield's name for inclusion on the All-Star ballot.
- In 1987, Winfield played all thirteen innings of the All-Star game. Yankee press packages highlighted his subsequent slump. Notes on Winfield's troubles began with "Since playing thirteen innings in the All-Star game, Winfield has..."
- Steinbrenner gave Winfield the nickname "Mr. May."

Born May 25, 1918
Johnny Beazley

Cardinal pitcher Beazley won two games, including the final one, against the Yankees in the five-game 1942 World Series.

MAY 26, 1907

Ed Walsh did not allow a hit, as the White Sox beat the Yankees in a five-inning game.

Walsh won a total of sixty-four games in 1907 and 1908. During this period, the Yankees had 181 losses. Given this mismatch, one might think the umpire invoked a mercy rule. Actually, rain stopped the game.

Greatest dominance by the American League leader in wins over the Yankee leader:

- Walter Johnson won thirty-six games, in 1913. Ray Fisher won eleven for the Yankees.
- Walsh had forty wins, in 1908, while Jack Chesbro had fourteen.
- In 1912, Joe Wood won thirty-four games. Russ Ford won thirteen.
- In 1990, Bob Welch had twenty-seven wins. Lee Guetterman had eleven.

(Dominance is expressed in terms of percentage. For example, Johnson's thirty-six wins is 327% of Fisher's eleven.)

Born May 26, 1964
Willie Fraser

Fraser was the winning pitcher, as the California Angels beat the Yankees 15-6. New York wasted five home runs in this 1988 game.

MAY 27, 1991

This date's edition of *Sports Illustrated* had the cover story, "Whatever Happened to the Yankees?"

Actor Dennis Hopper had the answer in an early-1990's shoe commercial, "bad things, man." For ten years, the Yankees had traded prospects for veterans who had a reputation, but little else. Steinbrenner had changed managers as frequently as Italy changed its governments. There was an atmosphere of an impossible owner, an overly critical media and vicious fans. Under these conditions, it was almost impossible to attract, or retain, quality players.

Some other *Sports Illustrated* covers for Yankee haters:

- August 19, 1996: *"The Team that Time Forgot."* On this cover, *SI* says, "The 1929 Philadelphia A's, not the '27 Yankees, may have been the greatest baseball club ever assembled."
- April 16, 1984: "Graig and the Goose: Two Ex-Yankees Find Sanity and Sanctuary in San Diego."
- July 31, 1978: *"Double, Double, Toil and Trouble."* This cover story dealt with Billy Martin's demise as Yankee manager.
- June 21, 1965: *"New York Yankees: End of an Era"*

Born May 27, 1893
Frank Snyder

Snyder was the Giants' leading hitter in their win over the Yankees in the 1921 World Series. He hit .364.

MAY 28, 1946

Washington won the first night game played at Yankee Stadium. The Senators did not fear the dark; they were facing a pitcher named "Cuddles" Marshall.

Winning pitcher Dutch Leonard had an easier time seeing than Tommy Henrich, Charlie Keller, and Joe Gordon did. Leonard drove in the winning run, while the Yankee trio had no hits in ten at bats.

During World War II, President Roosevelt had asked major-league teams to schedule more night games for the benefit of war workers. Unlike many other teams, the Yankees did not do so. General Manager Ed Barrow was too busy signing Yankee players for low salaries. He had no time for trivial matters like a request by the President of the United States.

Some other Yankee "fans come first" gestures:

- They prohibited radio broadcasts of any games during the 1930's.
- New York was among the last teams to sell merchandise like Yankee caps.
- Steinbrenner has threatened to move to New Jersey unless the Yankees get a new stadium. It seems the luxury boxes in Yankee Stadium are inadequate.

Born May 28, 1888
Jim Thorpe

Thorpe, not Babe Ruth, was voted the greatest athlete of the first half of the twentieth century. Thorpe won Olympic gold medals and was a professional baseball and football player.

MAY 29, 1944

In wartime baseball, the traditionally bad St. Louis Browns were good, as shown by their 11-3 win over the Yankees. One thousand, two hundred and six fans attended the game. Few St. Louis fans wanted to see the 1944 Yankees.

Some regulars with the 1944 Yankees:

- third baseman Don Savage
- shortstop Mike Milosovich
- outfielders Bud Methany and Hersh Martin
- catcher Mike Garbark
- pitcher Atley Donald

(Only Methany played after 1945, the last wartime season. He had three at bats in 1946.)

Died May 29, 1978
Carl Reynolds

Reynolds, an outfielder for the 1932 Senators, got into a fight with Bill Dickey. As a result of this fight, the Yankee catcher was suspended for thirty days.

MAY 30, 1951

Mickey Mantle struck out five times in five at bats. His Yankees lost a doubleheader, to the Red Sox. When he retired in 1969, Mantle had a major-league-record 1,710 strikeouts.

Former Yankee Reggie Jackson is the current record-holder. He has 2,597 strikeouts, 661 more than second-place Willie Stargell's total.

Members of the Hall of Fame whose 2,398 combined career strikeouts are less than Reggie Jackson's total:

- Al Simmons, 737
- Stan Musial, 696
- Johnny Mize, 524
- George Sisler, 327
- Joe Sewell, 114

Ended May 30, 1911
The New York Giants' tenancy at Hilltop Park

Because of a fire at the Polo Grounds, the Giants played at the Yankees' home field for several weeks. This gave the Yankees a chance to see how baseball should be played. They obviously did not pay attention. In 1911, the Yankees finished sixth, twenty-five games behind Philadelphia.

MAY 31, 1998

Scoring eleven runs in one inning, the Red Sox beat the Yankees 13-7.

Born May 31, 1943
Joe Namath

Namath guaranteed his Jets would win Super Bowl III. They did. Two decades later, another New York athlete, Don Mattingly, guaranteed a Yankee pennant. His team finished fifth in its division.

Yankee hating by the numbers, part twelve:

- **44.** Jersey number Hank Aaron wore when he hit his record-breaking 715th home run, against the Dodgers. Former Yankee Al Downing, who allowed this home run, also wore number forty-four.
- **45.** Hits by which one-time Yankee Willie Keeler fell short of a career total of three thousand.
- **46.** RBI Yankee cleanup hitter Mel Hall had in 1990. We should not be critical of the Yankees for using Hall as a cleanup hitter. Only two members of the 1990 Yankees had more RBI.
- **47.** Home losses, in seventy-four games, by the Yankees in 1913

JUNE 1, 1913

Poor play, not superstition, was responsible for the Yankees being in the middle of a thirteen-game losing streak. Six of these losses were at the Polo Grounds. These extended the Yankees' home-field losing streak to eighteen games.

When the streak ended, the Yankees had a 9-34 record. They were in last place, twenty-three games out.

Highlights of the thirteen-game losing streak:

- Philadelphia swept a four-game series, winning the last game 12-2.
- Boston won both games of a doubleheader.
- Allowing seven runs in the last three innings, the Yankees lost 8-2 to Cleveland.
- Cleveland's Joe Jackson hit a home run completely out of the Polo Grounds.

Born June 1, 1941
Dean Chance

Chance dominated the Yankees in 1964. In fifty innings pitched, the Angel pitcher allowed the Yankees one run on fourteen hits.

Chance was a dreadful hitter, with a lifetime batting average of .066. One suspects Chance learned how to hit watching the Yankees bat against him.

JUNE 2, 1979

A bad White Sox team beat the Yankees 7-0. With only one Yankee among the league's top thirty-five hitters, the failure to score should not have been a surprise.

In this game, Reggie Jackson hurt himself chasing a fly ball. This was clearly a case of overworking unused muscles.

Born June 2, 1933
Jerry Lumpe

Casey Stengel, Lumpe's manager, said of this Yankee infielder, "He's a great hitter until I play him."

Some other Casey Stengel descriptions of his players on the Yankees:

- "He (pitcher Bob Turley) don't drink, he don't smoke, he don't chase women and he don't win." Stengel said roughly the same thing of second baseman Bobby Richardson, with the punch line "he don't hit .250."
- "He ain't got it here." Stengel tapped his head, as he spoke of Mickey Mantle.
- "The way (first baseman Bill Skowron) was going, I'd be better off if he was hurt."
- "The only thing wrong with (pitcher Ralph Terry) is he ain't smart enough to cross the street."
- As Mets' manager, Stengel described Jimmy Piersall, who had emotional problems, ("You have to play him in a cage") and Chris Cannizzaro ("The only defensive catcher who can't catch").

JUNE 3, 1934

Yankee manager Joe McCarthy had been thrown out of a game for arguing with an umpire. Thinking the umpire only wanted him to get off the field, McCarthy remained on the Yankee bench. This possibly unintentional flouting of the umpire's authority cost the Yankee manager a three-day suspension.

Selected Yankee suspensions:

- Dale Berra was suspended for one year for using drugs. Several years later, Steve Howe received a lifetime ban for drug use, making Berra look almost angelic.
- Kid Elberfeld earned a five-day suspension for bumping an umpire, in 1908. For part of the 1908 season, Elberfeld was the Yankee player-manager. He was no good at either role, hitting .196 and compiling a 27-71 record. Had the rest of the American League been more alert, they would have demanded his suspension be replaced with a fine.
- In 1938, the American League suspended Jake Powell for ten days for his part in a brawl with the Red Sox.
- Bob Meusel incited a riot in Detroit, in 1924, by charging the mound. This cost him a ten-day suspension.

Born June 3, 1934
Jim Gentile

Recently, the Society for American Baseball Research found that Roger Maris had been incorrectly credited with a RBI during the 1961 season. This meant that Gentile tied Maris for the RBI title that year.

FRAZEE'S JUST REWARD (June 4)

JUNE 4, 1972

Chicago was trailing the Yankees 4-2, in the bottom of the ninth inning. In one of the more memorable moments in the history of Comiskey Park, the White Sox Dick Allen won the game with a three-run, pinch-hit home run.

Born June 4, 1939
Phil Linz

His harmonica playing on the Yankee bus led to an angry confrontation with manager Yogi Berra. Coach Frank Crosetti called this incident "the worst thing that happened to the Yankees." In his anger, Crosetti forgot far worse occurrences, like signing Joe Pepitone to a contract.

Two reflections on Harry Frazee, who died on this date in 1929:

(Frazee was the Red Sox owner who sold Babe Ruth and numerous lesser stars to the Yankees. He used the money in his other businesses. To this day, he is reviled in Boston.)

- Two tourists were reading an article in a Montreal newspaper on Nanette Workman, a singer who is especially popular in Quebec. The title of the article was *"Yes, Yes, Nanette,"* a turn on the famous play Frazee promoted. I overheard one say, "We're in another country, but we can't get away from that ____ Frazee."
- More than fifty years after Frazee's death, I was in a sports bar in Boston. Someone named Frazee appeared on the screen, with his name clearly shown. He was booed.

179

JUNE 5, 1989

Six Yankee errors gave Baltimore a league-record thirteen unearned runs. New York lost 16-3.

This day's amateur draft would not provide the help New York obviously needed. As the Yankees had traded their first pick, they could not select future stars like Mo Vaughn, Frank Thomas, and Chuck Knoblach.

A year later, the Yankees were worse. Some notes on the 1990 Yankee team:

- This team was last in the American League in runs scored, batting average, and slugging average.
- Of the fourteen American League teams, the 1990 Yankees were twelfth in ERA and in walks allowed.
- All five of the team's principal starters had ERA's in excess of 4.00.
- Not surprisingly, this Yankee team had the worst record in the American League, 67-95.

Born June 5, 1916
Eddie Joost

No fan of Casey Stengel, the A's shortstop said of the Yankee manager, "He was in the dugout, not having any idea what was going on."

JUNE 6, 1990

Justice occurred when Bucky Dent was fired in Boston (Dent's three-run home run had beaten the Red Sox in their famous 1978 playoff game). New York had an 18-31 record.

Dent did not say if he would try to revive his acting career. In 1979, he had starred in a made-for-television movie. Dent played a football player who fell in love with a Dallas Cowboys' cheerleader. The American Film Institute left this effort off its 1997 list of the one hundred greatest movies ever made.

Born June 6, 1953
Dave Bergman

Bergman's career with the Yankees consisted of twenty-one at bats. He had one hit.

Worst career batting averages by a Yankee:

- .025, Skeeter Shelton. Most managers would have realized Shelton could not hit once he was one-for-twenty. Yankee manager Wild Bill Donovan finally gave up when Shelton reached one-for-forty. Donovan was either stubborn or stupid. His 69-83 record in 1915 suggests the latter.
- .043, Kal Segrist
- .048, Bergman
- .050, Bill Otis
- .054, Kevin Elster

(Minimum of twenty at bats, excluding pitchers)

JUNE 7, 1968

California did not have to forfeit the next-day's game with the eighth-place Yankees. Angel players had been prepared to give up an almost-certain victory. They thought it inappropriate to play baseball during Robert Kennedy's funeral. In one of the two decisions he made as commissioner, William Eckert rendered the forfeit unnecessary. He ordered that the start of the game be delayed until after the funeral had ended.

Born June 7, 1884
George Moriarity

Moriarity had no home runs, in almost one thousand at bats, in his career with the Yankees. He later hit five with the Tigers. Detroit had players like Hall of Famers Ty Cobb and Sam Crawford. Given a chance to be around quality major-leaguers, Moriarity's hitting improved.

Most at bats as a Yankee without a home run:

- 982, Moriarity
- 843, Benny Bengough
- 695, Deacon McGuire
- 638, Leo Durocher
- 568, Roxy Walters

JUNE 8, 1987

Mark Salas, whom the Yankees had recently acquired from Minnesota, had trouble getting to Yankee Stadium. He told the cab driver to take him to the ballpark. Welcome to Shea Stadium, Mark.

A punctual Salas would not have made much difference. Toronto beat the Yankees 11-0.

Born June 8, 1944
Mark Belanger

Belanger, the Orioles' shortstop, hit home runs about as frequently as Steinbrenner accepted responsibility for his mistakes. One came in a 10-1 win in 1981. This win was part of Baltimore's three-game sweep of the Yankees.

High-priced players, whose misfortunes are not described elsewhere in this book, who did not work out for the Yankees:

- Steve Kemp had ninety RBI in two seasons with the Yankees. This was two fewer than he had the season before he joined the team.
- Jack Clark spent one season with the Yankees. His batting average dropped forty-four points from the prior year.
- Dave Collins hit .303 and stole seventy-nine bases for Cincinnati, in 1980. In 1982, his only season with the Yankees, he hit .253, with thirteen steals.

JUNE 9, 1990

New York's 10-1 loss, to Baltimore, was its eighth consecutive defeat. Prince Charles and Princess Diana's marriage was in better shape than the Yankees, who had an 18-35 record.

The worst starts ever by the Yankees:

- New York began the 1913 season by losing thirty-four of its first forty-three games.
- As noted above, the Yankees lost thirty-five of their first fifty-three games in 1990.
- In 1912, the Yankees lost twenty-nine of their first forty-four games, a .340 winning percentage. They then hit a slump, losing seventy-three of their final 108 games, a .324 percentage.
- A 4-16 start in 1966 helped the Yankees finish last that year.

Born June 9, 1931
Bill Virdon

Virdon played for Pittsburgh in the 1960 World Series. In the seventh game, he hit an apparent double play grounder. After the ball hit a pebble, it hit Tony Kubek's throat, knocking the Yankee shortstop out of the game. This started a five-run, eighth-inning rally that gave the Pirates a 9-7 lead.

Years later, Virdon became the first Yankee manager to be fired by Steinbrenner. This is like being the first woman to be propositioned by President Clinton.

JUNE 10, 1933

Philadelphia overcame Yankee leads and won both games of a double-header. Pinky Higgins drove in four runs in the first game, while Ed Coleman's heroics won the second. Coleman, who had homered earlier, singled home two runs in the bottom of the ninth inning.

Lefty Gomez, normally a starter, pitched in relief. With one pitch to Coleman, he earned a loss and a blown save. Outings like this one, and his 5-12 record as a reliever, make one wish Gomez had pitched in relief more frequently.

Now-defunct teams who have beaten the Yankees:

- Philadelphia (1901-1954) and Kansas City (1955-1967) A's
- Washington Senators (1901-1960, 1961-1971)
- Milwaukee Braves, Brooklyn Dodgers, and New York Giants (in various World Series)
- St. Louis Browns (1902-1953)
- Seattle Pilots (1969)

Born June 10, 1948
Bob Randall

Randall, the Twins' second baseman, beat Yankee pitcher Catfish Hunter in a 1977 cow-milking contest.

JUNE 11, 1925

There were six teams ahead of the Yankees in the standings after New York lost to Cleveland. The Yankees would finish seventh, with sixteen more losses than wins.

Died June 11, 1969
John L. Lewis

For many years, Lewis was the leader of the mineworkers. He could have had Yankee outfielder Roger Maris as a member. Describing his love of baseball, Maris had said, "If I could make more money down in the zinc mines, I'd be mining zinc."

Lewis was not related to comedian Joe E. Lewis, who said, "Rooting for the Yankees is like rooting for U.S. Steel."

Yankee hating by the numbers, part thirteen:

- **48.** Total games the Yankees finished behind Philadelphia, 1929-1931.
- **49.** Duration, in minutes, of the half-inning when the Tigers scored thirteen runs against the Yankees, in 1925.
- **50.** Salary, in thousands of dollars, offered to Roger Maris, the season after he hit sixty-one home runs. This was a 33 percent increase over his 1961 salary. Maris was not impressed.
- **51.** Number the Yankees' Bernie Williams wore when he struck out five consecutive times in a 1991 game.

JUNE 12, 1948

Cleveland made most of the 68,586 fans at Yankee Stadium unhappy. By sweeping a doubleheader, the Indians took over first place.

When the 1948 season ended, the Yankees were two games behind Cleveland. This made many of the 6,858,600 baseball fans in New York City unhappy. It made Yankee General Manager George Weiss upset enough to fire manager Bucky Harris. Weiss did not care that Harris had won the 1947 World Series. Harris's ninety-four wins in 1948 meant little to his general manager.

There must be something in the water at Yankee Stadium. Why else would men of German descent named George feel the need to fire successful managers?

Born June 12, 1971
Ryan Klesko

His home run gave the 1998 Braves twenty-five consecutive games with at least one home run. This tied a record shared by the Yankees and the Detroit Tigers.

How Yankee team records for home runs in a season were broken or tied:

- By hitting 158 home runs in 1927, the Yankees established a major-league record. Many thought this record would last for decades. In fairness, it did last until the next decade. In 1930, the Chicago Cubs hit 171 home runs.
- New York's hold on the American League record was almost as short-lived. In 1932, the A's hit 172 home runs.
- In 1947, the New York Giants obliterated the major-league record for home runs in a season, when they hit 227 (The Yankees had reclaimed the record, hitting 182 home runs in 1936). This record lasted until 1961, when the Yankees hit 240.
- In 1996, Baltimore, Seattle, and Oakland all broke this record.
- Seattle hit 264 home runs, in 1997, to set the existing mark.

JUNE 13, 1958

Detroit won the second of four straight games over the Yankees. No team has beaten the Yankees more frequently than the Tigers have.

Players who played in most of the Tigers' 884 wins over the Yankees, between 1903 and 1998:

- Ty Cobb, who was with the Tigers from 1905 to 1926
- Charlie Gehringer, 1924-1942
- George Kell, 1946-1952
- Al Kaline, 1953-1974
- Lou Whitaker, 1977-1995

Born June 13, 1922
Mel Parnell

Boston's Parnell pitched four shutouts against the Yankees in 1953.

Parnell won 123 games for the Red Sox during his eleven-year career. He had a .621 winning percentage. Parnell gave Boston an outstanding left-handed starter for over a decade.

Mel Queen pitched for the Yankees in the late 1940's. He shared a first name and little else with Parnell. His 9.00 ERA in 1947 followed one of 6.60 in 1946. Queen gave the Yankees a terrible right-handed pitcher for a fifth of a decade.

JUNE 14, 1927

Paul Waner was working on a remarkable streak. He would have fourteen consecutive games with at least one extra-base hit.

Waner's streak is a great retort when someone mentions Joe DiMaggio's fifty-six-game hitting streak. So is noting that, during DiMaggio's hitting streak, Ted Williams outhit the Yankee star, .412 to .408.

Since you are belittling DiMaggio's achievements, point out that his wife, actress Marilyn Monroe, never won an Oscar.

Died June 14, 1980
Johnny Hodapp

Cleveland's Hodapp twice had two hits in an inning, as the Indians beat the Yankees 24-6.

The Yankees' performance in the first year of interleague play:

- They lost their first interleague game, 2-1 to Florida. New Yorkers had the joy of reading about the game on this date in 1997.
- Their record in interleague play in 1997 was 5-10.
- National League teams outscored the Yankees 57-38.

JUNE 15, 1976

In a terrible deal, the Yankees traded Tippy Martinez, Scott McGregor, Rudy May, Dave Pagan, and Rick Dempsey to the Orioles. In return, New York received Ken Holtzman, Doyle Alexander, Elrod Hendricks, and Grant Jackson. Steinbrenner engineered the trade, reportedly on advice from his thirteen-year-old son. Unfortunately for the Yankees, the Orioles sought the advice of Earl Weaver, their forty-five-year-old manager.

Why the trade was terrible:

- Martinez, McGregor, May, and Pagan won 267 games and had 120 saves after the trade. Holtzman, Alexander, and Jackson won 203 games and had thirty-nine saves.
- Dempsey had 1,007 hits after the trade. This was 986 more than Hendricks had. Like Holtzman, Hendricks was at the end of his career.
- McGregor, Martinez, and Dempsey would spend most of their careers with the Orioles; Alexander and Jackson would spend most of their careers with other teams.

Born June 15,1972
Andy Pettite

In 1997, the Mets beat the Yankees 6-0, in their first-ever regular season game. Pettite was the losing pitcher.

JUNE 16, 1933 and 1986

In 1933, the last-place Red Sox won their fourth in a row over the Yankees. Fifty-three years later, Roger Clemens met Ron Guidry in a battle of ace pitchers. Boston won 10-1. This win started a three-game sweep by the Red Sox at Yankee Stadium.

Fun with numbers:

These are the leading winners on the Yankee pitching staff, from 1986 to 1998:

- 1986: Dennis Rasmussen (18-6)
- 1987: Rick Rhoden (16-10)
- 1988: John Candalaria (13-7)
- 1989: Andy Hawkins (15-15)
- 1990: Lee Guetterman (11-7)
- 1991: Scott Sanderson (16-10)
- 1992: Melido Perez (13-16)
- 1993: Jimmy Key (18-6)
- 1994: Jimmy Key (17-4)
- 1995: Jack McDowell (15-10)
- 1996: Andy Pettite (He had a 21-8 record, proving even the Yankees, if given enough time, could have a twenty-game winner.)
- 1997: Andy Pettite (18-7)
- 1998: David Cone (20-7)

These pitchers have an aggregate record of 211-113. Over the same period, Roger Clemens's record is 217-115.

Born June 16, 1923
Allie Clark

In 1948, Clark hit .310 to help the Indians win the pennant. Cleveland had obtained him for Red Embree, who appeared in twenty games for the Yankees.

JUNE 17, 1925

Detroit won 19-1 at Yankee Stadium. Let us savor the sixth inning of this game. Detroit got six hits, while seven batters walked. Two Tigers were safe on Yankee errors. Yankee pitchers allowed eleven runs before they retired a batter. When the inning was over, Detroit had scored thirteen runs. They did all of this on only one home run, a grand slam by Ty Cobb.

Other low moments of the 1925 season:

- Babe Ruth's illness and suspension caused him to miss fifty-six games.
- Cleveland scored six runs in the last of the ninth inning to beat the Yankees 10-9.
- Yankee shortstop Everett Scott was benched, ending his consecutive-games-played streak.
- New York finished with a 69-85 record.

Born June 17, 1928
Willard Nixon

In a 1955 game, the Yankees used four pinch hitters against Red Sox pitchers Nixon and Ike Delock. (Ike and Nixon formed a good combination in the 1950's.) All four struck out.

JUNE 18, 1977

Reggie Jackson was removed from a game for not hustling. As the game was nationally televised, millions of people saw Jackson leave the field in disgrace. His considerable ego offended, Jackson nearly came to blows with manager Billy Martin.

New York was in the process of losing three games at Fenway Park. In these games, Boston hit sixteen home runs and outscored the Yankees 30-9.

Other low moments in the co-existence of Billy Martin and Reggie Jackson:

- Martin started Paul Blair, rather than Jackson, in the final game of the 1977 American League Championship Series. Throughout his career, the slumping Jackson had difficulty hitting Kansas City's starter, Paul Splittorff.
- In a game in Kansas City, Jackson insisted on bunting when Martin wanted him to hit away. Jackson was suspended for his defiance.
- Jackson thought he worked for Steinbrenner, to whom he complained frequently about Martin.
- There was an embarrassing incident when Jackson's number was retired. As he read the other retired Yankee numbers, the stadium announcer omitted Martin's number one. While it might have recognition that Martin's number should not have been retired in the first place, it was bush.

Born June 18, 1939
Lou Brock

Several times, Brock, the St. Louis outfielder, stole more bases in a season than the Yankees did as a team.

Brock hit .300, with five RBI, against the Yankees in the 1964 World Series.

THE HUMILIATION OF REGGIE JACKSON (June 18)

JUNE 19, 1922

Babe Ruth earned his third suspension of the season. He verbally abused an umpire, as the Yankees lost their eighth consecutive game.

Ruth's five suspensions in 1922:

- Ruth missed the first six weeks of the season. Commissioner Landis had suspended him for going on an off-season barnstorming tour, in defiance of baseball's rules.
- Ruth was suspended for one game for going into the stands after a fan. He also lost his captaincy. Ruth's term as Yankee captain had lasted six games, all of which the Yankees lost.
- He earned his third suspension, three days, for verbally abusing an umpire.
- Ruth received a five-day suspension for threatening an umpire.
- Having not yet learned how to treat umpires, Ruth got into more trouble. He received a three-day suspension for arguing a called strike.

Born June 19, 1884
Eddie Cicotte

Cicotte was the winning pitcher, as the White Sox completed a three-game sweep of the Yankees, late in the 1920 season. This sweep, followed by a loss to the Browns, effectively eliminated the Yankees from the pennant race.

JUNE 20, 1953

Detroit pitcher Ted Gray was savoring his first win of the season. The previous day, Gray, who had lost his first nine decisions, had beaten the Yankees 3-2. Detroit's Jim Delsing, who is best known for pinch running for a midget, hit two home runs.

Born June 20, 1908
Bill Werber

In a 1935 game, Werber scored in an unusual manner. Yankee catcher Bill Dickey dropped a third strike. When Dickey threw to first to retire the batter, Boston's Werber scored from third base.

Besides purchasing Werber, steps the Red Sox took under Tom Yawkey, in the 1930's, to become more competitive:

- They acquired Lefty Grove and Jimmie Foxx from the A's, and Rick Ferrell from the Browns.
- Boston purchased Joe Cronin from the Senators.
- They spent a considerable amount of money refurbishing Fenway Park.

(All these players, who were acquired principally for cash, are in the Hall of Fame.)

JUNE 21, 1989

New York traded Rickey Henderson, who had at least ten great seasons left in a Hall of Fame-caliber career. They received Luis Polonia, who had a few ordinary seasons left. Will Polonia make the Hall of Fame? Maybe, if they decide to induct nine thousand more players.

Born June 21, 1918
Eddie Lopat

Chicago scored fifteen runs off Yankee pitchers Lopat and Don Johnson in a 1950 game. This embarrassment occurred at Yankee Stadium. Fifteen runs are the most allowed by the Yankees in a shutout loss.

Yankee hating by the numbers, part fourteen:

- **52.** Games Hall of Famer Robin Roberts won after the Yankees released him, in 1962. Most of these wins were for the Orioles, including the final game of a five-game sweep of the Yankees.
- **53.** Games the Yankees finished behind the Giants in 1912. This represents their greatest deficit to another New York City team. Early that season, these teams played a benefit game for the survivors of the *Titanic*. Proving their superiority, the Giants won 11-2.
- **54.** Combined home runs Roger Maris, Mickey Mantle, Elston Howard, and Joe Pepitone hit in 1965. These four were the heart of the Yankee batting order. Unfortunately for the Yankees, heart transplants were not available in 1965.
- **55.** Length, in minutes, of the fastest game in American League history. St. Louis made short work of the Yankees in 1926.

JUNE 22, 1965

Kansas City beat the Yankees 6-2. Yankee starter Jim Bouton gave up four runs while retiring only three batters.

Bouton would finish the 1965 season with a 4-15 record. In the 1960's, a performance like this was usually the first step back to your hometown. There you would shoot pool and talk about how you once pitched to Al Kaline.

Even the most pessimistic Yankee hater had concluded the Yankees were not going to win their sixth consecutive pennant. With their 28-36 record, the Yankees were in sixth place, ten games out.

Born June 22, 1903
Carl Hubbell

Hubbell, the ace of the Giants' pitching staff, beat the Yankees twice in World Series play. He was the best pitcher in New York in the 1930's.

A comparison of the careers of Hubbell and Lefty Gomez, the Yankees' best pitcher of the 1930's:

- Hubbell won 253 games; Gomez won 189.
- Hubbell had a 2.98 ERA; Gomez's was 3.34.
- Hubbell threw 258 complete games; Gomez threw 173.
- Hubbell struck out 1,678 batters; Gomez struck out 1,468.
- Hubbell had thirty-six shutouts; Gomez had twenty-eight.
- Hubbell was elected to Hall of Fame in 1947; Gomez in 1972.

JUNE 23, 1988

Billy Martin was fired for the fifth time as Yankee manager. This set a virtually impossible-to-beat record. Martin had previously established another dubious distinction. In 1978, he became the first manager of a World Series winner to be fired during the following season.

The reasons for the five Billy Martin firings:

#1. Martin said, "One's a born liar, and the other's convicted." He was describing, with at least 50 percent accuracy, Reggie Jackson and Steinbrenner.

#2. He punched a marshmallow salesman.

#3. Martin defied Steinbrenner, particularly by not holding a workout on an offday.

#4. There were numerous incidents, especially his fight with pitcher Ed Whitson. A losing streak that cost the Yankees the 1985 division title did not help.

#5. His drinking was close to being out-of-control. More importantly, Steinbrenner had gone almost eight months without firing a manager.

Died June 23, 1928
Mal Kitteridge

Kitteridge's career as a manager comprised eighteen games with the Senators in 1904. His only win was against the Yankees.

JUNE 24, 1933

Baseball announced that Al Simmons was the leading vote getter for the first All-Star game. He received more votes than Babe Ruth or Lou Gehrig did.

Twenty years later, Simmons won another election. He was chosen for the Hall of Fame, while Joe DiMaggio failed to receive a sufficient number of votes.

Comments on the initial All-Star voting:

- Ruth was not as good as Simmons was in 1933. He had sixteen fewer RBI than Simmons had. His batting average was thirty points lower than the White Sox outfielder's.
- Neither Gehrig, nor Simmons for that matter, deserved to be the leading vote getter. Philadelphia's Jimmie Foxx was clearly the best player in baseball. He would win the Triple Crown in 1933. Incredibly, his 1933 totals in each of the Triple Crown categories were less than in 1932. That year, he had fallen two hits short of winning the Triple Crown.

Born June 24, 1938
Don Mincher

In a 1966 game, Mincher was one of five Twins to hit a home run in a single inning. Only one original American League team, the Yankees, has not hit at least four home runs in an inning.

JUNE 25, 1933

Babe Ruth was benched for the first time in his career. Ruth was in a slump, with two hits in his previous seventeen times at bat. We do not know what the Babe did during the game. Did he sulk? Did he spend the time thinking of his future as Yankee manager?

Either activity would have been a complete waste of time.

Born June 25, 1906
Joe Kuhel

Kuhel hit .322, with 107 RBI, as his Senators finished seven games ahead of the Yankees in 1933.

New York had six Hall of Famers (Lou Gehrig, Tony Lazzeri, Joe Sewell, Babe Ruth, Earl Combs, and Bill Dickey) in its 1933 lineup. All except Ruth played in more than 130 games. Hall of Fame pitchers Lefty Gomez and Red Ruffing appeared in seventy games for New York. Yankee manager Joe McCarthy is also in the Hall of Fame.

This team is in the dictionary. You can find it next to the word "under-achieving."

Fewest wins at home, full season:

- twenty-seven, 1913
- thirty, 1908
- thirty-one, 1912
- thirty-three, 1907
- thirty-five, 1917 and 1966

JUNE 26, 1939

The Yankees played their first-ever night game. They lost, in Philadelphia, to an A's team that had players with names like Sep Gantenbein, Dee Miles, and Chubby Dean.

Born June 26, 1908
Debs Garms

Garms, another unusually named player, was the leading hitter on the 1938 Boston Braves. These Braves were the only National League team managed by Casey Stengel to win more games than it lost. In fairness, Stengel managed in the National League for only thirteen seasons.

Records of selected Yankee managers when their previous teams fired them:

- Art Fletcher had a record of 58-93 with the 1926 Phillies.
- Stengel was 47-60 with the 1943 Braves.
- Bucky Harris's 1943 Senators had a 38-52 record.
- Bill Virdon was 67-69 with the 1972 Pirates.

JUNE 27, 1986

Toronto won 14-7, in the first of three games against the Yankees. They would sweep the series, extending New York's losing streak at Yankee Stadium to ten games.

To avoid long losing streaks, you need a solid pitching staff. In 1986, New York had only one pitcher who had more than nine wins. This made their staff as effective at stopping losing streaks as trash talk is at stopping Michael Jordan.

Died June 27, 1992
Sandy Amaros

His superb catch started a key double play in the seventh game of the 1955 World Series. Brooklyn won the game 2-0.

Other key players in the seventh game of the 1955 World Series:

- Johnny Podres pitched a complete game and was the winning pitcher.
- Gil Hodges drove in both runs for the Dodgers.
- Roy Campanella doubled and scored the first run.
- Pee Wee Reese scored a run and threw out Elston Howard, on a ground ball, to end the Series.

JUNE 28, 1907

Washington stole a major-league-record thirteen bases against Yankee catcher Branch Rickey.

In 1907, Rickey hit .182 and had more errors than RBI. He was the Yankees' third-string catcher. Try to imagine how bad Walter Blair, the fourth-string catcher, must have been.

Other noteworthy base-stealing feats against the Yankees:

- Reggie Smith stole five bases in a doubleheader, in 1967.
- Rickey Henderson broke Lou Brock's career stolen-base record in 1991.
- Cincinnati stole seven bases against the Yankees in four games in the 1976 World Series.

Born June 28, 1941
Al Downing

Downing symbolizes the Yankees' 1965-1972 descent to an average team. He was one of the few African-Americans on the Yankees. Many cite the Yankees' reluctance to sign black players in the 1950's and 1960's as the key to the team's downfall.

Downing pitched in the 1964 World Series, because of another symbol of Yankee slippage, age and injuries. These rendered Whitey Ford unable to pitch. Downing lost the fourth game of this Series, giving up a grand slam to St. Louis's Ken Boyer.

Many Yankee fans hoped Hank Aaron would not break Babe Ruth's record for career home runs. There is irony in Downing, a symbol of Yankee decline, giving up Aaron's record-breaking home run.

JUNE 29, 1986

Boston acquired Tom Seaver from the White Sox. Seaver was a pitcher the Yankees badly needed. This trade, and the subsequent acquisition of Spike Owen and Dave Henderson, helped the Red Sox win the American League East title. Referring to the Owen-Henderson acquisition, Steinbrenner said, "My front office was asleep."

Years later, this office was barely awake, as the Yankees signed free agent Owen to a rich three-year contract. Owen was gone after one season. He had lost his job, as Yankee shortstop, to the legendary Mike Gallego.

Born June 29, 1936
Harmon Killebrew

In 1976, fans selected the greatest moment in their team's history. Minnesota fans chose the Twins' 1965 victory over the Yankees. Killebrew won this game with a home run in the bottom of the ninth inning.

Notable greatest moments for other teams, as selected by their fans in 1976:

- Pittsburgh fans chose Bill Mazeroski's 1960 World Series-winning home run.
- Houston's victory over the Yankees in the first-ever indoor game was the choice of Astro fans.
- Indians' fans selected Frank Robinson's debut as baseball's first African-American manager. Cleveland defeated the Yankees in this 1975 game.

JUNE 30, 1908

Cy Young enjoyed the best day any pitcher has ever had against the Yankees. He pitched a no-hitter, facing the minimum number of batters. Young had three hits, as Boston won 8-0.

Born June 30, 1945
Jerry Kenney

Kenney had a batting average of .193 for the 1970 Yankees. This is the worst-ever batting average by a Yankee with at least four hundred at bats. Yankee shortstop Gene Michael had the next-worst 1970 total, hitting .214. Combined, Kenney and Michael barely equaled a competent major-leaguer. They had six home runs and seventy-three RBI.

Ron Woods and Curt Blefary were not much better. They formed a useless outfield platoon on this Yankee team, hitting a combined .219.

In 1970, American League pitchers had to bat. Manager Ralph Houk must have considered having his Yankee pitchers bat sixth in the lineup. Tradition, certainly not the hitting talents of Kenney, Michael, and the buffoon platoon, kept Houk from doing this.

The Yankees' worst batting averages, by position:

- catcher, Jake Gibbs, .213 in 1968
- first base, Mickey Mantle, .237 in 1968
- second base, Fritz Maisel, .198 in 1917
- shortstop, Frank Crosetti, .194 in 1940
- third base, Kenney, .193 in 1970
- outfield, Tom Tresh, .219 in 1967; Dave Fultz, .232 in 1905; and Roy Hartzell, .233 in 1914
- designated hitter, Kevin Maas, .220 in 1991

(Minimum of four hundred at bats in a season)

JULY 1, 1953

In losing their ninth consecutive game, the Yankees had only four hits. Mel Parnell won his one-hundredth game, as the Red Sox shut out New York 4-0.

The longest Yankee losing streaks:

- They lost thirteen consecutive games in 1913.
- New York had a twelve-game losing streak in 1908.
- The Yankees have lost nine in a row several times, most recently in 1982.

Born July 1, 1945
Bill Rohr

In his first career start, at Yankee Stadium, Rohr allowed no hits through eight and two-thirds innings. He won his next start, 6-1 against the Yankees. You have just read about two of Rohr's three career wins.

JULY 2, 1943

Cleveland scored all twelve of its runs in one inning, as they shut out the Yankees.

Died July 2, 1903
Ed Delahanty

Playing for the Senators, Delahanty hit the first home run ever against the Yankees.

Yankee hating from A to Z, part four:

- **N.** Not there. Manager Lou Pinella was not in his hotel room to take a call from Steinbrenner, in 1987. An angry Steinbrenner issued a written statement critical of Pinella. In an appropriate ceremony, the players burned this statement.
- **O.** "Overdressed, uncomprehending autumn arrivistes." Roger Angell used this phrase to describe Yankee World Series fans in *The Summer Game*. (New York: Ballantine Books, 1984, 105.) Angell might have been thinking of the well-dressed fans who left during Don Larsen's perfect game. To them, it was a boring game. Brooklyn had not had a base runner. New York was not hitting either; the Yankees had two runs and five hits. Besides there was a wine-and-cheese party at the club that evening.
- **P.** Dallas Parks. He is the umpire who threatened to sue Steinbrenner for defamation of character. Steinbrenner, thinking the umpires were his employees, had criticized them accordingly.
- **Q.** Bob Quinn. His purchase of the Red Sox ended Harry Frazee's regime. Frazee is remembered, to this day, for selling star players, most notably Babe Ruth, to the Yankees.

JULY 3, 1978

On Steinbrenner's orders, catcher Thurman Munson was playing right field. Reggie Jackson, normally the right fielder, was the designated hitter. Because of injuries to New York's pitching staff, first baseman Jim Spencer was preparing to pitch.

It was probably a rumor that the peanut vendors were ushers. It was fact, not rumor, that Phil Rizzuto, normally a cheerleader, was broadcasting games.

The key events leading to Billy Martin's first firing as Yankee manager, July 1978:

* Martin was drinking heavily, particularly after learning of Steinbrenner's attempt to trade him for White Sox manager Bob Lemon.
* New York was two converted touchdowns behind the Red Sox in the standings.
* After taking a strike, Reggie Jackson twice ignored instructions to hit away. He struck out while unsuccessfully attempting to bunt. Jackson would be suspended.
* Martin uttered his famous line describing Jackson and Steinbrenner: "One's a born liar, and the other's convicted." He resigned shortly afterwards.

Died July 3, 1951
Hugh Casey

This Dodger reliever was the winning pitcher when Cookie Lavagetto broke up Yankee pitcher Bill Bevens's no-hitter. Two 1947 World Series games later, Casey earned a save in the game where Al Gionfriddo made his famous catch off Joe DiMaggio.

JULY 4, 1933

It was not a good holiday for the Yankees. Washington swept a double-header at Yankee Stadium. This was typical of the 1933 season. Despite having nine future Hall of Famers, the 1933 Yankees would finish seven games behind the Senators.

Born July 4, 1884
Jack Warhop

Yankee pitcher Warhop set a team record by hitting twenty-six batters in 1909. Warhop did not do much right that season. Thirty-five American League pitchers made more than fifteen starts in 1909. Warhop had the eighth-worst ERA and the fifth-most losses.

Other ways Yankee pitchers have hurt the team:

- Vic Raschi committed four balks in a game, in 1950.
- Jack Chesbro had fifteen errors in the 1904 season, establishing the American League record for errors by a pitcher.
- Tim Leary threw twenty-three wild pitches in 1990, the sixth-worst total ever.
- Jumbo Brown got fatter. Listed as weighing 260 pounds, this heaviest-ever Yankee might have weighed close to three hundred pounds. As Brown got heavier, his winning percentage declined. It was .200 in Brown's final season as a Yankee.

JULY 5, 1967

In one of his two major-league appearances, Yankee pitcher Cecil Perkins gave up five runs in three innings. His efforts helped the Twins complete a four-game sweep of the Yankees. Following this series, the Yankees had a team batting average of .219. This was close to the worst-ever, .212 by the 1910 White Sox.

Yankee hitters could not hit, and Yankee pitchers could not pitch. Maybe the team's demise was not entirely the fault of its former manager, Johnny Keane.

The top five Yankee hitters, and where they ranked in 1967:

- Horace Clarke, who hit .272, was twelfth.
- Joe Pepitone finished twenty-seventh, with a .251 average.
- Mickey Mantle was thirty-fifth, hitting .245.
- Steve Whitaker, who hit .243, wound up thirty-ninth.
- Charley Smith was the American League's fifty-seventh best hitter, with a .224 average.

(Ranking is among the sixty-one American Leaguers who had at least four hundred at bats.)

Died July 5, 1974
Duster Mails

Cleveland signed this pitcher late in the 1920 season. Although he had not pitched in the major leagues for four years, Mails won all seven of his decisions. These wins helped the Indians finish three games ahead of the Yankees.

DEFEAT IS AN ORPHAN (July 5)

JULY 6, 1933

For the first time, the best players in baseball met in the All-Star game. There have been sixty-eight of these games. With no Yankees on its teams, the National League has won forty times.

Yankee "lowlights" in the All-Star game, part one:

- In 1940, the National League won 4-0. Yankee pitcher Red Ruffing gave up a three-run home run to Max West. In 1942, Ruffing lost the final game of the World Series to Billy Southworth's Cardinals. Fortunately for Ruffing, he never faced Ron Northey or Hugh East.
- Manager Joe McCarthy played none of the six Yankees in his lineup in the 1943 game. This managerial wisdom helped the American League win.
- Joe DiMaggio hit into a double play to end the 1950 game.
- Whitey Ford gave up five runs, as the American League blew a 5-0 lead in 1955.

Born July 6, 1891
Steve O'Neil

O'Neil was the manager of the Detroit Tigers, who finished ahead of the Yankees in three consecutive seasons, 1944-1946.

JULY 7, 1951

Boston's Clyde Vollmer was on a tear. In successive games against the Yankees, he hit a two-run triple, a grand slam home run, and a two-run home run.

Boston won all three games. New York had yet to win at Fenway Park in 1951.

Died July 7, 1990
Don Bessent

Bessent was the winning pitcher in the second game of the 1956 World Series. Brooklyn overcame a six-run deficit to win 13-8. Tom Morgan, in his last appearance as a Yankee, was the losing pitcher.

J. Edgar Hoover ran the FBI for almost fifty years. He would send agents who displeased him to the Bureau's Butte, Montana office. There being no major-league team in Butte, Yankee General Manager George Weiss sent Morgan to the Kansas City A's.

Yankee "lowlights" in the All-Star game, part two:

- Bobby Richardson hit into two double plays in the 1963 game. The second double play ended the game.
- With the 1978 game tied, Rich Gossage allowed four eighth-inning runs, giving the National League a 7-3 win.
- In 1987, Dave Winfield played all thirteen innings. He went into a slump after this incredible feat of endurance.
- No Yankee pitcher started the game from 1970 to 1993.
- Each year, there is an award for the Most Valuable Player in the All-Star game. No Yankee has received this award since its inception in 1962.

JULY 8, 1969

Baltimore celebrated "Babe Ruth Day." Two Oriole wins over the Yankees added to the occasion. New York's pitchers started well, giving up ten runs in the first inning of the first game.

These teams were not evenly matched. Future Hall of Famers Brooks Robinson and Frank Robinson played for the Orioles; Bill Robinson and Frank Tepedino were with the Yankees.

Tepedino and Bill Robinson might make a Hall of Fame someday. I am presuming their high schools have such a means for honoring alumni.

Born July 8, 1941
Ken Sanders

Sanders had thirty-one saves for the Milwaukee Brewers in 1971. This was more than twice as many as the entire Yankee pitching staff had.

Greatest dominance by the American League leader in saves over the Yankee leader:

- Sanders had thirty-one saves to Jack Aker's and Lindy McDaniel's four in 1971.
- Chicago's Goose Gossage had twenty-six saves, while Tippy Martinez had eight in 1975.
- Minnesota's Ron Perranoski earned thirty-one saves to Jack Aker's 1969 total of eleven.
- In 1994, Baltimore's Lee Smith had thirty-three saves to Steve Howe's fifteen.

(Dominance is measured in terms of percentage. For example, Sanders's thirty-one saves is 775 percent of Aker's four.)

JULY 9, 1939

Boston completed a five-game sweep at Yankee Stadium. Almost exactly twenty years later, the Red Sox would win five straight against the Yankees at Fenway Park.

Highlights of the Red Sox sweeps:

- Boston won consecutive doubleheaders in 1939.
- Jimmie Foxx was the hitting star in 1939, with eight hits in nineteen at bats.
- In 1959, the Red Sox, who had a 33-45 record before the sweep, outscored the Yankees 50-18.
- Don Buddin's game-winning grand slam in the bottom of the eleventh inning was the most dramatic moment of the 1959 sweep.

Died July 9, 1951
Harry Heilmann

Heilmann won the 1927 American League batting title. By so doing, the Tiger outfielder prevented a member of the Yankees from leading the American League in every important batting category.

JULY 10, 1945

Wartime travel restrictions had canceled the All-Star game. This was not necessarily bad. Baseball fans were spared seeing Nick Etten, Snuffy Stirnweiss, or Monk Dubiel representing the fourth-place Yankees.

A series of crosstown exhibition games replaced the All-Star game. On this date, the Yankees were preparing for their game with the Giants. They needed the practice, having lost ten of sixteen games on a recent road trip.

Born July 10, 1945
Hal McRae

Kansas City's designated hitter had a .444 batting average against the Yankees in the 1977 American League Championship Series.

Nineteen seventy-seven was the fifth season American League teams used the designated hitter. New York still had not understood the second word of this concept. For 1976, and most of 1977, they used Carlos May as their designated hitter. In these two seasons combined, May had five home runs, fifty-seven RBI, and a .257 average. A team would accept these statistics from a second baseman, provided he fielded well.

Other Kansas City Royals who starred against the Yankees in their four playoff series between 1976 and 1980:

- George Brett and Frank White were the Royals' outstanding players.
- Paul Splittorff, Dennis Leonard, and Larry Gura won two games.
- Fred Patek hit .389 in 1976 and in 1977.
- Amos Otis hit .429 in 1978 and .333 in 1980.
- Dan Quisenberry had a win and a save in 1980.

JULY 11, 1979

Unlike the previous night, Yankee outfielder Lou Pinella was able to ignore the San Diego Chicken. Angered by the famous mascot, who was appearing as a guest in Seattle, Pinella had thrown his glove at it. For one of the rare times that season, he made an accurate throw.

Pinella could not ignore the score of the game. Seattle scored nine runs in the first inning and beat the Yankees 16-1.

Seattle versus the Yankees during the Mariners' first six seasons, 1977-1982:

- Seattle won twenty-seven of its sixty-two games against the Yankees. This .435 winning percentage exceeded the Mariners' .397 percentage against the rest of the league.
- The Mariners won thirteen of the teams' first sixteen games in Seattle.
- Their predecessors, the Pilots, lasted one season. This team also had a better winning percentage against the Yankees than against the rest of the league.

Born July 11, 1884
Harry Wolter

Wolter was the Yankee co-leader in home runs in 1913. He hit two.

JULY 12, 1990

Chicago's Melido Perez pitched a six-inning no-hitter against the Yankees. Rain ended New York's misery.

It is impossible to be certain if Perez would have completed the no-hitter. As the 1990 Yankees had the lowest team batting average in the American League, it is safe to assume he would have.

Other actions by a Perez that damaged the Yankees:

- In 1993, Melido was a Yankee. During a slump, Perez lost seven of eight decisions and had a 6.71 ERA.
- Pascual, a Yankee pitcher, was suspended for the 1992 season for drug use.
- Tony had the game-winning RBI in second game of the 1976 World Series. His Reds went on to sweep the Series from the Yankees.

Born July 12, 1938
Ron Fairly

Fairly had four hits, as Toronto beat the Yankees 19-3, in a 1977 game. (See September 10.)

JULY 13, 1969

New York lost both games of a doubleheader to the Senators. Washington scored five first-inning runs in the first game and built a 7-0 lead in the second game.

Born July 13, 1953
J.J. Cannon

Toronto's outfielder made a superb catch, as the awful Blue Jays won at Yankee Stadium. This loss spoiled Billy Martin's 1979 return as manager of the Yankees. Was the ever-patient Steinbrenner going to check with his "baseball people" about rehiring Martin's predecessor, Bob Lemon?

Yankee hating by the numbers, part fifteen:

- **56.** Number worn by Jim Bouton, who wrote *Ball Four*. This diary contains many unflattering comments about the Yankees.
- **57.** What Joe DiMaggio was trying to extend his hitting streak to, the night it was stopped. He was rumored to have had an endorsement deal with Heinz had the streak continued for one more game.
- **58.** Years since the previous time a team had scored as few runs as the four the Yankees scored in the 1963 World Series.
- **59.** Games the Yankees won during the 1981 strike-shortened season. Four other American League East teams won at least that many. It did not matter. Baseball had a split season in 1981. Teams, like the Yankees, with the best pre-strike records qualified for the playoffs. So did the teams with the best post-strike records. This split season was one of the dumber ideas of the 1980's. It ranks with Walter Mondale's idea for a campaign promise. He told voters that, if elected president, he would increase taxes.

JULY 14, 1979

Yankee relief ace Goose Gossage gave up three home runs. One of these, a three-run home run by Don Baylor, tied the game. California won the game in the twelfth inning.

The previous day, California's Nolan Ryan had taken a no-hitter into the ninth inning. He settled for a one-hit victory over the Yankees.

Born July 14, 1967
Robin Ventura

Yankee outfielder Jim Leyritz misplayed Ventura's bases-loaded fly ball into a three-run, three-base error. Moments later, Ventura scored on another error. Because of these miscues, Andy Hawkins lost a game in which he did not allow a hit.

In honor of Bastille Day, some players of French descent who did damage to the Yankees:

- Jim Bouton wrote *Ball Four.* (See July 15.) "Bouton" can be translated into English as "pimple." Because of his book, the Yankees told Bouton he was as welcome as this skin affliction.
- Max Lanier beat the Yankees in the fourth game of the 1942 World Series.
- Napoleon Lajoie had a lifetime batting average of .339.
- Urban Shocker kept the St. Louis Browns in the 1922 pennant race with the Yankees. He won twenty-four games.

(See notes on others like Bob Feller, Clem Labine, and Lou Boudreau elsewhere in this book.)

JULY 15, 1907

Chicago humiliated the Yankees 15-0. They would repeat this feat in 1950. These are the worst shutout losses ever suffered by the Yankees.

Born July 15, 1892
Eugene Hargrave

Of all the players who have played for the Yankees, "Bubbles" Hargrave had the least fear-inspiring nickname. That is with the possible exception of Julius (Julie) Wera and Elias (Liz) Funk.

Some of Jim Bouton's comments about the Yankees in *Ball Four*:

- Mickey Mantle pushed kids aside and closed bus windows on their hands when they wanted his autograph.
- Mantle's injuries might have healed more quickly if he had spent less time in bars.
- Whitey Ford cheated by doctoring the ball with his ring. Sometimes his catcher, Elston Howard, would help by putting mud on the ball.
- Roger Maris did not hustle. Bouton claimed Maris ran to first base as if he had sore feet.

JULY 16, 1953

Clint Courtney, Dick Kryhoski, and Jim Dyck hit consecutive home runs, tying a major-league record. These came in the first inning, as St. Louis beat the Yankees 7-3.

Born July 16, 1889
Shoeless Joe Jackson

Jackson set the American League record with twenty-six triples in 1912. This was twice as many as the Yankees hit, as a team, in 1988. No team has ever hit fewer triples in a season.

Comparing the ten Jacksons who had at least five hundred career at bats:

- Joe had the best batting average, .356, while Travis is second with .291. Reggie is fourth with a .262 average.
- Joe's career slugging average, .518, is twenty-eight points higher than Reggie's.
- Bo hit home runs the most frequently, once every 16.9 at bats.
- Joe's career postseason batting average is sixty-seven points higher than Reggie's.
- Reggie used phrases like "the magnitude of being me" more than all the other Jacksons combined.

JULY 17, 1923 and 1941

This was not the Yankees' day to be in Cleveland. In 1923, the Indians won 13-0, scoring all their runs off Carl Mays. This was just about the last thing Mays did for the Yankees.

Eighteen years later, Cleveland pitchers Al Smith and Jim Bagby stopped Joe DiMaggio's fifty-six-game hitting streak.

Pitchers who did not give up a hit to DiMaggio during his streak:

- Bill Beckman, Les McCrabb, A's
- Tommy Bridges, Johnny Gorsica, Tigers
- Joe Dobson, Charlie Wagner, Red Sox

(Minimum of 125 innings pitched in 1941)

Born July 17, 1917
Lou Boudreau

Player-manager Boudreau won the American League's Most Valuable Player award in 1948. He had led the Indians to the pennant.

While Boudreau had a great year, the National League MVP, Stan Musial, had a classic season. Musial led the National League in runs scored, hits, doubles, triples, RBI, batting average, and slugging average.

Admirers of Babe Ruth point to his 1921 season as the greatest-ever by a player. They ignore Musial's 1948 achievement. As noted, Musial led in seven, of the eight, major hitting categories. (If one long foul ball had been fair, Musial would have tied Ralph Kiner for the home run title.) In 1921, Ruth led in four. He was sixth in hits. Ruth lost the batting title to Harry Heilmann and the doubles title to Tris Speaker.

Howard Shanks won the triples title. Mindful of this feat, the Yankees acquired Shanks in 1925. He hit one triple in sixty-six games and left baseball. It is safe to assume he did not become a professional golfer.

224

JULY 18, 1995

In a loss to the White Sox, Yankee pitcher Jack McDowell gave up thirteen hits in four and two-thirds innings. As he left the mound, McDowell gestured to the crowd with an erect middle finger. This was not the way to win back fans who were still bitter over the 1994 players' strike.

Nor was adding Darryl Strawberry to the roster, as the Yankees did before the game. By 1995, Strawberry had become an underachieving, substance-abusing shell of the player he had been in the 1980's.

Fallout from McDowell's gesture:

- The Yankees fined him five thousand dollars.
- McDowell never apologized, limiting himself to calling his action stupid.
- Many opposing players thought, thank you, Jack, I have always wanted to do that to Yankee fans.

Born July 18, 1963
Mike Greenwell

He and Roger Clemens played on the four Red Sox teams that won the American League East over the Yankees, between 1986 and 1995.

JULY 19, 1987

Texas had twenty-two hits, as they beat the Yankees 20-3. They got five runs off each of four different Yankee pitchers. Only Rick Cerone, normally a catcher, was able to get the Rangers out. Not that Cerone was dominating. He barely missed giving up a grand slam home run that would have made the score 24-3.

Born July 19, 1888
Ed Sweeney

This Yankee catcher committed three errors in one inning, in a 1912 game.

Miscellaneous feats by catchers:

- In 1997, Sandy Alomar, Jr. drove in four runs, as Cleveland, who had trailed 9-2, beat the Yankees 10-9.
- Terry Humphrey, a terrible hitter, made his last major-league hit count. It led to the winning run, as Nolan Ryan and the Angels defeated Ron Guidry and the Yankees, in 1979.
- Charlie Lau had two pinch hits in an inning. These helped Baltimore score seven runs, after two were out, and beat the Yankees 9-8, in a 1964 game.
- Baltimore manager Paul Richards, a former catcher, invented the oversized mitt for catching knuckleball pitchers. In its first use, the mitt and Hoyt Wilhelm beat the Yankees 3-2, in 1960.

JULY 20, 1945

After losing a doubleheader to the Browns, the Yankees were in the second division. St. Louis's Boris "Babe" Martin homered to move to within 713 career home runs of George "Babe" Ruth. Martin finished his career with two home runs. This is almost certainly the major-league record for a player named Boris.

Most games the Yankees finished out of the first division, 1903-1968:

- thirty-three, 1908
- twenty-seven, 1912
- twenty-two, 1913
- fifteen, 1915
- thirteen, 1907

(Finishing in the "first division," that is among the upper half of the league, used to be considered the mark of a satisfactory season. It also meant league-paid bonus money for the players. When further expansion dictated six-team divisions in 1969, this concept disappeared.)

Born July 20, 1901
Heinie Manush

By winning the 1926 batting title, the Detroit outfielder kept Babe Ruth from winning the Triple Crown.

JULY 21, 1921

Cleveland extended its lead over the second-place Yankees by beating New York 17-8.

Died July 21, 1967
Jimmie Foxx

He was the most dangerous hitter on the 1929-1931 Philadelphia A's. This team won three consecutive pennants. In 1932, Foxx's fifty-eight home runs threatened Babe Ruth's single-season record.

Jimmie Foxx, Denny McLain, and other things:

- Foxx's and Hank Greenberg's fifty-eight home runs were the most hit in a season by a right-handed batter until Mark McGwire came along. Joe DiMaggio holds the Yankee record, with forty-six.
- Detroit's Denny McLain almost certainly grooved the pitch that Mickey Mantle hit to pass Foxx on the all-time home run list.
- McLain won his thirty-first game of the 1968 season against the Yankees. He is one of eighteen major-league pitchers to have won that many games in a season. Only one did it with the Yankees.

JULY 22, 1904

Chicago was in the process of winning three consecutive games in New York. These losses dropped the Yankees into third place.

It looked like the American League's effort to stack the Yankees might not be successful. For commercial reasons, the League wanted a strong team in New York City. League President Ban Johnson had arranged for the Yankees to acquire players like Patsy Dougherty, who had hit .331 for Boston.

Johnson should have provided the Yankees with a stepladder. One Yankee said New York catcher Red Kleinow needed this device to catch the wild pitch that Jack Chesbro threw to lose the 1904 pennant.

Born July 22, 1956
Scott Sanderson

Yankee pitcher Sanderson gave up four home runs in an inning. This brought back memories of one of Catfish Hunter's games with the Yankees.

Boston versus Catfish Hunter, the first inning of the June 17, 1977 game:

- Rick Burleson led off with a home run.
- Fred Lynn followed with a long home run.
- Three batters later, Carlton Fisk hit an even longer home run.
- This brought manager Billy Martin out to give Hunter advice. It helped. George Scott's home run did not go as far as Fisk's did.

JULY 23, 1950

Detroit scored two ninth-inning runs to beat the Yankees 6-5. Pitcher Saul Rogovin had the Tigers' biggest hit, a grand slam home run. Detroit remained in first place, two games ahead of the Yankees.

Jim Palmer pitched almost four thousand major-league innings without allowing a grand slam. Palmer, a Hall of Famer, knew how to pitch to poor hitters, like Rogovin, with the bases loaded. This would not seem to be a difficult skill for a major-league pitcher to learn.

Born July 23, 1936
Don Drysdale

Drysdale threw a three-hit shutout in the third game of the 1963 World Series. This victory set up the completion of the Dodgers' four-game sweep of the Yankees.

Fewest hits allowed against the Yankees in a World Series game:

- two, Warren Spahn, 1958
- three, Drysdale, 1963
- three, Jack Sanford, 1962
- three, Billy Pierce, 1962

JULY 24, 1983

George Brett hit a two-out, two-run home run in the ninth inning. It gave the Royals a one-run lead over the Yankees. Upon discovering Brett had too much pine tar on his bat, the umpire called Brett out, canceling the home run.

As the rules provided for only the bat to be thrown out, American League President Lee MacPhail overruled the umpires. He reinstated Brett's home run and ordered the game to be resumed at a later date. The Yankees tried to overturn this ruling by participating in a court challenge. Eventually, the teams completed the game, on August 18, with Kansas City winning.

The "prequel" to the Pine Tar Game:

- In a July 1975 game against Minnesota, Yankee catcher Thurman Munson hit a RBI single.
- Twins' manager Frank Quilici complained that Munson had too much pine tar on his bat.
- Umpire Art Frantz called Munson out and disallowed the run. Minnesota eventually won 2-1.
- As a result of this game, the rule was changed. In 1983, MacPhail cited this revised rule in overruling the umpires.

Born July 24, 1927
Preston Ward

His home run helped the Indians defeat the Yankees in an unusual game. Cleveland's Ward, Bobby Avila, Rocky Colovito, and Chico Carrasquel hit solo home runs to account for all the scoring in a 1956 game.

JULY 25, 1955

A 4-8 road trip left the Yankees only one game ahead of Cleveland and Chicago. One reason the pennant race was close was New York's pitching problems. These problems were so serious that the desperate Yankees signed Ted Gray. In the previous twelve months, three American League teams had let Gray go. Missing the message, the Yankees gave Gray a start. He lasted three innings.

Died July 25, 1986
Ted Lyons

Lyons was a reliable pitcher for twenty years against the Yankees. He won 260 games for the White Sox.

Pitchers who won more than 250 American League games, but none with the Yankees:

- Walter Johnson, 417
- Eddie Plank, 304 (Twenty-one of his 325 wins were in the Federal League.)
- Lefty Grove, 300
- Early Wynn, 300
- Jim Palmer, 268
- Bob Feller, 266
- Lyons, 260
- Red Faber, 254
- Jack Morris, 254
- Bert Blyleven, 253 (Thirty-four of his 287 wins were in the National League.)

JULY 26, 1952

Steve Souchock's ninth-inning grand slam home run gave the last-place Tigers a win over the Yankees. This was Souchock's second game-winning home run against the Yankees in as many days.

Born July 26, 1923
Hoyt Wilhelm

If you look hard enough, you will find that virtually every player holds some sort of major-league record.

Wilhelm allowed the fewest hits to the Yankees in games played in successive seasons. Pitching for Baltimore, Wilhelm threw a no-hitter in 1958 and a one-hitter in 1959.

Some serious errors in the movie, *The Babe Ruth Story,* which was released on this date in 1948:

- William Bendix, age forty-two, played the adult and the teenage Ruth.
- Bendix could not swing a bat in a manner even closely resembling a baseball player, much less Ruth. He was more credible pretending he was a teenage boy.
- According to the movie, Ruth received his famous suspension, in 1925, for going to the veterinarian with a sick dog. (See August 29 for the actual reasons.)
- In the movie, Ruth pointed, bat extended, toward the center field bleachers. He then hit his famous home run in the 1932 World Series. (There is considerable disagreement over what really happened. While Ruth might have made a gesture, he came nowhere near the emphatic pointing portrayed in this movie.)
- Moviegoers committed the most egregious error. They paid money to see this movie, rather than *Key Largo*, which was showing in other theaters.

HOLLYWOOD TELLS THE BABE RUTH STORY (July 26)

JULY 27, 1978 and 1956

Duane Kuiper tied a record with two bases-loaded triples, as Cleveland defeated the Yankees 17-5. Twenty-two years earlier, the Kansas City A's had twenty-six hits against the Yankees. Giving up twenty-six hits to the 1956 A's was like losing a battle to the 1991 Iraqis.

Died July 27, 1985
Smokey Joe Wood

As a Red Sox pitcher, Wood had two one-hitters against the Yankees. With Cleveland in 1918, pitcher-turned-outfielder Wood hit a home run in the nineteenth inning. Wood's hit gave the Yankees their longest-ever loss.

Longest losses by the Yankees:

- Cleveland beat the Yankees 3-2, in nineteen innings, in 1918.
- Boston defeated New York 12-11, in eighteen innings, in 1927.
- In 1967, the Twins beat the Yankees 3-2, in eighteen innings.
- Washington won 2-1 over the Yankees. This 1970 game lasted eighteen innings.

JULY 28, 1975

The third of three consecutive shutout losses effectively ended any Yankee pennant hopes. Boston's Bill Lee and Roger Moret, and Detroit's Vern Ruhle blanked the slumping Yankees.

Born July 28, 1949
Vida Blue

Blue might have won the majority of his eighteen wins in 1976 for the Yankees. Fortunately, Commissioner Bowie Kuhn voided the Yankees' purchase of the A's pitcher.

Without Blue, the Yankees had no useful left-handed starters for the playoffs. They chose not to use Ken Holtzman. He had won only six postseason games and obviously was inexperienced.

Colorful contributors to problems for the Yankees:

- Brooklyn's Joe Black beat them in the first game of the 1952 World Series.
- Kansas City's Frank White hit .545 against New York in the 1980 American League Championship Series.
- Bobby Brown had one hit in twelve postseason at bats for the Yankees, in 1980 and 1981.
- Dallas Green was fired as manager of the Yankees, with the team in sixth place, in 1989.
- Labatt Blue is a major brand of Labatt Breweries, who co-owned the Toronto Blue Jays during their most successful years.

JULY 29, 1928

The seventh-place Indians beat the Yankees 24-6. Cleveland scored seventeen runs in the first two innings. Fatigued from all this base running, the Indians scored only seven runs in the final seven innings.

Died July 29, 1954
Babe Borton

Babe ("Don't call me Ruth") Borton hit .130 for the Yankees in 1913. This is the worst-ever for a Yankee with at least one hundred at bats. A writer was so unimpressed with Borton that he called him an "onion." This is early twentieth-century slang for "lemon."

Other Babes who have caused problems for the Yankees:

- Loren Babe came close to a truly dubious achievement in 1952. His combined batting average (.095) and fielding average (.906) was almost less than 1.000.
- Red Sox pitcher Babe Ruth had a 17-5 record against the Yankees.
- A few days short of his twenty-first birthday, Fernando Valenzuela pitched for the Dodgers. He threw a complete game victory over the Yankees in the 1981 World Series.
- Some Yankees probably used this term to describe the woman who caused an uproar when she got her derriere autographed on the Yankee team bus.

JULY 30, 1990

Steinbrenner agreed to resign as managing general partner of the Yankees. Ever the negotiator, Steinbrenner bargained a potential two-year suspension from baseball into a lifetime ban. He had paid an undesirable character for incriminating information on Yankee star Dave Winfield.

What happened at Yankee Stadium when Steinbrenner's resignation was announced:

- There was a ninety-second standing ovation.
- Fans chanted "No more George!"
- Everyone forgot, for the moment, that the 1990 Yankees were one of that franchise's worst-ever teams.

Died July 30, 1962
Steinbrenner's hopes of owning a NBA team

Steinbrenner owned the Cleveland Pipers of the American Basketball League. Motivated by its desire to put a rival league out of business, the NBA was prepared to accept Steinbrenner and the Pipers. (Look up "Devil, deals with" in the encyclopedia.) Fortunately for the NBA, Steinbrenner was unable to raise the entry fee, which was due on this date.

JULY 31, 1992

With a 13-2 win, Toronto increased its lead over the Yankees to thirteen games. Off the field, the Yankees could not acquire Jim Abbott, a starting pitcher they needed badly. Abbott would have replaced Tim Leary. Pitching like drug guru Dr. Timothy Leary, the dropout as a Yankee starter gave up six runs to the Blue Jays.

Born July 31, 1893
Alan Russell

Russell and Slim Lowe became the first pitchers to allow a switch-hitter to homer from both sides of the plate in a single game. Philadelphia's Wally Schang did it against these Yankee pitchers in 1916.

John Lucadello, of the St. Louis Browns, was the next American Leaguer to accomplish this feat. His home runs came in a 16-4 win over the Yankees, in September 1940. This loss put the Yankees four games behind two teams, with two weeks remaining in the season.

Where the Yankees' most prominent switch-hitter, Mickey Mantle, ranks among switch-hitters:

- He is tenth in hits, behind Pete Rose, Eddie Murray, Frank Frisch, George Davis, Max Carey, Ted Simmons, Ozzie Smith, Tim Raines, and Red Schoendeinst.
- He is second to Eddie Murray in RBI.
- Rose and Murray have more total bases.
- Mantle is fourth in career batting average, behind Frisch, Roberto Alomar, and Rose.

AUGUST 1, 1903

Rube Waddell struck out thirteen Yankees. Only Kid Elberfeld got a hit off the A's pitcher.

Waddell could be forgiven for not concentrating on Elberfeld. Future Hall of Fame pitchers do not worry about career .271 hitters. This is particularly true when the hitter weighs 135 pounds and is depressed over being traded from Detroit.

Admitted as a state August 1, 1876
Colorado

In 1993, the Colorado Rockies drew more fans than the Yankees and the Mets combined.

Some comments on Steinbrenner:

- "(Steinbrenner is) congenitally unsuited to be in the sporting world." (*Cleveland Press*, in its issue of this date in 1962)
- "He has the qualities of a local Aztec volcano." (*Time* magazine, 1982)
- "What has he ever done except sit up in the stands and second guess?" (Billy Martin)
- "When you see his mouth move." (White Sox owner Jerry Reinsdorf on how you can tell Steinbrenner is lying.)

AUGUST 2, 1975

At a press conference, the Yankees announced that Billy Martin would replace Bill Virdon as Yankee manager.

Few were surprised. News of Martin's hiring had been leaked. Virdon, who was unaware of his fate, had had the pleasure of denying what he thought were rumors.

Born August 2, 1924
Carroll O'Connor

O'Connor was the star of the classic television series, *All in the Family*. His character, Archie Bunker, a New York City resident, was a Mets fan.

Some actors whose television characters supported Yankee opponents:

- In *Magnum, P.I.*, Tom Selleck's character was a Tiger fan.
- Victor French wore an Oakland A's cap in *Highway to Heaven*.
- As Corporal Klinger in *M*A*S*H*, Jamie Farr wore a Toledo Mud Hens' cap. This was actually a Texas Rangers' cap.
- Ted Danson played Sam Malone, a former Red Sox pitcher, in *Cheers*.

AUGUST 3, 1978

Reggie Jackson had no hits in ten at bats, as the Yankees lost a double-header. This was hardly a unique experience for Jackson. He would do it again in 1979.

Born August 3, 1964
Kevin Elster

In 1994, Elster had twenty at bats without getting a hit. This is the most in a season for a Yankee non-pitcher. Elster improved in 1995. He had two hits in seventeen at bats, to increase his batting average as a Yankee to .054.

Some stoppers of Yankee streaks:

- Lefty Grove shut out the Yankees on this date in 1933. New York had scored at least one run in 308 consecutive games.
- Carl Hubbell was the winning pitcher in the first game of the 1936 World Series. This stopped the Yankees' World Series winning streak at twelve games.
- Larry Hisle hit the key home run, as the Twins beat Ron Guidry in 1978. This ended Guidry's streak of twelve consecutive wins.
- Norwood Gibson was the winning pitcher when the Red Sox ended Jack Chesbro's winning streak at fourteen, in 1904.
- Yankee pitcher Whitey Ford had not allowed a run in the World Series in thirty-two and two-thirds innings. San Francisco's Jose Pagan ended that nonsense by driving in Willie Mays, in the 1962 Series.

AUGUST 4, 1929

Cleveland beat the Yankees 14-6. After two were out, the Indians scored nine runs in the top of the ninth inning. Imagine the reactions of Yankee fans. They would have gone from "only one more out," to "let's hold them," to "the Yanks can come back," to "where did I park my car?"

Died August 4, 1983
The Unknown Seagull

Dave Winfield was throwing in a between-innings warmup. One of his throws struck this bird, killing it. Toronto police arrested the Yankee outfielder and charged him with cruelty to animals. They subsequently dropped this charge. Had the case gone to trial, Winfield's attorney could have proved reasonable doubt. Winfield had only five assists in 151 games in 1983, indicating he rarely threw accurately.

Confusion and panic during the 1982 season:

- Clyde King became the Yankees' third manager of the season, on this date in 1982. His appointment followed New York's 14-2 loss to the White Sox.
- Besides three managers, the Yankees had three batting instructors and five pitching coaches.
- Steinbrenner had advertised the 1982 Yankees as a team built around speed. New York would rank ninth in the league in steals.
- Forty-seven different players played for the Yankees that season.

AUGUST 5, 1967

Kansas City, who had ceased being New York's virtual farm club, beat the last-place Yankees.

Kansas City's previous owner, Arnold Johnson, had business dealings with the Yankee owners. His profit came from the attendance when the Yankees came to town. Beholden to the Yankees, he had sent players, like Roger Maris, to New York. No longer. By 1967, the A's had talent. Bert Campaneris, Joe Rudi, Catfish Hunter, and other young players would become part of the Oakland A's dynasty of the 1970's.

Died August 5, 1978
Jesse Haines

Pitching for the Cardinals, Haines beat the Yankees in the third and seventh games of the 1926 World Series. Haines did something in that Series that only Babe Ruth was able to do for the Yankees. He hit a home run.

The best batting averages by a pitcher against the Yankees in the World Series:

- Haines hit .600 in 1926.
- Jack Bentley had a .600 average for the Giants, in the 1923 Series.
- In 1921, Jesse Barnes hit .444 for the Giants.
- San Francisco's Jack Sanford hit .429, in 1962.
- Warren Spahn had a .333 average for the Braves, in 1958.

(Minimum of five at bats)

AUGUST 6, 1994

After the 1981 players' strike, Steinbrenner made a promise. He said we could bury him at home plate if another strike ever occurred. People were hopeful of such an interring, as the players struck.

As every cloud has a silver lining, some benefits from the 1994 players' strike:

- We did not have to watch the Yankees in the playoffs. When play stopped, the Yankees had a six-game lead in the American League East.
- There was no race for the batting title between Yankee teammates Paul O'Neil and Wade Boggs.
- Jimmy Key could not improve on his 17-4 record.
- Steinbrenner would not get richer.

Born August 6, 1926
Clem Labine

Dodger pitcher Labine threw a shutout in the sixth game of the 1956 World Series. He limited the Yankees to seven hits over ten innings.

Primarily a relief pitcher, Labine had only one complete game in the 1956 regular season. This was a case of history repeating itself. In the 1952 World Series, Joe Black had a complete game victory. This Dodger reliever had one such victory during the regular season.

Emergency starters should not beat a good team twice in five World Series. This should occur about as frequently as Lesley Gore's *You Don't Own Me* is played at weddings.

BURYING STEINBRENNER (August 6)

AUGUST 7, 1956

Tommy Byrne walked Ted Williams, with the bases loaded, to give Boston a 1-0 win. This was one of Byrne's 763 walks, in 994 innings, as a Yankee pitcher. Let us put Byrne's wildness into perspective. Nolan Ryan, who holds the record for walks in a career, walked 516 batters every 994 innings.

Born August 7, 1886
Bill McKechnie

McKechnie left the Yankees for the Federal League, where he got his first job as a manager. He succeeded in this role. McKechnie was elected to the Hall of Fame before legendary Yankee manager Miller Huggins was.

Terrible managerial efforts by former Yankees:

- Under Eddie Lopat, the 1963 Kansas City A's finished eighth, thirty-one games out.
- Ben Chapman's 1947 Phillies were seventh, forty-three games behind Brooklyn.
- Jerry Coleman managed the 1980 Padres, who finished last. There is a pattern to Coleman's career in baseball. He went from an average player, to a bad broadcaster, to a dreadful manager. Fantasy: Coleman becomes the general manager of the Yankees.
- With Joe Gordon as manager, the 1969 Royals lost ninety-three games. They finished thirty-one games behind Baltimore.

AUGUST 8, 1948

Cleveland's Satchel Paige became the first African-American pitcher to beat the Yankees.

Baseball did not integrate until 1947. This was eighty-four years after the Gettysburg Address. In this speech, President Lincoln reminded Americans that all men are created equal. The Yankees waited until 1955 to integrate. They figured their general manager, George Weiss, knew more about human rights than Lincoln did.

Born August 8, 1913
Cecil Travis

Travis, the Senators' shortstop, hit .359 in 1941. Despite a fifty-six-game hitting streak, Joe DiMaggio did not do as well. He hit .357 that season. Ted Williams surpassed both players, hitting .406.

Comparisons between Ted Williams and Joe DiMaggio:

- Williams had a career batting average of .344; DiMaggio's was .325.
- Williams hit 521 home runs; DiMaggio hit 361.
- Williams had 1,839 RBI; DiMaggio had 1,537.
- Williams's on base average was .480; DiMaggio's was .395.
- Williams won fourteen batting, home run, and RBI titles, DiMaggio won six.

AUGUST 9, 1987

Detroit beat the Yankees 15-4. Earlier in the series, the Tigers had won 12-5 and 8-0. These losses started the Yankees on the slide that took them from first to fourth place.

How the Yankees fell out of contention in 1987:

- Following the sweep by the Tigers, the Yankees worked their way down to five games out of first place by September 7.
- On September 8 and 9, they lost to the Red Sox. In the first of these losses, they had to endure a three-hour rain delay and a six-run Red Sox lead.
- September 10 was a travel day. One presumes Steinbrenner, who had never played, coached, or managed professional baseball, advised Yankee manager Lou Pinella on the appropriate lineup.
- In Toronto, the Yankees proved they could lose close games, as well as blowouts. Ernie Whitt's tenth-inning home run won the first game; numerous Blue Jays helped win the second 13-1. Following the game, Pinella announced he would begin giving playing time to the Yankee rookies. This was not to get them ready for postseason play.

Born August 9, 1919
Fred Sanford

Yankee General Manager George Weiss called acquiring Sanford the worst deal he ever made. New York gave up future All-Star catcher Sherman Lollar, two players, and one hundred thousand dollars. Sanford won twelve games in three seasons with the Yankees.

Redd Foxx played a character named Fred Sanford in the television series *Sanford and Son*. Like Weiss, he worked with garbage.

AUGUST 10, 1980

Baltimore moved to within two games of New York by sweeping a series at Yankee Stadium. John Lowenstein's RBI single in the first game was the key play of this series. This hit followed a controversial call against the Yankees.

Died August 10, 1966
Chuck Dressen

Commissioner Chandler suspended Dressen for accepting a job as a Yankee coach. Dressen had broken an oral agreement to remain in Brooklyn.

There are hundreds of thousands of lawyers in this country. Why has not one argued this case is a precedent for getting Steinbrenner suspended? (Steinbrenner has broken more than a few oral commitments.) Is personal injury work really that much fun?

The Yankees and the Leo Durocher suspension:

- Commissioner Chandler had ordered Dodger manager Durocher not to associate with numerous gamblers.
- Durocher saw Yankee co-owner Larry MacPhail with some of these characters.
- Durocher told his boss, Branch Rickey, who complained to Chandler. As background, Rickey knew of MacPhail's interest in hiring Durocher as Yankee manager. Rickey saw New York's hiring of Dressen as a coach as a preliminary step in this process.
- MacPhail asked for an investigation into the affair.
- Durocher was suspended for a year, for reasons that are still not clear. Chandler fined the Yankees, who were hardly blameless, two thousand dollars.

AUGUST 11, 1950

Joe DiMaggio was benched, officially because he needed a rest. He was hitting .270. Cliff Mapes, his well-rested replacement, had two hits in fourteen at bats. Gene Woodling, Mapes's replacement, did not do much better.

Realizing he needed a rest from these phony DiMaggios, manager Casey Stengel reinstated the real one.

Born August 11, 1913
Bob Scheffing

Scheffing was replaced, as Cubs' manager, by rotating coaches. Cubs' owner Phil Wrigley figured this committee of coaches was superior to a single manager. Steinbrenner effectively instituted the same system with the Yankees.

Yankee hating by the numbers, part sixteen:

- **60.** Career batting average (.060) of Ryne Duren. He nevertheless drove in the tying and winning runs, as the expansion Angels beat the Yankees, in 1961.
- **61.** American League victories by Earl Hamilton, who pitched for the Browns from 1911 to 1917. Two of these wins were one-hitters against the Yankees.
- **62.** The most Hall of Fame votes that Thurman Munson has received. (Approximately four hundred votes are needed for induction.) Some journalists, their brains softened by their grief over the Yankee catcher's tragic death, wanted the five-year waiting period waived for Munson.
- **63.** Games Fritz Peterson and Mike Kekich started for the Yankees in 1972. Their "life-swapping" during the off-season limited their effectiveness in 1973. (See March 5.)

AUGUST 12, 1945

New York lost the first of two consecutive doubleheaders to Detroit. These losses left the Yankees seven games behind the Tigers, effectively eliminating New York from the 1945 pennant race. In the second doubleheader, the Tigers scored twenty-six runs.

Born August 12, 1892
Ray Schalk

In 1920, the Yankees won ninety-five games. Chicago won one more, primarily because Schalk, their catcher, helped four pitchers win at least twenty games. The Yankees have never had more than two twenty-game winners in a season.

Yankee hating by the numbers, part seventeen:

- **64.** RBI by Bill Mazeroski for the Pirates in the 1960 season. He had five critical ones against the Yankees in the 1960 World Series.
- **65.** Games Bob Lemon managed in 1979 before Steinbrenner fired him. He was the second manager to be fired during the season after he managed a World Series winner. Billy Martin became the first, when Steinbrenner fired him during the previous season.
- **66.** In 1966, the Yankees finished tenth.
- **67.** Of the first seventy-three members of the Hall of Fame, the number who spent the bulk of their careers with teams other than the Yankees.

AUGUST 13, 1964

CBS bought the Yankees. During their eight full seasons of ownership by the network, the Yankees never won anything. They finished an average of twenty games out of first place.

This network seems to have operated the Yankees as ridiculously as it ran the sleeping arrangements on the *Dick Van Dyke Show.* CBS had Rob and Laura Petrie, a married couple, sleeping in twin beds.

CBS had problems in its own business. In six of the eight seasons CBS owned the Yankees, another network had the top-rated series on television.

The most popular television series during the period CBS owned the Yankees:

- *Bonanza* (NBC), 1964-1965*, 1965-1966, 1966-1967
- *Andy Griffith Show* (CBS), 1967-1968
- *Rowan and Martin's Laugh-In* (NBC), 1968-1969, 1969-1970
- *Marcus Welby, M.D.* (ABC), 1970-1971
- *All in the Family* (CBS), 1971-1972

Source: *TV Facts*

* 1964-1965, for example, refers to the television season running from September 1964 to August 1965.

Born August 13, 1964
Jay Buhner

In a terrible deal, the Yankees sent Buhner and two minor-leaguers to Seattle for Ken Phelps. As a Mariner, Buhner has hit at least forty home runs three times. Phelps played in 131 games for the Yankees. New York eventually traded him to Oakland, for what turned out to be valueless consideration.

YANKEES IN CBS LAND (August 13)

AUGUST 14, 1960

Twenty-four innings of play resulted in two Yankee losses to Washington. Senators' pitcher Camilo Pascual showed why he was a good batter by hitting a grand slam home run. New York's Ralph Terry showed that he might not be a reliever by walking in the winning run.

Born August 14, 1944
Mike Ferraro

Kansas City led 3-2, in the second game of the 1980 American League Championship Series. There were two outs in the eighth inning. With Willie Randolph on first base, New York's Bob Watson doubled. As it was clear that Willie Wilson's throw was going to miss the cutoff man, third base coach Ferraro directed Randolph to try to score. George Brett, the backup cutoff man, caught the throw and threw Randolph out.

Steinbrenner blamed Ferraro when the Yankees lost the Series. This was unfair. Even his "baseball people" would have told him that sending a fast runner, with two outs, on an apparent misplay, made sense. One presumes Steinbrenner spoke with his "shipbuilding people" before criticizing Ferraro.

Speaking of base running, the greatest dominance by the league leader in steals versus the Yankee leader:

- Rickey Henderson had 130 steals in 1982, to Willie Randolph's sixteen.
- Bert Campaneris stole fifty-one bases in 1965; Bobby Richardson stole six.
- Henderson had 108 steals in 1983, to Don Baylor's seventeen.
- Kenny Lofton stole fifty-four bases in 1995; Luis Polonia stole ten.
- George Case stole sixty-one times in 1943; Snuffy Stirnweiss did it eleven times.

(Dominance is expressed in terms of percentage. For example, Henderson's 130 steals are 813 percent of Randolph's sixteen.)

AUGUST 15, 1991

Reverting to the 1960's, the Yankees benched their best player, Don Mattingly. He had refused to get a haircut.

Some low moments in the Steinbrenner-Mattingly relationship:

- In 1988, Steinbrenner called Mattingly "the most unproductive .300 hitter in baseball." Twenty-five other major-league teams were prepared to offer Steinbrenner their most productive .200 hitter in exchange for Mattingly. They would even guarantee the player would have well-trimmed hair.
- When Mattingly said he needed a "mental rest," Steinbrenner told him to "get a real job."
- After Mattingly won at arbitration in 1987, Steinbrenner blasted him. (See February 17.)
- Following the 1995 season, the Yankees did not offer Mattingly a contract. He ended up retiring from baseball.

Born August 15, 1859
Charles Comiskey

Comiskey built the 1906, 1917, and 1919 American League champion Chicago White Sox. Some feel the 1919 White Sox might have been the best team in the history of baseball.

AUGUST 16, 1981

Kirk Gibson hit a three-run home run in the bottom of the ninth. Detroit stunned the Yankees 5-4.

Born August 16, 1952
Al Holland

In 1986, the Yankees were so desperate for starting pitchers that Holland, a relief pitcher, started a game. So did Mike Armstrong, Brad Arnsberg, and Alfonso Pulido. Meanwhile, Phil Niekro, whom the Yankees had released, started thirty-two games for Cleveland. This is twelve more starts than the four Yankee pitchers mentioned in this paragraph had in their combined careers.

The Aaron brothers:

- Hank and Tommie Aaron hit 768 home runs between them. Tommie died on this date in 1984.
- This is more home runs than the three DiMaggio brothers (573 by Joe, Dom, and Vince) or the two Dickey brothers (206 by Bill and George) hit.
- Hank and Tommie Aaron's total is almost as many as the other two families combined.

AUGUST 17, 1925

New York waived Bobby Veach, who was hitting .353. With this average, he was overqualified for a team that had the second-worst batting average in the league. While with the Yankees, Veach had pinch hit for Babe Ruth. This should not be surprising. Veach outhit Ruth by sixty-three points that season.

Other obscure Yankees who outhit Babe Ruth:

- Ben Paschal outhit him by seventy points in 1925.
- Myril Hoag's 1932 batting average was twenty-nine points higher than Ruth's was.
- In 1926, Roy Carlyle outhit the Babe by five points.
- In 1922, Wally Schang had a batting average that was four points higher than Ruth's was.

Born August 17, 1892
Johnny Rawlings

His bench-jockeying in the 1922 World Series contributed to Babe Ruth's .118 batting average. Ruth was so upset that he went after Rawlings. When Rawlings's teammates prevented a fight, Ruth lectured Rawlings. Ruth said he did not mind being called certain ten and twelve-letter words, but Rawlings should not use certain racial epithets.

AUGUST 18, 1989

Dallas Green became the sixteenth manager to be fired by Steinbrenner. No longer content to fire just the manager, Steinbrenner also axed four coaches.

Born August 18, 1920
Bob Kennedy

Kennedy hit a grand slam, as the Orioles beat the Yankees 10-0, in a 1954 game.

Highlights of the conclusion of the Pine Tar Game, on this date in 1983:

- Yankee manager Billy Martin knew a different umpiring crew had been working when George Brett hit his controversial home run. Martin alleged that Brett had failed to touch all the bases, twenty-five days earlier. Fully prepared for such a challenge, the umpires produced affidavits. In these, the original umpires attested that Brett had run the bases properly.
- First baseman Don Mattingly played second base, while pitcher Ron Guidry was in center field for the Yankees.
- Only 1,245 fans bothered to attend.
- Three youths had sued the Yankees for the right to use their ticket stubs from the first part of the game. They felt paying a separate admission was unfair. A court actually granted an injunction stopping the game. On appeal, this injunction was reversed. Since the cost of the separate admission was $2.50, one can easily understand why so much court time was necessary.

AUGUST 19, 1951

Bill Veeck arranged for Eddie Gaedel, a midget, to bat for the St. Louis Browns. The reaction from the baseball establishment was predictable. Midgets were banned, as they made "a travesty of the game."

In response, Veeck asked if five-foot-six-inch-tall Yankee shortstop Phil Rizzuto was a small player or a tall midget.

Born August 19, 1935
Bobby Richardson

Richardson led the Yankees with seven stolen bases in 1965. New York had not adjusted to the running game. Between 1946 and 1968, the Yankees did not have a player who stole more than twenty-five bases in a season.

Teams with most players stealing twenty-five or more bases in a season, 1946-1968:

- Dodgers, nineteen
- White Sox, fourteen
- Braves, eight
- Browns/ Orioles, seven

AUGUST 20, 1964

Chicago completed a four-game sweep of the Yankees. New York was in third place, four games behind the White Sox.

Born August 20, 1908
Al Lopez

Lopez led two teams, the Indians and the White Sox, to pennants over the Yankees in the 1950's. His fifty-sixth birthday must have been particularly enjoyable, as he was the manager of the 1964 White Sox.

The Yankees' Lopezes, Hector and Art:

- Hector and Art (no relation to Al, or to each other) were Yankee teammates in 1965.
- In 1961, Hector hit .222, while playing with one of the Yankees' more powerful lineups.
- Hector, who was not a gifted outfielder, had a fielding average of .936 in 1965. He had more than twice as many errors as assists.
- Art, who was not a gifted part-time outfielder and pinch hitter, had a career slugging average of .143.
- In forty-nine career at bats, Art failed to drive in a run. He received only one base on balls. One would bet this was not an intentional walk. (We have all felt bitterness and disappointment at losing out to someone who we knew was decidedly our inferior. As misery loves company, we take comfort in noting that somewhere there is someone whom Art Lopez beat out for a job with the Yankees.)

AUGUST 21, 1946

With yet another victory, the Montreal Royals were seventeen games ahead of the Newark Bears, the Yankees' top minor-league team. Yankee fans had become less smug about their farm team being better than many major-league teams were.

Born August 21, 1920
Gerry Staley

In Staley's short stay with the 1956 Yankees, he had an ERA of 108.00. This meant he would allow twelve earned runs per inning pitched.

To Yankee haters, Staley's time as a Yankee was a brief, shining moment.

The worst ERA's for a single season by a Yankee pitcher:

- Staley's 1956 ERA is the worst by a Yankee.
- In 1908, Art Goodwin's ERA was 81.00.
- Jim Lewis was only half as ineffective as Staley was. In 1982, he had an ERA of 54.00.
- In 1961, Duke Maas had an ERA of 54.00.

AUGUST 22, 1959

After a loss to Kansas City, the Yankees were as close to last place as they were to first place. Their day was made worse. St. Louis management vehemently denied rumors of a Stan Musial- for- Yogi Berra trade. Yankee catcher Johnny Blanchard probably felt worst of all. Thieves had broken into his Bronx apartment.

Died August 22, 1968
Heinie Groh

Groh hit .474, as his Giants swept the Yankees in the 1922 World Series. With their .203 batting average in this Series, the Yankees hit like Henry Knight Groh's nickname.

Highest batting averages against the Yankees in the World Series:

- Johnny Bench hit .533, for Cincinnati, in the 1976 World Series.
- San Diego's Tony Gwynn hit .500, in the 1998 Series.
- In the 1938 Series, Chicago's Joe Marty hit .500.
- Tim McCarver had a .478 average, for St. Louis, in the 1964 Series.
- Groh hit .474, for the Giants, in 1922.

(Minimum of ten at bats)

AUGUST 23, 1974

Steinbrenner pleaded guilty to a felony, making illegal campaign contributions.

Separate explanations Steinbrenner gave for the actions that led to his conviction:

- His lawyer orchestrated the whole thing, setting up Steinbrenner as a patsy.
- Herbert Kalmbach, a fund-raiser for President Nixon, pressured Steinbrenner.
- Steinbrenner made the contributions because he feared the wrath of Nixon and his gang.
- Steinbrenner was responsible. (This is implicit in a guilty plea.)
- He was contributing to the democratic process. Fortunately, this process, like baseball, has been strong enough to withstand Steinbrenner's contributions.

Born August 23, 1911
Nels Potter

Late in the 1944 season, Potter pitched a 1-0 shutout for the Browns. This completed a doubleheader sweep, during which the Yankees were eliminated from the pennant race.

AUGUST 24, 1961

Despite five hits by Bobby Richardson, the Yankees lost to the expansion Los Angeles Angels. This brought back memories of the 1960 World Series, which the Yankees lost, as Richardson hit .367. Another pleasant reminder was Ted Bowsfield starting for the Angels. Bowsfield, then a rookie with the Red Sox, beat the Yankees three times in 1958.

Born August 24, 1960
Cal Ripken, Jr.

Baltimore's shortstop shattered Lou Gehrig's consecutive-games-played streak. Gehrig's streak had been 2,130 games; Ripken's ended at 2,632 games.

Some things Gehrig did to maintain his streak that Ripken did not do:

- Gehrig played first base, a position less susceptible to injury.
- When he needed a rest, Gehrig would bat in the top of the first inning. He would then sit out the rest of the game.

AUGUST 25, 1956

Yankee General Manager George Weiss had a question for shortstop Phil Rizzuto. Whom did Rizzuto think should be released to make room for the newly acquired Enos Slaughter?

Rizzuto made several suggestions, all of which Weiss declined. It was a charade. Weiss knew all along that the released player was going to be Phil Rizzuto. As it was Old Timers' Day, the release embarrassed Rizzuto in front of his current and former teammates.

Other bits of silliness on Old Timers Day:

- In 1978, the Yankees announced that the recently forced-out Billy Martin would return as Yankee manager in 1980.
- Jim Bouton, the author of *Ball Four*, was not invited to the game until 1998. This was thirty years after he left the Yankees.
- Yogi Berra has refused to attend as long as Steinbrenner owns the Yankees.

Born August 25, 1939
Dooley Womack

His name and 15-16 record made him a symbol of Yankee ineptitude in the late 1960's. In *Ball Four*, Jim Bouton wrote of being told he was having a better spring than Dooley Womack. Bouton asked if his manager was referring to *the* Dooley Womack.

AUGUST 26, 1962

Baltimore completed a five-game sweep of the Yankees. The Orioles, who had been 61-64 prior to this series, outscored New York 34-14. These losses left the Yankees just three games ahead of the Los Angeles Angels, who were in their second year in the league.

Born August 26, 1892
Jesse Barnes

Giants' pitchers Barnes, Phil Douglas, and Art Nehf held the Yankees to one run in the last twenty-four innings of the 1921 World Series.

Yankee hating by the numbers, part eighteen:

- **68.** Consecutive innings the Yankees went without an extra-base hit, in April 1967.
- **69.** In 1969, the Mets won the World Series, outdrawing the Yankees by more than a million fans.
- **70.** Number by which the Braves' Hank Aaron and Eddie Mathews broke the Ruth-Gehrig record for home runs as teammates. Aaron and Mathews hit 863 home runs; Ruth and Gehrig had hit 793.
- **71.** Total hits by Minnesota's Darrell Brown in 1984. Brown had promised Joe DiMaggio that he would not surpass the Yankee Clipper's fifty-six-game hitting streak. And I promise that I will not accept more than one Nobel Prize.

AUGUST 27, 1977

Texas hit five home runs and beat the Yankees. Two of these were consecutive, inside-the-park home runs, by Bump Wills and Toby Harrah. This was only the second time a team had hit two inside-the-park home runs in a major-league game.

Born August 27, 1875
Ed Hahn

Partway through the 1906 season, Hahn, a Yankee outfielder, had a .136 slugging percentage. This was unacceptable, even for the Yankees. They sent Hahn to the White Sox. Hahn became an everyday outfielder on Chicago's 1906 World Series-winning team.

Worst slugging averages, single season, by a Yankee:

- Skeeter Shelton slugged .025, in 1915.
- Kal Segrist had an .043 slugging average, in 1952.
- In 1989, Jamie Quirk's slugging average was .083.
- Angel Aragon had a slugging average of .089, in 1917.
- In 1919, George Halas slugged .091.

(Minimum of twenty at bats, excluding pitchers)

AUGUST 28, 1973

New York lost its seventh consecutive game. With twenty-one losses in thirty games, the Yankees had dropped out of the pennant race. They fell further back the next night, as California's Nolan Ryan pitched a one-hitter.

Highlights of the eight-game losing streak:

- This streak was part of the Yankees' descent from first place to fourth place, seventeen games behind Baltimore.
- Kansas City, Oakland, and California swept their series with the Yankees.
- The Yankees scored three runs in their final five losses.
- New York went twenty-two innings without scoring.

Born August 28, 1896
Aaron Ward

Playing for the Yankees, Ward participated in an unusual double play to end the 1921 World Series. He tried to go to third base on an infield out. Ward did not make it. Giants' first baseman George Kelly completed the 4-3-5 (second baseman-to first baseman-to third baseman) double play with a perfect throw.

A baseball maxim is never make the final out of an inning at third base. Ward figured circumstances justified his action. His team was losing 1-0 and had not scored in sixteen innings. Six Yankee starters were hitting .200 or less. By being on third base, Ward could take advantage of the Yankees' best hope of scoring, a wild pitch.

AUGUST 29, 1925

The Yankees fined Babe Ruth five thousand dollars and suspended their star player indefinitely. Ruth had "broken training." This was the term used, at the time, to describe excess womanizing, drinking, and/or partying.

Ruth had not merely broken training. He treated it like Rome treated Carthage. He destroyed it, then salted the earth in hopes it would not rise again.

Born August 29, 1928
Mickey McDermott

McDermott was the winning pitcher, as the Red Sox beat the Yankees 14-10 in 1953. At the time, it was the longest nine-inning game in baseball history.

A 1997 game set the current record. Baltimore beat the Yankees in a game that lasted four hours and twenty-two minutes.

Numerology:

- The Yankees have never won the World Series in a year ending in four or five. We will not talk about years ending in eight.
- Other than in 1950, the Yankees have never won the World Series in a year with a zero in it. This is another reason to look forward to the new millennium.

AUGUST 30, 1910

Tom Hughes, a Yankee pitcher, allowed no hits through nine innings. He gave up five runs in the eleventh inning to lose the game.

Born August 30, 1918
Ted Williams

Williams lost five seasons to military service. Assume he spent those seasons in baseball and averaged thirty-nine home runs and seventy-five RBI per season. If this had occurred, the Red Sox star would have surpassed Babe Ruth's career records in these two categories.

Winning percentages of teams in the New York City area, 1914-1915:

- Newark Peppers (Federal League), .526
- Brooklyn Dodgers, .506
- New York Giants, .500
- Brooklyn Tip-Tops (Federal League), .480
- New York Yankees, .459

(Tom Seaton, born on this date in 1887, won thirty-seven games for the Tip-Tops. Neither this team nor the Federal League survived. With team names like "Peppers" and "Tip-Tops," the Federal League could not have expected long-term survival.)

AUGUST 31, 1968

It had been thirty-four innings since the Yankees had scored a run. These things happen when your RBI leader is tied for fifteenth in the league, and your second-best hitter has a .245 batting average.

Some comments on the 1968 Yankees, or why only soccer teams had more trouble scoring:

- New York had a team batting average of .214, the Yankees' worst ever.
- They had the fewest hits of any team in the American League.
- Andy Kosco was second on the team in RBI. This would have been acceptable if the Yankees were playing in the minor leagues.
- Rocky Colovito and Mickey Mantle were the Yankees' two best power hitters. This would have been acceptable if the Yankees were playing in 1963.

Born August 31, 1935
Frank Robinson

His debut as the first African-American manager in baseball history was successful. One of his better players, designated hitter Frank Robinson, hit a home run. Robinson's Cleveland Indians defeated the Yankees, in this 1975 game.

SEPTEMBER 1, 1990

Mike Greenwell hit an inside-the-park, grand slam home run, as the Red Sox defeated the Yankees 15-1. A few weeks previously, Cleveland had beaten the Yankees 17-3. Small wonder the Yankee pitching staff had a 4.21 ERA in 1990.

Born September 1, 1900
Hub Pruett

Pruett was the St. Louis Browns' pitcher who frustrated Babe Ruth. By far the biggest of Pruett's twenty-nine career wins came late in the 1922 season. This win moved the Browns into a virtual tie for first place with the Yankees.

Babe Ruth's first five games against Pruett:

- strikeout, walk
- strikeout *
- three strikeouts, walk
- three strikeouts, ground out
- strikeout *

(Ruth struck out thirteen times in his first twenty-one at bats against Pruett.)

* relief appearance by Pruett

SEPTEMBER 2, 1989

Fay Vincent became baseball's acting commissioner. He would have the pleasure of reading the following statement: "Mr. Steinbrenner has agreed to resign, on or before August 20, 1990, as the General Partner of the New York Yankees. From then on, Mr. Steinbrenner will have no further involvement in the management of the New York Yankees or in the day-to-day operations of the club."

Born September 2, 1933
Marv Throneberry

This one-time Yankee symbolized the ineptitude of the early Mets. He became one of dozens of athletes who did clever commercials for Miller Lite, in the 1970's and 1980's. Unlike Mickey Mantle, Throneberry never defected to a rival brand.

Moments from Miller Lite commercials for Yankee haters:

- Mediocre-player-turned-announcer Bob Uecker pretended he was Yankee Hall of Famer Whitey Ford. People believed him.
- Steinbrenner fired Yankee manager Billy Martin. They had disagreed whether the beer was less filling or tasted great.
- Martin claimed he was not the kind of guy to ever get into an argument. With laughter in the background, a beer bottle fell over.
- Off camera, one-time Yankee Bobby Bonds was fired. He had overstated his career stolen base total in one of these commercials.

SEPTEMBER 3, 1952

Harry Byrd pitched a one-hitter against the Yankees. Philadelphia won the game 3-0. Nine years later, New York had more trouble with another ornithologically-named pitcher. Cincinnati's Joey Jay beat the Yankees, in the second game of the 1961 World Series.

Jay was the first former Little Leaguer to make it to the major leagues. In his 1961 victory, Jay made the New York Yankees look like the Jerry's Bicycle Shop Yankees. He limited them to four hits.

Born September 3, 1951
Alan Bannister

In a 1982 game, the Indians scored four ninth-inning runs to beat the Yankees. It was New York's ninth consecutive loss. Cleveland scored the winning run when the Yankees misplayed Bannister's ground ball.

Postseason grand slams against the Yankees:

- Chuck Hiller hit one, for the Giants, in the fourth game of the 1962 World Series. Marshall Bridges, who died on this date in 1990, was Hiller's victim.
- Ken Boyer's won the fourth game of the 1964 World Series, for the Cardinals.
- Edgar Martinez hit one for Seattle. It won the fourth game of the 1995 Division Series.
- Cleveland's Jim Thome hit a grand slam in the sixth game of the 1998 American League Championship Series. It made a 6-1 game a 6-5 game.

SEPTEMBER 4, 1960

By completing a three-game sweep against the Yankees, Baltimore took a two-game lead in the American League pennant race. Oriole pitchers Milt Pappas, Jack Fisher, and Chuck Estrada threw twenty-five consecutive scoreless innings.

New York had prepared for this series by being shut out by Kansas City's Ned Garver. Being shut out by the 1960 A's was like being shut out in bowling.

Born September 4, 1950
Frank White

White hit .545 and fielded superbly in the 1980 American League Championship Series. He was named the Most Valuable Player, as Kansas City defeated the Yankees.

The name "Yankees" might not be great, but "Highlanders" was worse. Some comments:

- Hilltop Park, where the team played, was at the highest point on Manhattan Island. This is not a region known for its mountain ranges.
- "Highlanders" was too long for sports editors, who often used "Yankees."
- The team's owners liked the name because it was similar to the Gordon Highlanders, a Scottish army regiment. They did not take into account that there were far more people of Irish than of Scottish descent in New York City.
- Following their 102-loss 1912 season, the team dropped "Highlanders." It helped. In 1913, the Yankees lost only ninety-four games.

SEPTEMBER 5, 1908

Walter Johnson pitched the second of what would be three shutouts in four days against the Yankees. This was a terrible mismatch. Many consider Johnson the greatest pitcher in baseball history. In 1908, the Yankees were dreadful, losing 103 games.

Born September 5, 1873
Al Orth

Orth, nicknamed the "Curveless Wonder," lost twenty-one games for the 1907 Yankees. He had a .133 winning percentage the following season. Early in the 1909 season, Orth became the "Jobless Wonder."

Orth did win some games during his career. He was the winning pitcher, as Washington defeated New York in the Yankees' first-ever game, in 1903.

Worst winning percentages in a season by a Yankee pitcher:

- With a 1-9 record, Fred Talbot had a .100 winning percentage, in 1968.
- Orth earned his .133 percentage with a 2-13 record.
- Catfish Hunter's 1979 record was 2-9, for a .182 percentage.
- Ray Fisher, Hippo Vaughn, and Jose Rijo all had 2-8 records. These gave them winning percentages of .200. Fisher and Vaughn did it in 1912, while Rijo pitched for New York in 1984.

(Minimum of ten decisions)

SEPTEMBER 6, 1928

Philadelphia was on a tear that would take them into first place on September 8. This completed a remarkable comeback. Philadelphia had trailed the Yankees by thirteen games.

Born September 6, 1889
George Kahler

Kahler was the winning pitcher in an unusual game in 1910. Cleveland did not get a hit against the Yankees until the tenth inning. In the eleventh inning, the Indians remembered they were facing Tom Hughes. He was the fifth-best starter on the league's third-worst pitching staff. Cleveland scored five runs to win the game.

Yankee hating by the numbers, part nineteen:

- **72.** Decline in the number of runs scored by the Yankees from 1958 to 1959, as the team fell to third place.
- **73.** Innings Whitey Ford was able to pitch in 1966. Injuries and age had caught up to the ace of the Yankee staff.
- **74.** Percentage of games the 1902 Pittsburgh Pirates won. They are one of three teams with a better winning percentage than the 1998 Yankees. (The others are the 1906 Cubs and the 1954 Indians.)
- **75.** Percentage of at bats in the 1990 World Series, where Cincinnati's Billy Hatcher hit successfully. His .750 batting average surpassed Babe Ruth's record .625.

SEPTEMBER 7, 1974

As Yankee Graig Nettles swung at a pitch, the end came off his bat. Both Nettles and the doctored bat were removed from the game.

Years later, Nettles would swing more successfully. He punched a Yankee teammate, Reggie Jackson, at a postseason party.

Died September 7, 1984
Joe Cronin

Cronin was involved in one of the more unusual plays of the 1933 season. Playing shortstop, the Senators' Cronin relayed outfielder Goose Goslin's throw to catcher Luke Sewell. Sewell tagged out Yankees Lou Gehrig and Dixie Walker, who were in a virtual dead heat to see who could score first.

Contributions by players involved in this play:

- Goslin played on five teams (the 1924, 1925, and 1933 Senators, the 1934 and 1935 Tigers) who beat out the Yankees for the pennant.
- Sewell managed the 1944 American League champion St. Louis Browns. This team won the pennant and eliminated the Yankees by sweeping a season-ending, four-game series with New York.
- Cronin managed the 1933 Senators and the 1946 Red Sox. Both teams won the American League pennant.

SEPTEMBER 8, 1916

Poor Connie Mack. His A's were the worst team in American League history. His competitors, the Phillies, were in a pennant race. It was a dreary weekday afternoon. With all of these factors against him, he could not have expected a large crowd. As he checked the schedule, he was hoping for an attractive opponent. Perhaps it would be Ty Cobb and the Tigers, or Shoeless Joe Jackson and the White Sox. How his heart must have sunk to see it was the Yankees.

Twenty-three people attended the game at Shibe Park.

Lousy crowds drawn by the Yankees for home games:

- 217 attended a game at the Polo Grounds, on September 21, 1915.
- 413 were at Yankee Stadium for a 1966 game. (See September 22.)
- Only 23,154 saw Roger Maris hit his record-breaking sixty-first home run.
- 38,093 attended the seventh game of the 1926 World Series. (This was some 23,000 fewer fans than saw the first game.)

Ended September 8, 1998
Yankee ownership of the single-season home run record

St. Louis's Mark McGwire hit his sixty-second home run. (For the few remaining members of baseball's Flat Earth Society, McGwire broke the record in fewer than 154 games.) He wound up with seventy home runs, and ownership of the single-season record, which a Yankee had held since 1920.

SEPTEMBER 9, 1990

Oakland completed a sweep of its season series with the Yankees.

Highlights of Oakland's 1990 sweep:

- Oakland won twelve games, outscoring the Yankees 62-12.
- In one game, the A's scored ten runs in an inning.
- This sweep continued Oakland's recent domination of the Yankees. In 1989, the A's won nine of the twelve games played.
- Tim Leary and Andy Hawkins each lost three of these games.

Died September 9, 1924
Frank Chance

In an attempt to compete with the New York Giants, the Yankees hired Chance. He was the arch-rival of Giants' manager John McGraw. Chance's Cubs had won four pennants over McGraw's Giants.

Chance left his talents in Chicago. He also left his good players. Instead of the Cubs' double play combination of Tinker-to-Evers-to-Chance, the Yankees had Zeider-to-Hartzell-no chance. After almost two seasons as a seventh-place team, the Yankees fired Chance in 1914.

SEPTEMBER 10, 1977

The Toronto Blue Jays, who would win only fifty-four games in 1977, won 19-3 at Yankee Stadium. This was the most runs scored against the Yankees in fifty-two years. Roy Howell, who would drive in forty-four runs all season, had nine RBI for the Blue Jays.

Born September 10, 1963
Randy Johnson

Johnson won two games, as Seattle beat the Yankees in the best-of-five Division Series in 1995. Johnson struck out sixteen Yankees in ten innings. (His appearance in the final game was in relief.) This performance brings the word "overmatched" to mind.

Worst career World Series batting averages by a Yankee:

- .125, Bernie Williams
- .158, Willie Randolph
- .163, Joe Collins
- .174, Frank Crosetti
- .175, Andy Carey
- .187, Roger Maris, who was born on this date in 1934

(Minimum of forty at bats, excluding pitchers)

SEPTEMBER 11, 1955

Nothing in baseball is more fundamental than pitching and catching the ball. In consecutive games, the Yankees had trouble with this basic skill. They lost on a wild pitch, and then on a passed ball.

Wild pitches occasionally happen, even to a great pitcher like Whitey Ford. Passed balls invariably happen when you have Hank Bauer, an outfielder, catching for the first time in his career.

Obviously, Bauer should not have been catching. However, with Yogi Berra ill, Casey Stengel had substituted for Elston Howard and Charlie Silvera. It takes managerial wisdom to run out of catchers.

Born September 11, 1964
Ellis Burks

His three-run home run helped the Red Sox win three-of-four games from the Yankees, late in the 1988 season. New York had had visions of moving into contention with a four-game sweep. Not this decade.

Teams with three players, each hitting forty or more home runs in one season:

- Burks, Vinny Castilla, and Andres Galarraga did it for the 1996 Rockies.
- In 1997, Colorado's Castilla, Galarraga, and Larry Walker repeated this feat.
- Dave Johnson, Hank Aaron, and Darrell Evans were the first to achieve this. They did it for the 1973 Atlanta Braves.

(No Yankee teammates have ever come close to accomplishing this feat.)

SEPTEMBER 12, 1954

A doubleheader with Cleveland represented the Yankees' last chance to get back in the 1954 pennant race. New York lost both games.

Born September 12, 1917
Russ Christopher

This Indians' relief pitcher, a Yankee castoff, led the American League in saves in 1948.

Perhaps the Yankees let Christopher go because he was sickly. (He would die of a heart problem at age thirty-seven.) They preferred players who looked like Frank Hiller. This pitcher was tall (six feet), strong (two hundred pounds), and lousy. In three seasons as a Yankee, in the late 1940's, Hiller had a 5-6 record, with a 4.26 ERA.

Some milestones achieved against the Yankees:

- Boston's Carl Yastrzemski got his three-thousandth hit, on this date in 1979.
- In 1914, Cleveland's Napoleon Lajoie had his three-thousandth hit.
- Tom Seaver won his three-hundredth game. It spoiled Phil Rizzuto Day in 1985. Seaver was pitching for the Chicago White Sox.
- Seattle's (briefly) Gaylord Perry got his three-hundredth win, in 1982.

SEPTEMBER 13, 1985

The Yankees began an eight-game losing streak that took them out of the 1985 pennant race.

Highlights of the Yankees' eight-game losing streak:

- New York lost three straight games to Toronto. With these losses, the Yankees fell five games behind the Blue Jays.
- New York led Cleveland 5-3, after eight innings. With ace reliever Dave Righetti available, Yankee manager Billy Martin let Brian Fisher give up six runs.
- Ron Guidry allowed five home runs in a loss to Detroit.
- In another loss to Detroit, the Yankees had two runners on base. There were two outs. Mickey Mahler, a left-hander, was pitching. Martin ordered left-hand-hitting Mike Pagliarulo to bat right-handed. Pagliarulo began and ended his major-league career as a right-handed batter by striking out.
- Martin inadvertently put the winning run in scoring position, as Baltimore beat the Yankees. He did not cancel the pitchout signal before scratching his itchy nose.

Born September 13, 1949
Rick Dempsey

Dempsey got into a fight with Yankee teammate Bill Sudakis. It is not necessarily a bad idea to try to injure a marginal player like Sudakis, a .232 hitter. You should not do it when your team trails Baltimore by a game, with two to play, in the 1974 season.

Bobby Murcer, New York's best player, was injured breaking up the fight. He could not play the next day. With Murcer out, the Yankees lost. When the Orioles won, the Yankees were eliminated.

SEPTEMBER 14, 1972

Four teams, including the Yankees, were in a tight race for the division title. Unfortunately for the company that had hoped to sell playoff souvenirs at Yankee Stadium, the Yankees lost eleven of their last sixteen games. New York finished fourth, six games behind Detroit.

Born September 14, 1966
Mike Draper

Draper set a Triple A record with thirty-seven saves, for a Yankee farm team in 1992. Was he the next great Yankee reliever? Hardly. In 1993, his only major-league season, Draper had one win, no saves, and a 4.25 ERA.

Besides Draper, some speculative picks of Yankees that did not work out for Rotisserie Leaguers:

- In 1992, Gerald Williams had three home runs and six RBI in twenty-seven at bats. Those who picked him in 1993 had extrapolated a great season. They got a .149 average and no home runs. They were also told to leave words like "extrapolated" at the office.
- John Ramos had a .308 average in twenty-six at bats, in 1992. Ramos was injured and missed the 1993 season.
- Vic Mata hit .329 in seventy at-bats in 1985. His 1986 "owners" got one hit and tons of abuse for picking him.
- Like the real Yankees, many Rotisserie League teams thought Hensley Meulens was a "can't miss" prospect. In 1991, Meulens hit .222, with six home runs and twenty-nine RBI. This was his best season.

SEPTEMBER 15, 1950

Despite Johnny Mize's three home runs, the Yankees lost to Detroit. Ex-Yankee Hank Borowy pitched four innings of one-hit relief, as the Tigers moved into first place.

Born September 15, 1787
The U.S. Department of State

Throughout American history, this Department has made statements on crucial issues. Before the 1996 baseball playoffs, Department spokesman Nicholas Burns said, "This is an official statement by the United States Department of State. Anybody but the New York Yankees."

Speaking of Washington, highlights of the 1924 pennant race:

- On August 28, the Senators beat the Yankees to move into first place. This was the last game between the teams that season.
- Washington benefited from two streaks. Walter Johnson had a fourteen-game winning streak that lasted well into September. Sam Rice kept his hitting streak going until the last week of the season, when this streak reached thirty-four games.
- Joe Dugan's throwing error cost the Yankees a crucial game.
- New York lost late-season games, to Detroit and Philadelphia, on wild pitches.
- Washington won the pennant by defeating the Red Sox. According to contemporary accounts, the Fenway Park crowd cheered the Senators to victory. The enemy of my enemy is my friend.

SEPTEMBER 16, 1982

Baltimore completed a five-game sweep of the Yankees. New York went oh-for-Maryland in 1982, losing all seven games with the Orioles. Unfortunately, Annapolis did not have an American League team.

Best records in a season series against the Yankees:

- 12-0, Oakland A's, 1990
- 19-2, Red Sox, 1912. If Yankee-Red Sox games that year had been boxing matches, no commission would have sanctioned them. Boston had thirty-four-game-winner Joe Wood and Hall of Famers Tris Speaker and Harry Hooper. Jack Lelivelt was the best of the forty-four players the Yankees used in 1912. Yankee manager Harry Wolverton, who is to managing as Albania is to countries, used this .362 hitter in only thirty-six games.
- 11-2, Orioles, 1982
- 10-2, Twins, 1969
- 10-2, White Sox, 1990. Chicago completed an unusual double against the Yankees in 1990. They won a game in which they allowed no hits, and another in which they had no hits.

Born September 16, 1945
Hector Torres

Mexican-born Torres hit the first American League grand slam in Canada. This home run, with NAFTA (North American Free Trade Agreement) elements, helped the Blue Jays beat the Yankees in a 1977 game.

SEPTEMBER 17, 1944

Philadelphia beat New York twice at Yankee Stadium. Former Yankee Larry Rosenthal had the key hit, a game-winning, ninth-inning home run. At the beginning of the day, the Yankees were in first place; at its end, they were in third. With all fourteen remaining games on the road, the Yankees were in trouble.

Their accountants began preparing an analysis. It would show how the proceeds from the team's sale of Rosenthal would offset the loss of World Series revenue.

How Joe McCarthy's Yankees did in close pennant races:

- They never won one.
- In 1944, they finished third, two games behind St. Louis.
- They were third, two back of Detroit, in 1940.
- In 1935, the Yankees finished second, three behind Detroit.
- New York ended up fourth in 1945, six games behind Detroit.

Born September 17, 1937
Orlando Cepeda

Cepeda gave haters of the new designated hitter rule cause to reconsider their position. He hit a game-winning home run against the Yankees. This gave the Red Sox a sweep of the 1973 season-opening series. (American League teams first used the designated hitter that year.)

SEPTEMBER 18, 1979

Cleveland celebrated the twenty-fifth anniversary of the 1954 Indians' clinching the American League pennant. They beat the Yankees 16-3. Paul Mirabella, Rick Anderson, Bob Kammeyer, and Don Hood all pitched for the Yankees. This most unfearsome foursome would win a combined fifty-three major-league games.

Died September 18, 1922
Jake Stahl

Stahl was the manager of the Red Sox, when they won eighteen in a row in New York, between 1911 and 1913.

Yankee hating by the numbers, part twenty:

- **76.** Length, in minutes, of the fastest shutout in American League history. Philadelphia beat the Yankees 10-0, in 1925.
- **77.** Hits former Yankee Reggie Jackson had in 1983, when he whiffed his way to a .194 batting average.
- **78.** RBI total of Yankee-leader Jesse Barfield in 1990. He had fifty-four fewer RBI than the league-leader, Cecil Fielder of Detroit.
- **79.** World Series games the Yankees have lost.

SEPTEMBER 19, 1981

Boston scored seven runs in the eighth inning to beat the Yankees 8-5. Rick Miller, who rarely hit home runs, hit one with two men on base to provide the winning margin. For the second consecutive weekend, Boston's hero was a lesser-known player.

During the previous weekend, Red Sox rookie Bob Ojeda had taken a no-hitter into the ninth inning. He retired twenty-two consecutive Yankees in his victory at Yankee Stadium.

Born September 19, 1926
Duke Snider

Snider's Dodgers were in four World Series against the Yankees in the 1950's. In these Series, Snider hit .324 with ten home runs and twenty-four RBI.

Players with two hits in an inning against the Yankees in a World Series game:

- Ross Youngs did it for the Giants, in the 1921 Series.
- In 1937, Hank Leiber, of the Giants, had two hits in a single inning.
- St. Louis's Stan Musial did it, in the 1942 Series.

SEPTEMBER 20, 1982

A Yankee team, which would finish one game out of last place, lost its ninth consecutive game. This streak included two losses to Milwaukee by a combined score of 28-1.

In 1982, the New York Jets could go two games without allowing twenty-eight points. New York's American Football Conference team had a major advantage over New York's American League baseball team. It had talent.

Born September 20, 1937
Tom Tresh

Tresh had power and a baseball player's name. Because his father, Mike, had been a major-league catcher, genetics should have been on Tom's side. Sadly for the Yankees, Tresh inherited the wrong genes. Tom-Hardly-Terrific wound up playing like his mother.

Tom Tresh's declining batting averages, with the Yankees, 1965-1969:

- .279 in 1965
- .233 in 1966
- .219 in 1967
- .195 in 1968
- .182 in 1969

SEPTEMBER 21, 1956

Usually a team wins when it gets fifteen hits, nine walks, and benefits from five errors. Not the Yankees. They set a major-league record by leaving twenty of these runners on base. Boston beat New York 13-7.

Born September 21, 1942
Sam McDowell

Longtime Cleveland pitcher McDowell had a 6-14 record as a Yankee. "Sudden Sam's" sentence in New York ended when he jumped the team, in 1974.

Pitchers you might be surprised to learn rank in the top twenty-five in career strikeouts:

- Frank Tanana is fifteenth, with 2,773 strikeouts.
- Jerry Koosman ranks eighteenth, with 2,556.
- Jim Kaat has 2,461 strikeouts, to rank twenty-third.
- McDowell is twenty-fourth, with 2,453.

(Tommy John is the highest-ranked pitcher who spent at least five years of his career with the Yankees. He ranks thirty-fifth.)

SEPTEMBER 22, 1966

There were 413 people at Yankee Stadium to see the Yankees and White Sox. Chicago made Mike Burke's first day as president of the Yankees complete by winning 4-1.

One of Burke's first decisions was to fire Red Barber, the legendary broadcaster. Barber had thought the smallest crowd in the history of Yankee Stadium was an event worth mentioning.

Some other classless firings by the Yankees:

- Mel Allen was fired, after twenty-five years as a Yankee broadcaster. There was no explanation given.
- Yankee managers Bob Lemon and Yogi Berra were fired early in the season. Steinbrenner's promise that each would have a full season as manager meant little.
- Mel Stottlemyre had received assurances that he could prepare for the 1975 season at his own pace. When the Yankees did not like this pace, they released Stottlemyre. He had anchored their pitching staff for eleven seasons.

Born September 22, 1929
Harry Bright

Bright was Sandy Koufax's record-breaking fifteenth strikeout victim in the first game of the 1963 World Series. Bright said, "If (striking out) isn't bad enough, sixty-nine thousand people were rooting against me, hoping I'd strike out."

SEPTEMBER 23, 1993

With no game scheduled, the Yankees were preparing for their series with the Blue Jays. They did not prepare well enough. Toronto won the first two games and extended their lead, in the American League East, to seven games. These losses effectively eliminated the Yankees from contention.

Born September 23, 1920
Mickey Rooney

Dan Topping and the frequently married actor could have compared notes. Topping, who co-owned the Yankees from 1946 to 1964, married six times.

Dan Topping and the chit-signing caper:

- Mickey Mantle, Whitey Ford, Billy Martin, and the other usual suspects ran up a $250 tab in a nightclub.
- As a joke, they signed Topping's name to the bill.
- When Topping learned of this, he had George Weiss, the Yankee general manager, summon the players to Weiss's office.
- Acting for Topping, Weiss threatened to charge the players with forgery. He fined each player five hundred dollars. This was considerably more than each player's share of the tab would have been.
- Topping did not care that the players had been celebrating winning the 1952 pennant.

DAN TOPPING, SERIAL BRIDEGROOM (September 23)

SEPTEMBER 24, 1954

Yankee pinch hitters Lou Berberet, Gus Triandos, and Frank Leja established a dubious pinch-hitting record. They struck out, consecutively, in the ninth inning.

Only 2,032 fans were at Yankee Stadium. These fans, who obviously could not unload their tickets, saw the Yankees lose to Philadelphia.

Yankee attendance, first home game after elimination, during their dominant years:

- 8,945 in 1945
- 24,051 in 1946 (This Sunday doubleheader was the first Yankee home game in two weeks.)
- 7,702 in 1954
- 11,641 in 1959

(Elimination occurred after the Yankees had played their final home games of the 1940, 1944, and 1948 seasons.)

Died September 24, 1969
Illusions that the Yankees were New York's
number one baseball team

Boston won 1-0, as the Yankees failed to score a run in fourteen innings. Only the players' friends and family cared. Most of New York was celebrating the Mets' clinching of the National League East pennant.

SEPTEMBER 25, 1954

The Cleveland Indians won their 111th game, fittingly by an 11-1 score. This win broke the American League record, established by the 1927 Yankees. Cleveland's .721 winning percentage remains the best in American League history.

Born September 25, 1917
Johnny Sain

In August 1951, the Yankees sent Lew Burdette, and fifty thousand dollars, to the Braves for Sain. Between 1952 and 1962, Burdette averaged sixteen wins and 232 innings pitched per season. Sain pitched for the Yankees for a little over three seasons.

There is also the small matter of Burdette's three wins against the Yankees in the 1957 World Series.

Key moments in the 1906 pennant race:

- In August, the White Sox won nineteen consecutive games to move into contention.
- On this date in 1906, Chicago won to tie the Yankees for first place.
- On the following day, the Yankees gave away a game. Detroit won 2-0, scoring their runs on a walk, a single, and two Yankee errors.
- New York lost four of its next seven games, as twenty-four-game winner Jack Chesbro lost twice.
- A 3-0 loss to Philadelphia eliminated the Yankees. Harry Davis hit what was meant to be intentional ball three for a three-run home run.

SEPTEMBER 26, 1907

For the second consecutive day, the Yankees had only one hit against Cleveland's pitching.

Born September 26, 1925
Bobby Shantz

Shantz was the most prominent player the Yankees lost in the 1961 expansion draft. He had been an effective pitcher in his four years with the team.

Yankee hating from A to Z, part five:

- **R.** Roger Repoz. New York's farm director described Repoz as "the next Yankee star, no question about it." Neither Repoz nor this farm director will ever be honored with a plaque at Yankee Stadium.
- **S.** Toots Shor. He was a saloonkeeper and marriage counselor. When Joe DiMaggio was in a funk over the breakup of his marriage to Marilyn Monroe, Shor asked him, "What do you expect when you marry a whore?"
- **T.** Gus Triandos. His home run was the only run in Hoyt Wilhelm's no-hitter against the Yankees. It tied Yogi Berra's record for most home runs in a season by an American League catcher.
- **U.** Cecil Upshaw. Someone with absolutely nothing to do could make two lists. One would list all Yankee relief pitchers in order of talent, beginning with the best. The second list would put these pitchers in alphabetical order. Upshaw's name would be in roughly the same place on both lists.

SEPTEMBER 27, 1940

Philadelphia's Johnny Babich beat New York for the fifth time in 1940. This loss officially eliminated the Yankees from the pennant race. Babich's five wins over the Yankees represented almost 10 percent of Philadelphia's fifty-four wins that season.

Given the choice of keeping Babich or Marv Breuer, the Yankees had waived Babich. In fairness to the Yankees, Breuer did win almost as many games as he lost in 1940.

Pitchers we are fortunate A's manager Connie Mack did not start against the Yankees in this crucial game:

- George Caster had a 4-19 record in twenty-four starts.
- Herman Besse pitched in seventeen games, starting five. Nobel Prize-winning author Hermann Hesse might have been a better pitcher. Besse had an ERA of 8.83.
- Chubby Dean lost thirteen games, while winning only six. His 6.62 ERA did not help.
- Potter Vaughan had a 2-9 record and a 5.36 ERA in eighteen games.

Born September 27, 1930
Dick Hall

Commissioner Frick had ruled that Roger Maris had to break Babe Ruth's single-season home run record in 154 games. If Maris did it in more games, his record would be treated as a separate, implicitly inferior, mark.

Hall was one of three Oriole pitchers who faced the Yankee slugger in New York's 154th game of the 1961 season. Maris was one home run short of Ruth's record when the game ended.

SEPTEMBER 28, 1948

New York lost to Philadelphia, in a game where a win was all but essential. Following this loss, the Yankees were two games behind Cleveland, with four games remaining in the season.

The next five days of the 1948 pennant race:

- On September 29, Cleveland, Boston, and New York all won. Cleveland had a 95-56 record; New York and Boston were 93-58.
- With the Indians idle, Boston and New York won on September 30.
- Cleveland lost on October 1, while the Red Sox and Yankees did not play.
- Boston eliminated the Yankees on October 2, as Ted Williams hit a two-run home run. Cleveland won to go to 96-57. Boston was 95-58; New York had a 94-59 record.
- In the last scheduled games of the season, the Red Sox beat New York, while the Indians lost. This set up a playoff game, which Cleveland would win.

Died September 28, 1978
Pope John Paul I

John Paul's predecessor, Pope Paul VI, had died in August. Yankee broadcaster Phil Rizzuto reported the news. According to Rizzuto, the Pope's death put a damper on even a Yankee win.

SEPTEMBER 29, 1944

St. Louis eliminated the Yankees from the pennant race by beating them in the first game of a doubleheader. Proving they were a better team, the Browns also won the second game. New York scored one run in the two games.

Even though they were better than the Yankees, the 1944 Browns were not a good team. They are the only American League champion not to have a Hall of Famer, or potential Hall of Famer, on its roster.

Died September 29, 1902
The first American League Baltimore Orioles

These Orioles were the forerunners of the New York Yankees. On this date in 1902, they played their last game. Baltimore finished the 1902 season in last place, thirty-four games behind Philadelphia.

Dubious feats by the Orioles during their 1901-1902 existence:

- Baltimore finished fifth in 1901, and last in 1902. They spent a total of three days in first place.
- They tied a league record by losing eleven consecutive games.
- In 1902, Oriole pitchers gave up 128 more runs than the next-worst American League pitching staff did.
- Baltimore had a 50-88 record in 1902. One of these losses was by forfeit. That day, the Orioles set an unofficial major-league record for the fewest players available for a game, five.
- They drew 141,952 fans in 1901, their better season in Baltimore. Despite playing in the league's smallest city, the last-place Milwaukee Brewers attracted almost that many (139,034).

SEPTEMBER 30, 1966

New York clinched last place by losing to the White Sox. In a desperate attempt to finish ninth, the Yankees used their best starting pitcher, Mel Stottlemyre, in relief. It did not work. Stottlemyre lost his twentieth game of the season.

Born September 30, 1932
Johnny Podres

During his career, Dodger pitcher Podres won three World Series games against the Yankees. None was more important than his 2-0 victory in the seventh game of the 1955 Series.

Pitchers with the most World Series wins against the Yankees:

- Milwaukee's Lew Burdette, a former Yankee, won four.
- Burdette's Braves' teammate, Warren Spahn, had three victories.
- Podres won three.
- Burt Hooton, of the Dodgers, beat the Yankees three times.
- Art Nehf won three games for the New York Giants.

OCTOBER 1, 1974

It looked like the 1974 division race would go down to the final day of the season. The Yankees, who trailed Baltimore by a game, led Milwaukee 2-0. In the eighth inning, Lou Pinella misplayed a fly ball into a triple, and the Brewers tied the score.

By the tenth inning, the Yankees knew Baltimore had won. They did not know how to pitch to Jack Lind, a .135 career hitter. He singled. When Lind scored on George Scott's hit, Milwaukee had won, and the Yankees were eliminated from contention.

Born October 1, 1963
Mark McGwire

During the first week of the future home run king's life, the Dodgers swept the Yankees in the World Series. McGwire could not have noticed that the Yankees hit only two home runs in this Series. Only two teams since have hit fewer. One was the 1976 Yankees.

No matter how good someone is at a sport, they will have an occasional loss of concentration. Such a lapse will make a pool champion scratch on an easy shot. This explains how Cincinnati pitching allowed Jim Mason to hit the Yankees' only home run of the 1976 Series.

Home run records, held by Yankees, that McGwire broke:

- most home runs in a season: seventy in 1998 (Roger Maris had sixty-one in 1961.)
- most home runs in two consecutive seasons: 128 in 1997-1998 (Babe Ruth hit 114 in 1927-1928.)
- most home runs in three consecutive seasons: 180 in 1996-1998 (Ruth hit 161 in 1926-1928.)
- fewest at bats per home run, career: 11.23 (Ruth had 11.76 at bats per home run.)

OCTOBER 2, 1958

By beating the Yankees 13-5, the Milwaukee Braves took a two-games-to-none lead in the World Series. Braves' pitcher Lew Burdette beat the Yankees for the fourth consecutive time in World Series play. Showing he had another skill the Yankees lacked, Burdette hit a three-run home run.

Biggest leads against the Yankees in a World Series game:

- During their 13-5 win in 1958, the Braves had an eleven-run lead.
- In the first game of 1996 World Series, the Braves built and held an eleven-run lead, winning 12-1.
- Los Angeles led 10-0 in the fifth game of the 1977 Series.
- With a 12-4 lead in the third game in 1921, the New York Giants had an eight-run advantage.
- St. Louis was up by eight runs, when they led 9-1 in the sixth game in 1926.

Died October 2, 1967
Orville Armbrust

Armbrust, a Washington Senators' pitcher, defeated the Yankees in Babe Ruth's last game with the team. It was Armbrust's only win in a three-game major-league career.

OCTOBER 3, 1947

It was the fourth game of the 1947 World Series. Brooklyn trailed the Yankees 2-1 in the bottom of the ninth inning. Two Dodgers were on base, thanks to Yankee pitcher Bill Bevens. He had issued his ninth and tenth walks of the game. Bevens had not allowed a hit. Cookie Lavagetto hit a two-run, game-winning double. This hit prevented years of having to listen to Yankee fans describe a ten-walk, no-hit effort as a well-pitched game.

Died October 3, 1995
Nippy Jones

New York led the 1957 World Series, two games to one. Jones was pinch hitting for the Braves in the bottom of the tenth inning. Although Tommy Byrne's pitch hit Jones on the foot, the umpire did not see it. Jones persuaded the umpire to inspect the ball. Seeing shoe polish, the umpire awarded Jones first base. Jones became the tying run, as the Braves rallied to win the game on Eddie Mathews's home run.

Nobody who lived in Milwaukee in 1957 has ever complained about having to shine his shoes.

A Yankee-free listing of baseball's greatest moments:

- On this date in 1951, Bobby Thomson hit a three-run home run, in the bottom of the ninth inning, to win the National League pennant.
- Francisco Cabrera's two-run, two-out, ninth-inning single won the seventh game of the 1992 National League Championship Series. This was the first time that one at bat decided which team won a postseason series.
- Washington's Earl McNeely hit a twelfth-inning single to win the seventh game of the 1924 World Series.
- Carlton Fisk's twelfth-inning fair-foul-fair-foul-fair ball won the sixth game of the 1975 World Series. More than just a game-winning home run, this hit was the culmination of a series of exceptional plays in an extraordinary game.

306

OCTOBER 4, 1955

Johnny Podres pitched a 2-0 shutout in the seventh game of the 1955 World Series. Brooklyn fans needed no special reason to savor this win, which is described in detail elsewhere. (See June 27.) That it came against the hated Yankees made it special.

Howard Cosell must have been overjoyed. Remember his speeches on the Dodgers during his stint on *Monday Night Baseball* in the 1970's? Cosell would say something like "I can still see the diminutive one, Dodger captain Pee Wee Reese, turning the double play with the unconquerable Jackie Robinson and the silent one, the great Gil Hodges. Hodges, of course, drove in two runs in the final game of the 1955 World Series and later managed the Mets to the world's championship in 1969, the year of Neil Armstrong, who will be Barbara Walters's special guest, tomorrow night on A-B-C."

Born October 4, 1910
Frank Crosetti

Crosetti still co-holds the team record for most errors in a World Series. He had four in 1932.

It is unlikely anyone ever asked Crosetti to write a book on good career moves. He left the Yankees to become a coach for the Seattle Pilots, who lasted one season.

Yankees who first achieved dubious marks:

- Crosetti was the first Yankee to strike out one hundred times in a season.
- By losing 103 times, the 1908 Yankees became the first Yankee team to lose one hundred games in a season.
- Bill Hogg became to first Yankee pitcher to issue one hundred walks in a season, in 1905.

OCTOBER 5, 1942

St. Louis won the World Series four games to one. A low moment for the Yankees occurred in the ninth inning of the final game. Trailing 4-2, the Yankees had runners on first and second with nobody out. Joe Gordon, the runner on second, was picked off base by Cardinal catcher Walker Cooper.

Joe Gordon's performance in the 1942 World Series:

- He showed great alertness on the bases, as noted above. Gordon is almost certainly the only MVP to be picked off second base, by the catcher, in the final game of the World Series. He might be the only human being to suffer this fate in any inning.
- The Yankee second baseman hit .095.
- Gordon struck out seven times.
- Hardly living up to his nickname, "Flash," Gordon did not steal a base.

Died October 5, 1912
The Yankees' era at Hilltop Park

During their ten seasons at this field, the Yankees never won a pennant. They finished last twice and had an average record of 76-79.

A hospital is now on this site. Somehow, this seems appropriate. After the Yankees spent ten years making the lives of New Yorkers worse, there is an institution making their lives better.

OCTOBER 6, 1978

Kansas City's George Brett was at his postseason best, hitting three home runs against the Yankees. Brett's blasts came in the third game of the American League Championship Series.

Brett hit .358 in four playoff series against the Yankees. His three-run home run in the eighth inning tied the fifth game in 1976. Another three-run home run won the 1980 Championship Series.

His brother, pitcher Ken Brett, also had his moments against the Yankees. Ken had three hits, as Boston beat the Yankees in a 1969 game.

Born October 6, 1965
Ruben Sierra

Sierra had the worst batting average, .174, of any Yankee regular in the 1995 Division Series.

Most important World Series home runs against the Yankees:

- Bill Mazeroski's ninth-inning home run won the 1960 World Series. Earlier, Hal Smith had a three-run home run. Smith's hit capped a five-run eighth inning and gave the Pirates a 9-7 lead.
- Eddie Mathews's tenth-inning home run, on this date in 1957, gave the Braves a 7-5 win. It tied the 1957 Series at two games each.
- Whitey Kurowski's ninth-inning home run won the fifth, and final, game of the 1942 Series for St. Louis.
- Tim McCarver's tenth-inning, three-run home run gave the Cardinals a three-games-to-two lead in the 1964 World Series.
- Steve Yeager's home run gave the Dodgers a 2-1 win and a three-games-to-two lead in the 1981 Series.
- Casey Stengel hit two game-winning home runs for the Giants in the 1923 World Series.

OCTOBER 7, 1922

The Yankees lost to the Giants 4-3 and trailed the World Series three games to none.

All games of the 1921 and 1922 Yankee-Giant World Series were played at the Polo Grounds. As home team, the Yankees drew about two thousand fewer fans per game than the Giants did. Affected by this lack of support, the Yankees won only three of the thirteen games played.

Lowest attendance, season, by the Yankees:

- 211,808 in 1903
- 242,194 in 1912
- 256,035 in 1915
- 282,047 in 1918

Died October 7, 1991
Leo Durocher

His last act as a Yankee player was telling Yankee General Manager Ed Barrow to go f___ himself.

OCTOBER 8, 1922

By winning 5-3, the Giants completed their sweep of the 1922 World Series. (There was one tie game.) Of the forty-six innings played in this Series, the Yankees led after only seven. Four of the eight Yankee regulars hit below .200. It makes one wish videotape had been invented earlier.

Some comments on Babe Ruth's .118 batting average in the 1922 World Series:

- Ruth had a single and a double in seventeen times at bat.
- His average was the lowest of any player, excluding pitchers, on either team.
- He was hitless in the last three games of the Series, all of which the Yankees lost.
- Ruth described his performance as a "deep disappointment."

Born October 8, 1902
Paul Schreiber

Schreiber is a symbol of how desperate the Yankees were for players during World War II. He pitched in two games in 1945. These were his first major-league appearances since 1923. Despite twenty-two years rest, Schreiber allowed four hits, walked two, and had an ERA of 4.15.

OCTOBER 9, 1921

The New York Giants beat the Yankees in the fourth game of the 1921 World Series. George Burns drove in the winning run, with a double off the Yankees' Carl Mays.

There have been rumors that gamblers paid Mays to let up in key situations in the 1921 Series. No one has ever proved this, though circumstantial evidence exists. Mays did give up late-inning winning runs twice in this Series.

Perhaps Mays was merely an innocent choker. It is hard to pitch well with both hands wrapped around your neck.

Born October 9, 1898
Joe Sewell

In a 1920 game, Mays had accidentally killed Cleveland shortstop Ray Chapman with a pitched ball. Sewell replaced Chapman. His .329 batting average helped the Indians prevail over the Yankees in that season's pennant race.

Players who played for two different franchises that beat the Yankees in the World Series:

- Clem Labine and Don Hoak played for the 1955 Dodgers and the 1960 Pirates.
- Roger Craig won games for the 1955 Dodgers and for 1964 Cardinals.
- Dick Groat and Bob Skinner were with the 1960 Pirates and the 1964 Cardinals.

OCTOBER 10, 1957

By winning the seventh game at Yankee Stadium, on Lew Burdette's shutout, the Braves won the 1957 World Series. Burdette, the Braves' second-best pitcher, pitched on two-days' rest. Whitey Ford, the Yankees' best pitcher, could not do the same.

Yankee manager Casey Stengel forgot that Ford had won a World Series game, pitching on two-days' rest. It had happened way back in 1956.

Died October 10, 1946
Walter Clarkson

Clarkson gave up seven runs, as the Yankees lost to the Red Sox 13-2. This win gave Boston a half-game lead over the Yankees. Boston and New York had three games to play, all against each other, to decide the 1904 pennant race.

Clarkson died on the forty-second anniversary of the death of the Yankees' 1904 pennant hopes. Boston won on Jack Chesbro's wild pitch in the second of these three games. (See January 16.)

Heroes of the 1926 World Series, which the St. Louis Cardinals won on this date:

- Grover Cleveland Alexander won two games and saved another. (See February 26.)
- Tommy Thevenow, who had a .417 average, hit one of his three major-league home runs.
- Jesse Haines won two games and batted .600.
- Jim Bottomley hit .345 with five RBI.

OCTOBER 11, 1978

Los Angeles took a two-games-to-none lead in the World Series, by beating the Yankees 4-3. In the game's most memorable moment, Reggie Jackson faced Dodger rookie Bob Welch. There were two runners on base with two outs in the ninth inning. Six minutes and nine pitches later, Jackson struck out swinging.

Born October 11, 1945
Bob Stinson

Seattle beat the Yankees 6-5, in a 1979 game. Stinson and Dan Meyer hit pinch-hit home runs in the eighth inning. Two pinch-hit home runs in an inning equaled a major-league record.

Excluding this game, Stinson and Meyer were a combined one-for-twelve as pinch-hitters for the Mariners in 1979.

Some terrible Yankee pinch-hitters:

- Bernie Allen did not have a hit in twenty pinch-hit at bats in 1972.
- Tommy Byrne was a pinch out from 1956 to 1958. He had no hits in twenty-four at bats. (Byrne found inventive ways to hurt the Yankees as a pinch hitter. As a member of the White Sox, Byrne hit a pinch-hit, grand slam home run to beat the Yankees.)
- Over two seasons, 1958 and 1959, Marv Throneberry had one hit in twenty-seven at bats.
- Mike Pagliarulo got one hit in twenty-six at bats, from 1986 to 1988.
- Bud Methany had one hit in twenty-one at bats between 1943 and 1946. As we have noted (March 13), the Yankees gave Babe Ruth's number three to this career .247 hitter. Perhaps the number affected Methany. Ruth had a .194 batting average as a pinch hitter.

OCTOBER 12, 1977

Ron Cey, Steve Yeager, and Reggie Smith hit home runs in the first three innings, as Los Angeles tied the World Series with a 6-1 win.

Catfish Hunter lost his third consecutive postseason game for the Yankees. In losing, he proved he could throw gopher balls in the postseason at a slightly higher rate than he did in the regular season.

Born October 12, 1955
Jim Lewis

In a 1982 game, Lewis gave up seven runs in two-thirds of an inning. Sadly, this was his only game with the Yankees.

A Columbus Day salute to the Yankee scouts, who could not sign these New York City natives:

- Hank Greenberg
- Sandy Koufax
- Frankie Frisch
- Ken Singleton

OCTOBER 13, 1960

Bill Mazeroski won the World Series with a home run in the bottom of the ninth inning. New York is the only team to lose a seventh game of the World Series on a last-inning home run.

This home run concluded a memorable Series for the Pirate second baseman. Mazeroski hit .320. His two-run home run won the first game. In the fifth game, he had a two-run double, as the Pirates won 5-2.

Somehow, Yankee second baseman Bobby Richardson won the World Series' Most Valuable Player award. And you wonder why people bought this book?

Born October 13, 1954
George Frazier

In 1981, this Yankee pitcher became the only honest man to lose three games in a World Series.

Some comparisons between Frazier and the only other man to lose three games in the World Series:

- Gamblers paid Lefty Williams, one of the Black Sox, to lose games.
- Williams achieved his feat in a Series that lasted eight games. Frazier required only six.
- Frazier's ERA of 17.18 was almost three times Williams's 6.61.
- Williams played with Shoeless Joe Jackson, a humble superstar. Frazier played with Reggie Jackson, who has never been in the same time zone as either humble or superstar.
- No actor will ever play George Frazier in a movie.

OCTOBER 14, 1892

A game between Washington and Boston was postponed. There was a football game scheduled on the Senators' field.

Twelve years later, the Yankees and Red Sox met in a five-game series to decide the American League pennant. Since the Yankees' management had leased their field for a college football game, two of these games were moved to Boston. Playing two scheduled road games at home helped the Red Sox win the pennant.

As a student, Yankee co-owner Bill Devery must have had trouble with English. Words like "priority" probably confused him.

Died October 14, 1988
Vic Raschi

In 1950, this Yankee pitcher committed four balks in a game.

In *Goldfinger,* the title character tells James Bond that once was happenstance, twice was coincidence, and three times was enemy action. One wonders how Goldfinger would have described Raschi's fourth balk.

Yankee pitchers who gave up notable home runs to Hank Aaron:

- As a Cardinal, Raschi gave up Aaron's first career home run.
- Al Downing, while pitching for the Dodgers, allowed Aaron's record-breaking 715th home run.
- Don Larsen surrendered Aaron's first postseason home run.

OCTOBER 15, 1964

St. Louis won the seventh game of the World Series. They took a 6-0 lead, before winning 7-5. Three of their runs resulted from four bad fielding plays by the Yankees. Actually, there were three bad plays and one stupid play. New York allowed a double steal. Mike Shannon stole second while Tim McCarver stole home. These two Cardinals had combined for six stolen bases during the 1964 season.

Highlights of the 1964 World Series:

- Ken Boyer hit a grand slam, as the Cardinals won the fourth game 4-3.
- Cardinal catcher Tim McCarver hit a tenth-inning, three-run home run to win the fifth game.
- Bob Gibson won the fifth and seventh games. He struck out thirty-one Yankees in the Series.
- Roger Craig and Dick Groat picked Mickey Mantle off second base in the fourth game.

Born October 15, 1945
Jim Palmer

Oriole pitcher Palmer won twenty or more games eight times in the 1970's. The entire Yankee pitching staff did this five times.

Palmer put his eloquence and his good looks to productive use. He has worked as a broadcaster, and as a model for an underwear manufacturer. Try to imagine former Yankee catcher Yogi Berra in either role.

OCTOBER 16, 1921

Yankee players Babe Ruth and Bob Meusel left on their barnstorming tour. This was in defiance of Commissioner Landis's orders. (Baseball had a rule prohibiting players on World Series' teams from playing in postseason exhibitions.) Ruth's tour was a flop.

Ruth, who showed more stubbornness than brains in this matter, paid for flouting Landis's authority. He and Meusel were suspended for the first six weeks of the following season.

Born October 16, 1941
Tim McCarver

McCarver hit .478 against the Yankees in the 1964 World Series. This was in addition to the heroics described with yesterday's entries.

Steals of home against the Yankees in the World Series:

- McCarver, 1964
- Monte Irvin, 1951
- Jackie Robinson, 1955

OCTOBER 17, 1976

Cincinnati beat the Yankees in the second game of the World Series. Tony Perez's single, in the bottom of the ninth inning, won the game for the Reds.

Riverfront Stadium in Cincinnati has an artificial playing surface. If you try hard enough, you can find something good to say about almost anything. For example, artificial turf is not all bad. The Yankees are the only team to have lost every World Series game they have played on this surface.

Stadiums where the Yankees have lost every postseason game they have played:

- Riverfront Stadium (Cincinnati)
- The Kingdome (Seattle)

Born October 17, 1908
Red Rolfe

Only a few players have committed two errors in an All-Star game. Rolfe, a Yankee third baseman, did it in the 1937 game.

Rolfe was influenced by the play of his fellow Yankee infielders. Lou Gehrig would lead American League first basemen in errors in 1937. Shortstop Frank Crosetti and second baseman Tony Lazzeri had led their peers in errors during the previous season.

OCTOBER 18, 1960

At a badly handled press conference, the Yankees tried to claim manager Casey Stengel was retiring. He was not, as his statements made clear. Or do you think Stengel's comments like "I was told my services were no longer desired" and "You're damn right I was fired" are ambiguous?

Born October 18, 1935
Howie Nunn

In their first-ever meeting, the Mets beat the Yankees. Nunn was the winning pitcher, in this 1962 preseason game.

Nunn was not good enough to make the Mets that season. These Mets were perhaps the worst team in baseball history.

Comparisons of the Yankees' and the Mets' attendance:

- In 1964, the Mets, who finished last, outdrew the pennant-winning Yankees by more than four hundred thousand fans.
- In 1965, the Mets increased this excess to half a million fans.
- By 1969, the difference was more than a million fans.
- By 1972, the Mets' attendance was double the Yankees'.

OCTOBER 19, 1990

Two years after his second firing by the Yankees, Lou Pinella was the manager of the Reds. Cincinnati was in the process of sweeping the World Series against the heavily favored Oakland A's.

That week, Steinbrenner hosted the television program, *Saturday Night Live*. His first line was "I just bought the Cincinnati Reds." Controversial Reds' owner Marge Schott suddenly became very popular.

Born October 19, 1961
Tim Belcher

Belcher was the Yankees' first pick in the amateur draft. Due to a screwup, Belcher would win his 136 games, through 1998, for other teams.

Oakland had the right to select a player from any other team's list of unprotected players. They picked Belcher after the Yankees erroneously failed to designate him as a protected player.

Imagine the bumbling Yankee executive explaining this error to the understanding, forgiving Steinbrenner. It makes the last time you were blasted by your boss seem almost tolerable, doesn't it?

Yankee hating by the numbers, part twenty-one:

- **80.** Games that former Yankee manager Casey Stengel's 1962 Mets finished below .500.
- **81.** Errors the unfortunately-named Yank Robinson committed in the 1889 season.
- **82.** Times the Yankees were caught stealing in 146 attempts in 1920.
- **83.** Points, of 140, that Yankee reliever Sparky Lyle did not get in the 1977 Cy Young Award voting. He is one of the few winners who did not receive a majority of the points available.

OCTOBER 20, 1964

Johnny Keane became the manager of the Yankees. He had recently resigned as manager of the Cardinals. It is virtually certain that Keane had agreed to manage the Yankees several weeks previously. This hiring concluded a five-day period during which the Yankees had lost the World Series and had fired manager Yogi Berra.

Some comments made about the Berra-Keane fiasco:

- Hall of Fame manager Leo Durocher (See March 1.): "What are you going to do if you're managing one team in the World Series, and you have already agreed to manage the team you're playing against? You keep quiet about it, that's what you do. If it was me, I'd have ended up out of baseball." (*Nice Guys Finish Last.* New York: Simon & Schuster, Inc, 1975, 307.)
- Cardinal broadcaster Harry Caray: "Somewhere in there (the 1964 World Series), there had to be a conflict of interest. But you sure couldn't find one from the way the teams played on the field." (*Holy Cow.* New York: Berkley Books, 1989, 147.)

Born October 20, 1931
Mickey Mantle

Mantle had been the youngest player to hit a home run in the World Series. Andruw Jones, aged nineteen, hit two home runs to break Mantle's record. He hit these for the Braves, on this date in 1996.

L'AFFAIRE JOHNNY KEANE (October 20)

OCTOBER 21, 1976

Cincinnati completed its sweep of the Yankees in the World Series.

Occasionally, someone wins an election in a landslide. Analysts point out how the winner swept virtually every important component of the vote. Cincinnati had a landslide of a World Series sweep. The Reds outscored the Yankees 22-8. They had more hits, doubles, triples, home runs, RBI, and stolen bases than the Yankees had. Seven of Cincinnati's nine starters hit better than .300. As noted below, they led in all but a few innings.

If this World Series were an election, it would not be Nixon-McGovern. It would be one of North Korea's.

The longest periods during which the Yankees did not trail in the 1976 World Series:

- three innings in the fourth game,
- two innings in the second game,
- one and a half innings in the second game, and
- one inning in the first game.

(The Yankees' only lead was for two innings in the fourth game.)

Born October 21, 1917
Frank Papish

Papish won only two of ten decisions in 1948. One of these was a late-season win over the contending Yankees. Papish drove in a run, as the White Sox won for only the forty-seventh time in 144 games. This loss prevented the Yankees from moving into a first-place tie with Boston and Cleveland.

OCTOBER 22, 1985

The 1985-86 hockey season was underway. It would end with the Montreal Canadiens winning their twenty-third Stanley Cup. This broke the Yankees' record for championships won in North American professional sports.

Born October 22, 1882
Birdie Cree

Cree played eight seasons for the Yankees. He would have been better off on the golf course. Cree's Yankee teams had a cumulative record of 535-682. This is a .440 winning percentage.

Some of Billy Martin's more memorable fights:

- On this date in 1979, Martin punched a marshmallow salesman. This resulted in Martin's second firing as manager of the Yankees.
- Martin was badly beaten in a "gentlemen's club" in 1988. Shortly thereafter, he was fired for the fifth time as Yankee manager.
- In 1969, he beat up one of his own players, twenty-game-winner Dave Boswell. Martin was fired as manager of the Minnesota Twins after that season.
- He got into a fight with, and lost badly to, Ed Whitson, one of his Yankee pitchers. Martin was more selective this time; Whitson was only a ten-game winner. This fight contributed to Martin's fourth firing in 1985.

OCTOBER 23, 1986

To the presumed delight of Joann Barrett, the Mets were playing in the World Series. Ms. Barrett had said, "I'm a Mets fan now" after being shot at Yankee Stadium in 1985.

Born October 23, 1931
Senator Jim Bunning

Bunning pitched 268 innings in 1961. This was the most by an opposing pitcher without giving up a home run to Roger Maris.

Consider some of the alleged pitchers who helped Maris pad his record that season. Ed Palmquist, of the Angels, had a career record of 1-3. Detroit's Jerry Casale was finished as a major-leaguer before he turned thirty. He had a career record of 17-24, with a 5.07 ERA.

Then there was Eli Grba. Maris likely remembered Grba's 6.48 ERA for the 1959 Yankees. Grba won twenty-eight games in the major leagues. He was last seen auditioning for *Wheel of Fortune*. He wanted to buy a vowel.

A complete listing of players who have hit more than fifty-five home runs in a season, but fewer than three hundred in their careers:

- Roger Maris, 275,
- Hack Wilson, 244, and
- Sammy Sosa, 273 home runs. Sosa will not be on this list much longer.

OCTOBER 24, 1981

Los Angeles tied the World Series at two games each, by overcoming a 6-3 Yankee lead. Jay Johnstone's two-run pinch-hit home run was the big hit.

Born October 24, 1941
Omar Moreno

Nicknamed "Omar the Outmaker," Moreno hit .250, .259 and .197 in his three seasons with the Yankees. Moreno, the Yankee leadoff hitter, had twenty-seven walks in 573 at bats.

The leading "outmakers" in a season for the Yankees:

- Frank Crosetti made 440 outs in 1940 (546 at bats- 106 hits).
- Roger Peckinpaugh accounted for 421 outs in 1915 (540- 119).
- In 1966, Tom Tresh made 412 outs (537- 125); in 1968 he was responsible for 408 (507- 99).
- Wid Conroy made 406 outs in 1907 (530- 124).
- In 1939, Babe Dahlgren equaled Conroy's futility (531- 125). Dahlgren replaced Lou Gehrig, who had contracted a fatal disease. Given Dahlgren's performance, the Yankees might have been better off with the dying Gehrig.

(Based on 125 or fewer hits)

OCTOBER 25, 1981

Steinbrenner said he was involved in a fight in an elevator. He claimed he administered Billy Martin-style justice to two individuals who had insulted New York and the Yankees. Or did he? One would search law libraries in vain to find *Steinbrenner v. Otis* or *Client of Contingency Fee Attorney v. Steinbrenner.* What actually occurred remains a mystery. Perhaps, frustrated over his team's performance in the World Series, Steinbrenner punched two guys named "Up" and "Down."

Various comments on the elevator incident:

- Steinbrenner: "There are two guys in this town looking for their teeth."
- Billy Martin, in a telegram to Steinbrenner: "I understand exactly how you must have felt in that elevator.... By the way, the marshmallow man I hit was saying bad things about New York and the Yankees."
- Orioles' owner and famed attorney Edward Bennett Williams: "If the fight really took place the way George says it did, this is the first time a millionaire has ever hit someone and not been sued."
- Reggie Jackson: "He probably did punch out those fans, as long as they were nine and ten."

Born October 25, 1939
Pete Mikkelson

Yankees pitcher Mikkelson lost the first indoor baseball game, a 1965 exhibition meeting between the Yankees and the Astros.

OCTOBER 26, 1960

The American League announced the Washington Senators would move to Minnesota and become the Twins. This move would make a weak franchise competitive.

Minnesota got off to a fine start in 1961. In the season opener, the Twins beat the Yankees 7-0.

Died October 26, 1991
Bill Bevens

Bevens had a .350 winning percentage in 1947. This is almost impossible for a pitcher with a meaningful number of decisions on a pennant-winning team. "Passenger" would have been a good nickname for this man.

A comparison of Bevens's World Series one-hitter with the other World Series one-hitters:

- Bevens lost the game, allowing ten walks and three runs.
- Claude Passeau won 3-0, walking one, in 1945.
- In 1967, Jim Lonborg won 5-0, issuing only one walk.
- Tom Glavine and Mark Wohlers shared a one-hitter in 1995. They won 1-0, walking three.

(Ed Reulbach is credited with pitching a one-hitter in the 1906 World Series. There is considerable evidence he allowed two hits.)

OCTOBER 27, 1985

Steinbrenner, feeling that baseball (i.e. Steinbrenner) was not getting enough attention, fired Billy Martin as Yankee manager. Unfortunately for Steinbrenner, the media ignored Martin's fourth firing. It paid more attention to the seventh game of the World Series.

Born October 27, 1922
Ralph Kiner

Kiner's .279 batting average is the second-worst of any outfielder in the Hall of Fame. It is still seventeen points better than Reggie Jackson's.

Jackson's rank among Hall of Famers:

- His batting average is the worst among outfielders. It is the seventh-worst among those who were elected primarily for what they achieved as players. These six other players were good fielders.
- Jackson is tied for last in Gold Gloves won, with none.
- Jackson is not among the top thirty-five leaders in career slugging average. He trails players like Jeff Heath, Bob Johnson, and Darryl Strawberry, none of whom will ever make the Hall of Fame.
- Reggie is first in strikeouts. He has 661 more than second-place Willie Stargell.

OCTOBER 28, 1981

After losing the first two games of the World Series to the Yankees, the Dodgers won their fourth straight to take the Series.

Some events that cost the Yankees the 1981 World Series:

- In the sixth game, Yankee manager Bob Lemon lifted Tommy John for a pinch hitter. It was only the fourth inning. This took John and his 0.69 World Series ERA out of a 1-1 game. Los Angeles scored seven runs in the next two innings.
- Pedro Guerrero and Steve Yeager hit consecutive home runs, as the Dodgers won the fifth game 2-1.
- Yankee base runner Larry Milbourne was caught off base, following Ron Cey's catch of a foul ball. This was the turning point in Fernando Valenzuela's win in the third game. Cey had a good day, hitting a three-run home run in the first inning.
- There were no outs in the seventh inning of the fourth game. Los Angeles had the bases loaded. Lemon passed up relief ace Goose Gossage. He brought in Tommy John, who had made twelve relief appearances in the previous fourteen years. John gave up the eventual winning run.
- Jerry Mumphrey, a good outfielder, was benched in the fourth game. His replacement, Bobby Brown, made an error to put the winning run in scoring position.

Observed October 28
The feast of St. Jude

Jude is the patron saint of lost causes. With the Yankees in first place, Steinbrenner said, "I'm not ready to give up on this team yet."

OCTOBER 29, 1919

Baseball's governing body, the National Commission, withheld the Yankees' third-place money. This meant the club would have to use its own funds to pay player bonuses.

Some saw this as vengeance for the Carl Mays affair. Mays, one of baseball's better pitchers, had quit the Red Sox. American League President Ban Johnson had warned that no team should sign Mays. Figuring that sending Boston two players of little value entitled them to ignore Johnson's ruling, the Yankees had signed Mays.

Born October 29, 1954
Jesse Barfield

In 1990, Barfield became the first Yankee to strike out at least 150 times in a season. That year, the Yankees came within sixteen strikeouts of their worst-ever total, 1,043 in 1967.

Imagine the Yankees' 1990 total if, as in 1967, their pitchers had been required to bat. Surprisingly, it might have been lower. In 1990, the Yankees used Steve Balboni, Deion Sanders, Wayne Tolleson, Mike Blowers, Claudell Washington, and Brian Dorsett as designated hitters. These designated outmakers struck out once every three and one-half times at bat.

Yankee strikeout performances:

- most in a game: five, by Johnny Broaca and by Bernie Williams
- most in a season: 156, by Danny Tartabull, in 1993
- most in a career: 1,710, by Mickey Mantle
- most in a postseason: thirteen, by Derek Jeter in 1996, and by Bernie Williams in 1998

OCTOBER 30, 1980

Although the Yankees had won 103 games in the recently completed season, Steinbrenner was not happy. "Sources close to the Yankees" (which often meant Steinbrenner) confirmed that he was thinking of replacing manager Dick Howser. He did not feel Howser was tough enough with the Yankee players. Steinbrenner's model for disciplining players was the way U.S. Olympic hockey coach Herb Brooks had controlled his team. This was a group of collegians in their early twenties, none of whom had guaranteed contracts.

Steinbrenner ultimately replaced Howser with Gene Michael. Brooks presumably was not available.

Born October 30, 1941
Jim Ray Hart

Hart was the designated hitter for the Yankees in 1973. His batting average ranked ninth among the twelve American League DH's who appeared in at least seventy-five games.

The worst designated hitters in Yankee history:

- Steve Balboni had a .192 average and thirty-four RBI, in 1990.
- Kevin Maas hit .248, in 1992, and drove in thirty-five runs.
- Carlos May had three home runs and forty RBI, in 1976.
- In 1988, the Yankees used pitcher Rick Rhoden as a DH in one game. This occurred because Rhoden was not a bad hitter and (choose one):
    - (a) Yankee designated hitters were either injured or, like forty-year-old Jose Cruz, were pathetic,
    - (b) the Yankee manager forgot he had the option of using a designated hitter, or
    - (c) Steinbrenner dictated the lineup.

(The correct answer is (a), although (b) and (c) are acceptable responses.)

OCTOBER 31, 1979

Baltimore's Mike Flanagan was a near-unanimous selection as the winner of the American League's Cy Young Award. Voters were not impressed by Tommy John's twenty-one victories for the Yankees.

Born October 31, 1882
Bert Daniels

Daniels was the Yankees' leading base stealer in 1912. Conceding they could not drive in runs (Hal Chase, their leading RBI man, ranked twentieth in the league), the Yankees stole home eighteen times. This strategy helped them lose 102 games.

Yankee hating by the numbers, part twenty-two:

- **84.** Wins by Jim Deshaies, after the Yankees traded him. New York received Joe Niekro, who won fourteen games for the Yankees.
- **85.** Wins in the career of Lew Burdette, at the start of the 1957 World Series. He had eighty-eight when the Series ended.
- **86.** RBI total no Yankee exceeded until 1911. By that year, other American League players had done this twenty times.
- **87.** Games in which pitcher Roy Sherid appeared, 1929-1931. It is unfortunate Sherid did not pitch more often. His winning percentage was ninety-two percentage points below the Yankees' in those years.

NOVEMBER 1, 1979

New York traded Damaso Garcia to the Blue Jays. In his twenty-nine games with the Yankees, Garcia made eight errors and hit .228. With the Blue Jays, he became an All-Star second baseman, twice hitting over .300.

Former players the Yankees wished they still had in 1982:

- Garcia hit .310 as Toronto's starting second baseman.
- Chris Chambliss hit .280, with twenty home runs, for Atlanta.
- Willie McGee had a .296 batting average for St. Louis.
- Reggie Jackson drove in 101 runs for the Angels.
- LaMarr Hoyt won nineteen games for the White Sox.

(Without these players, the Yankees finished one game out of last place in 1982.)

Born November 1, 1917
Pat Mullin

In 1949, this Tiger outfielder hit five of his twelve home runs against the Yankees.

NOVEMBER 2, 1947

The Secret Life of Walter Mitty was in theaters. There was a sign in Ebbets Field advertising this movie. Cookie Lavagetto's game-winning, no-hitter-ruining hit in the 1947 World Series had bounced off this sign.

Walter Mitty daydreamed about being glamorous, heroic characters. Bill Bevens, who gave up Lavagetto's hit, might have been fantasizing that he had a future in baseball.

Three days after allowing Lavagetto's hit, Bevens threw his last pitch in the major leagues. He was thirty years old.

Born November 2, 1958
Willie McGee

The Yankees traded this future World Series hero for Bob Sykes. McGee was successful in the regular season as well, winning two batting titles and a Most Valuable Player award. Sykes never threw a pitch for the Yankees.

The performances of other players acquired by the Yankees in major trades in the 1980's:

- Mike Witt (acquired for Dave Winfield) won eight games for the Yankees.
- Luis Polonia (acquired for Rickey Henderson) was with the Yankees briefly. He spent almost as long, sixty days, in prison, for having sex with a minor. (*Interviewer*: Let's talk about your record with the Yankees, Luis. *Polonia*: As I keep telling people, I've done my time. Leave me alone.)
- Lance McCullers (acquired for Jack Clark) had five wins and three saves in sixty-three games for the Yankees.

NOVEMBER 3, 1992

Bill Clinton was elected president. By 1998, he was in the middle of a scandal involving adultery, for which he apologized repeatedly. A friend of Mrs. Clinton joked that the First Lady found these embarrassing, sometimes self-serving, apologies harder to accept than the act itself.

Speaking of remorse that was hard to take, there was Steinbrenner's apology following the 1981 World Series.

Some comments on Steinbrenner's apology:

- Steinbrenner said, "I want to sincerely apologize to the people of New York and to fans of the New York Yankees everywhere for the performance of the Yankee team in the World Series."
- His words and tone suggested that his real purpose was blasting his team.
- Perhaps we should be more sympathetic. Steinbrenner was not used to apologizing. His apologies for some of his other offensive actions were, at best, low-key and, at worst, non-existent. These actions included his criminal conviction, his comments about umpires and league officials, his treatment of Dave Winfield, and his hiring of Bill Virdon as Yankee manager.

Born November 3, 1956
Bob Welch

Welch, a Dodger rookie, struck out Reggie Jackson to save the second game of the 1978 World Series. Twelve years later, Welch won twenty-seven games for the Oakland A's. This team won all twelve games it played against the Yankees that season.

338

November 4, 2001

The Yankees lost game 7 of the World Series to the Arizona Diamondbacks (only 4th year in the league), denying them 4 straight championships and 5 out of 6 years. Feeling comfortable going into the bottom of the 9th inning with a 2-1 lead and their ace closer * Mariana Rivera (career postseason ERA 0.70), pitching, the Yankees were given a taste of their own medicine (The Yankees tied games 4+5 with 2 outs in the bottom of the 9th inning, games they eventually won in extra innings). Arizona dominated Rivera with a leadoff single followed by an errant throw from Rivera to 2nd on a bunt play which led to a game-tying single by Arizona's Womack and game-winning single (series winning) by Gonzalez. The Yankees proved they shouldn't have been there, batting < .150 as a team. Boy, do they suck!!

NOVEMBER 4, 1948

Jake Powell, a Yankee outfielder from 1936 to 1940, committed suicide. He was in a police station, following his arrest for writing bad checks. Given his action, Powell probably was not innocent of the charge.

Other Yankees who killed themselves:

- Skeeter Shelton played briefly for the Yankees in 1915. His batting average and slugging average were both .025. These are the worst of any major-league player who had at least one hit during his career.
- George Davis died in 1961, one year short of the fiftieth anniversary of his only season with the Yankees. He had a 1-4 record, with a 6.50 ERA.
- Hugh Casey pitched briefly for the Yankees in 1949.
- Harvey Hendrick appeared in seventy-seven games with the Yankees in 1923 and 1924. No source refers to these teams as the Ruth-Meusel-Hendrick Yankees.

Source for names: *Baseball Babylon* by Dan Gutman (New York: Penguin Books, 1992)

Born November 4, 1968
Carlos Baerga

Cleveland's second baseman had quite a game against the Yankees in 1993. He became the first major-leaguer to hit home runs from both sides of the plate in the same inning.

NOVEMBER 5, 1954

Joe DiMaggio, Frank Sinatra, and a private detective broke down an apartment door. They were expecting to catch DiMaggio's estranged wife, Marilyn Monroe, with a lover. It was the wrong door. Our heroes settled out of court with the astonished tenant.

Died November 5, 1970
Charlie Root

Root refused to portray himself in *The Babe Ruth Story*. Legend had Ruth pointing to center field just before hitting Root's next pitch for a home run. When Root learned that the movie would not only accept, but would exaggerate this story, he turned down the proffered part.

Comments on Ruth's "called shot" home run in the 1932 World Series:

- Root: "(Ruth) pointed in my direction and yelled 'you still need one more (strike), kid!'" Root also maintained that if Ruth had actually pointed, he would have knocked Ruth "on his butt."
- Ruth: "I didn't exactly point to any spot....I just sort of waved at the whole fence."
- Yankee manager Joe McCarthy: "I'm not going to say he didn't do it. Maybe I didn't see it. Maybe I was looking the other way."
- Yankee outfielder Ben Chapman claimed Ruth said he did not point.
- Ruth's ghostwriter Ford Frick: "He never said he did and he never said he didn't."

NOVEMBER 6, 1935

"Sad Sam" Jones retired from baseball. Jones was also a carrier of sadness. During his 1922-1926 stay with the Yankees, this pitcher had a winning percentage that was thirty-one points less than the team's was. Jones's worst year was 1925. He lost twenty-one games that season.

Born November 6, 1887
Walter Johnson

An extraordinary pitcher, Johnson was also an excellent hitter. In 1925, his best season, Johnson hit .433. No Yankee with more than forty at bats in a season has ever had this high an average.

Pitchers who outhit the Yankees' best hitter in a season:

- In 1925, Johnson hit .433. Ben Paschal led the Yankees with a .360 average.
- Boston's Mickey McDermott hit .364 in 1950. This was forty points higher than Phil Rizzuto's average for New York.
- Orel Hersheiser had a .356 batting average for Los Angeles in 1993. Dion James's was .332 for the Yankees.
- In 1958, Milwaukee's Warren Spahn hit .333. New York's Elston Howard had a .314 average.

(Minimum of forty at bats)

NOVEMBER 7, 1997

A record Atlanta crowd saw the Chicago Bulls play the Hawks. In their next visit to Atlanta, the Bulls drew the largest crowd in NBA history.

Both games were played in a stadium designed for football. Many fans willingly bought seats with no view of the game. They were happy to be in the same building as Michael Jordan. "His Airness" had become the most popular athlete ever, beyond Babe Ruth or any other Yankee.

Born November 7, 1938
Jake Gibbs

Gibbs, the Yankee catcher, had a .213 batting average in 1968. This approximated the team's .214 batting average, which was the Yankees' worst ever.

Contributors to the Yankees' .214 team batting average in 1968:

- Tom Tresh hit .195.
- Dick Howser had a .153 batting average.
- Ruben Amaro hit .122.
- With his .117 average, Steve Whitaker assured he would never be asked to be a designated hitter.
- Denny McLain won thirty-one games for Detroit, and Luis Tiant had a 1.60 ERA for Cleveland.

JAKE GIBBS AND THE HOLE-IN-THE-BAT GANG
(November 7)

NOVEMBER 8, 1966

Mickey Mantle received five points in the voting for the American League's Most Valuable Player award. This was the most of any Yankee. Mantle's five points were 275 fewer than Baltimore's Frank Robinson received in winning this award.

Some players who received more points in this election than Mickey Mantle did:

- Stu Miller, whom Baltimore did not use in winning the 1966 World Series, received twenty-seven points.
- Jack Aker had twenty-two points.
- Bill Freehan, who might have been Detroit's sixth-best player in 1966, obtained nine points.
- Bobby Knoop, who hit .232, got six points.

Born November 8, 1909
Katherine Hepburn

Hepburn starred in *Guess Who's Coming to Dinner*, a 1967 movie about interracial marriage. In this movie, Spencer Tracy's character accepts what was then a controversial matter.

A mere twenty-three years later, Steinbrenner suggested that the white lawyer investigating him had done something wrong by adopting black children.

NOVEMBER 9, various years

As the weather worsened, people preferred indoor activities, such as watching the movie *Field of Dreams*.

Like the character in the movie, the real Moonlight Graham appeared in one game, without batting. Graham was with the 1905 New York Giants, who became the first New York City team to win the World Series. Eighteen years passed before the Yankees won their first World Series.

Born November 9, 1935
Bob Gibson

Gibson won the fifth and seventh games of the 1964 World Series. In this Series, the Cardinal pitcher struck out thirty-one Yankees.

Some Yankees who did especially poorly against Gibson in the 1964 World Series:

- Mickey Mantle, Mel Stottlemyre, and Elston Howard struck out five times.
- Tom Tresh and Clete Boyer fanned three times.
- Joe Pepitone was an equal-opportunity dud. He hit .154 against all Cardinal pitchers. Pepitone had an identical average against Dodger pitchers in the 1963 Series. Yankee manager Ralph Houk did not use Pepitone in the 1962 Series. This decision probably prevented a Yankee loss to the Giants.

NOVEMBER 10, 1967

Radio stations were playing "Summer Rain," a song by Johnny Rivers.

Summer rain cost the Yankees an important win in August 1978. New York led 5-3 in bottom of the seventh inning. Rain ended the game before Baltimore could complete its time at bat. Under the rules at the time, the score reverted to the previous inning, giving the Orioles a 3-0 win.

Some other Johnny Rivers' hits and possible Yankee tie-ins:

- "Poor Side of Town": Steinbrenner has a franchise that is printing money. It is playing in the most historic stadium in America. Steinbrenner does not like the neighborhood, the parking, or the relative lack of luxury boxes. He is threatening to move when his lease expires.
- "Secret Agent Man": Howard Spira was like Maxwell Smart, the bumbling secret agent in the television series *Get Smart*. Spira, Steinbrenner's agent, wound up getting Steinbrenner thrown out of baseball.
- "Memphis": New York Giant Bill Terry was from this city. He outhit Lou Gehrig, his Yankee contemporary at first base, .341 to .340 over their careers.

Born November 10, 1934
Norm Cash

Cash, the Tiger first baseman, led the American League in batting in 1961. Cash hit .361; Roger Maris and Mickey Mantle, who got all the publicity that year, hit .269 and .317, respectively.

NOVEMBER 11, 1918

World War I ended. With the Armistice, the Chicago White Sox would get back players like Shoeless Joe Jackson, Eddie Collins, and Lefty Williams. Not surprisingly, they won the 1919 American League pennant.

With the end of the War, the Yankees would have to find a way to get rid of some of their returning bums. One was pitcher Walt Smallwood, who had an ERA of 4.56 in an eight-game major-league career.

Other stars of Yankee rivals who returned to baseball as a result of Armistice Day:

- Harry Heilmann would win four batting titles for Detroit.
- Urban Shocker would have twenty-four wins for the 1922 Browns.
- Ken Williams and Baby Doll Jacobson teamed with Jack Tobin to form the Browns' outfield. Each of these players would hit over .300 in every season, but one, between 1919 and 1925. In 1924, Tobin would slip to .299.
- Herb Pennock would continue his Hall of Fame career with the Red Sox. Pennock eventually became one of far too many players that Red Sox owner Harry Frazee sold to the Yankees.

Born November 11, 1892
Al Schacht

We can accurately say that a clown can beat the Yankees. Schacht, the "Clown Prince of Baseball," beat New York in 1920. This was one of his fourteen major-league wins, all for the Senators.

NOVEMBER 12, 1920

Judge Kenesaw Mountain Landis was elected commissioner. Unlike later commissioners, he was not a tool of the owners, charged with selling naming rights to second base. He had real power.

Decisions by Landis that hurt the Yankees:

- Landis suspended Yankee stars Babe Ruth and Bob Meusel for the first six weeks of the 1922 season. (See October 16.)
- He suspended Yankee catcher Bill Dickey for thirty days, for slugging the Senators' Carl Reynolds.
- Landis located his office in Chicago. This made it less convenient for the Yankee owners to make their "for the good of the game" suggestions.
- In one of his later acts, Landis prevented Bill Veeck from buying the Phillies in 1944. (He did this for a terrible reason. Landis did not want Veeck to stock the team with black players.) Had Veeck bought the Phillies, he would not have become the owner of three different American League teams. In this role, Veeck excelled at tormenting the Yankees.

Born November 12, 1968
Sammy Sosa

In 1998, he and Mark McGwire chased the single-season home run record. Both surpassed Yankee Roger Maris's former mark. McGwire finished the season with seventy home runs, four more than Sosa hit.

NOVEMBER 13, 1981

Baseball held its draft of free agents. (Under this now-defunct process, clubs claimed the right to sign players whose contracts with their current teams had expired.)

Seven clubs selected Reggie Jackson. This was surprising. Given his batting average for the Yankees in 1981 (.237), his age (thirty-five), and his ego (legendary), it was hard to believe that any team would have been interested.

Born November 13, 1941
Mel Stottlemyre

Yankee fans tell how Stottlemyre joined the team late in the 1964 season. He posted a 9-3 record, leading the team to the pennant.

One has to wonder why Ralph Houk, the Yankee general manager, left Stottlemyre in the minors until August. Was it to protect a roster spot for Ralph Terry and his 7-11 record?

The bestseller *The Peter Principle* posits that someone rises to the level of his or her incompetence. Houk was a successful manager. Given his performance as a general manager, this book could have been called *The Ralph Rule.*

Most career losses by a Yankee pitcher:

- Stottlemyre lost 139 games. He ranks sixth in wins.
- Bob Shawkey had 131 losses.
- Red Ruffing suffered 124 defeats as a Yankee.
- Whitey Ford and Fritz Peterson had 106 losses.

NOVEMBER 14, 1966

George Weiss resigned as general manager of the Mets. In Weiss's five seasons as general manager, the Mets lost 547 games. No team in baseball history has lost that many games over a comparable period.

This experience was good for the former Yankee general manager. He learned new skills, like how to return phone calls, and how to trade players who might actually have a future in baseball.

Some of George Weiss's more endearing actions as Yankee general manager:

- He continually signed Yankee players for less money than comparable players on other teams received. (Weiss received a bonus based on how he controlled player salaries. The thought of club revenue going to a cold-blooded manager, rather than to Yankee players, is not pleasant.)
- Weiss, whose name means "white" in German, instructed his scouts not to sign black players.
- Weiss had private detectives follow Yankee players. He used the information these detectives obtained as leverage in salary negotiations.
- In 1950, the Yankees won the World Series in four games. Weiss added to the festivities by making a speech. He announced that the short Series meant less revenue for the owners, and lower player salaries the following season.

Born November 14, 1929
Jim Piersall

Playing for the Indians in 1961, Piersall punched two Yankee fans who had run onto the field. A few years earlier, his home run off New York's Johnny Sain had helped the Red Sox overcome a seven-run deficit and defeat the Yankees.

NOVEMBER 15, 1978

Sparky Lyle was working on *The Bronx Zoo*, his diary of the 1978 season. In it, the Yankee relief pitcher wrote some unflattering things about his team. For example, Lyle accused Yankee center fielder Mickey Rivers of not always giving a 100-percent effort. This is like accusing wrestling of being fixed.

Died November 15, 1969
Billy Southworth

As a Cardinal player, Southworth hit .345 against the Yankees in the 1926 World Series. As a manager, he led the Cardinals to a win over the Yankees in the 1942 Series.

Other players who hurt the Yankees, after playing on teams that beat them in the World Series:

- Tom Lasorda played for the 1955 Brooklyn Dodgers. Lasorda managed the Los Angeles Dodgers when they beat the Yankees in the 1981 World Series.
- Gil Hodges, of the 1955 Dodgers, was the manager of the Mets when they won the 1969 World Series. This win converted many New Yorkers into Mets fans, costing the Yankees attendance.
- Ron Taylor was an effective relief pitcher for the Cardinals in the 1964 World Series. He became Dr. Ron Taylor, the Blue Jays' team doctor. Years after he retired, Taylor was still working to help defeat the Yankees.
- Ken Griffey played right field for the 1976 Reds. He is the father of Ken Griffey, Jr., who starred in the 1995 Division Series against the Yankees.

NOVEMBER 16, 1965

Ford Frick stepped down as commissioner. His most memorable act was ruling that Roger Maris had to break Babe Ruth's single-season record for home runs in 154 games. When Maris needed 162 games to break the record, there was a sense of failure. Still, many felt that Ruth no longer held the record. Frick, with one ruling, lessened the achievements of the two Yankees.

Died November 16, 1987
Jim Brewer

Brewer, a pitcher, sued Billy Martin for more than a million dollars following a 1960 brawl. Nine years later, Martin paid twenty-two thousand dollars to settle the case. This represented a significant percentage of the future Yankee manager's salary.

Yankee hating from A to Z, part six:

- **V.** Pete Vuckovich. Pitching for the Brewers, Vuckovich had a win and a 0.00 ERA against the Yankees in the 1981 playoffs.
- **W.** Early Wynn. He was the winning pitcher, as Cleveland completed a sweep of a 1954 doubleheader with the Yankees. With these wins, the Indians virtually clinched the pennant.
- **X.** The middle initial of Duane Xavier Pillette. By being the winning pitcher in a 1953 Yankees-Browns game, Pillette helped end two streaks. New York had won eighteen in a row, while Pillette's St. Louis Browns had lost fourteen consecutive games.
- **Y.** Yen. This was the currency that Bill Gullickson would get to know in 1988. Following the 1987 season, Gullickson decided he would rather play in Japan than return to the Yankees.
- **Z.** Zeb Eaton. This Detroit pitcher hit a pinch-hit, grand slam home run off New York's Hank Borowy in 1945.

NOVEMBER 17, 1981

Aurelio Rodriguez's career as a Yankee ended, as he was traded to Toronto. This career .237 hitter had pinch hit for Reggie Jackson in the 1981 World Series.

Died November 17, 1985
The Dallas Cowboy mystique

At Texas Stadium, the Chicago Bears humiliated the Cowboys 44-0. (Whoops, next book!)

Since you are wondering, the worst losses in Cowboy history:

- 44-0, to the Chicago Bears in 1985
- 54-13, to the Minnesota Vikings in 1970
- 48-7, to the Cleveland Browns in 1960
- 43-3, to the Minnesota Vikings in 1988
- 38-0, to the St. Louis Cardinals in 1970
- 45-7, to the Baltimore Colts in 1960

NOVEMBER 18, 1967

On this Saturday morning, millions of children watched cartoons on television. These featured Bugs Bunny, Popeye, and, only on six-year-old Don Mattingly's television, Babe Ruth. Mattingly later admitted "I thought Babe Ruth was a cartoon character. I really did. I wasn't born until 1961."

Died November 18, 1979
Fred Fitzsimmons

At age forty, Fitzsimmons pitched seven scoreless innings against the Yankees in the 1941 World Series. Unfortunately, this Dodger pitcher had to leave the game with an injury.

Yankee hating by the numbers, part twenty-three:

- **88.** Percent of chances Orioles' third baseman Roger Bresnahan handled successfully in 1902. He had an .880 fielding average for the Yankees' predecessors.When the Orioles became the Yankees, they kept their ineptitude at third base. Wid Conroy had the second-worst fielding average of any American League third baseman in 1903.
- **89.** The most Hall of Fame votes Yankee pitcher Lefty Gomez received, as he failed to be elected to the Hall of Fame during his initial period of eligibility. (This was about half the number of votes needed for election.) Overlooking the fact that Gomez won less than two hundred games, the Veterans' Committee eventually chose him.
- **90.** Points (.462 to .372) by which the Cardinals' Ken Boyer outslugged his brother, the Yankees' Clete, in the 1964 World Series.
- **91.** Percent of Mike McNally's career hits that were singles. This lifetime .238 hitter once pinch hit for Babe Ruth.

NOVEMBER 19, 1979

Nolan Ryan, a free agent, signed with the Astros. Despite their wealth and need for pitching, the Yankees were never able to obtain Ryan. In his twenty-seven Yankee-free seasons, Ryan won 324 games and struck out 5,714 batters.

Born November 19, 1908
Joe Glenn

Glenn was the second-best catcher to wear number nine for the Yankees in 1933. Art Jorgens outhit Glenn by seventy-seven points. No one is saying that Jorgens's .220 average was any great achievement.

Some useless Yankee backup catchers, 1921-1964:

- Jorgens had .238 career average. In his eleven years with the Yankees, he averaged twenty-eight games a season. It seems that every organization has an Art Jorgens. There is someone, with no apparent talent, who has worked in the finance department or the chemistry faculty for years. He or she draws a moderate salary, never offends anyone, but never gets anything done. North American organizations might consider recognizing these employees with an annual Art Jorgens award.
- Ed Kearse had a .192 average, in eleven games, in 1942.
- In 1945, Herb Crompton hit .192, in thirty-six games.
- Darrell Johnson batted .217, in twenty-one games, in 1957.

NOVEMBER 20, 1962

Pittsburgh traded Dick Stuart to Boston. One year, the Pirates voted Stuart a partial share of postseason money, while voting a full share for the bat boy. When Stuart was asked about this, he replied, "he's a very good bat boy."

In 1976, the Yankees did not have this generous attitude. They voted not to give any postseason money to their bat boys.

Born November 20, 1945
Rick Monday

"What if " is fun to play. Consider if Monday had not hit a home run against the Montreal Expos to win the 1981 National League pennant.

Would the Expos, like Monday's Dodgers, have beaten the Yankees in the World Series? Montreal had no World Series experience. Their relief pitching was ineffective. Jim Fanning, their recently hired manager, had not managed at any level in nineteen years.

These weaknesses might not have been serious. Yankee relief pitching in the World Series was abysmal. George Frazier lost three games, while Ron Davis had a 23.50 ERA. Yankee manager Steinbrenner, who used Bob Lemon to execute his decisions, had last managed baseball on a playground.

Bad first picks by the Yankees in the amateur draft (Monday was the first pick in the first-ever amateur draft.):

- With Johnny Bench and Nolan Ryan available, the Yankees made Bill Burbach their first-ever pick. Bench might have been a better pitcher than Burbach, who had a 6-11 record in the major leagues.
- John Elway
- Bo Jackson
- Billy Cannon, Jr. These last three picks suggest the Yankees were putting far too much emphasis on their touch football team.

NOVEMBER 21, 1980

One of the braver World Series decisions occurred in 1968. Detroit manager Mayo Smith used center fielder Mickey Stanley as his shortstop. Stanley had played nine major-league games at this position.

Smith needed to get Al Kaline's bat into the lineup. He also had to replace shortstop Ray Oyler, one of the worst hitters in major-league history.

In 1968, only one major-leaguer, with at least 150 at bats, had a lower slugging average than Oyler's .185. This player was a reserve Yankee infielder named Dick Howser.

On this date in 1980, Howser resigned as the manager of the Yankees. He went on to manage the Kansas City Royals. Howser's Royals won the World Series in 1985, and were in the postseason three times.

Born November 21, 1969
Ken Griffey, Jr.

Griffey had five home runs and batted .391, as Seattle beat the Yankees in the 1995 Division Series.

If Griffey can remain healthy, he has an excellent chance of passing Babe Ruth for second place in career home runs. Griffey would need to average thirty-four home runs a season, over the next eleven seasons, to accomplish this.

Some achievements by Stan Musial (born on this date in 1920):

- He had 3,630 hits, 757 more than Babe Ruth had.
- With 6,134 total bases, Musial had 341 more than Ruth's total.
- His 1,377 extra-base hits are twenty-one more than Ruth's.

NOVEMBER 22, 1975

Oscar Gamble became a Yankee. Of Gamble, San Diego owner Ray Kroc said, "I signed Oscar Gamble on the advice of my attorney. I no longer have Oscar Gamble, and I no longer have my attorney."

Born November 22, 1926
Lew Burdette

Burdette, a former Yankee, beat the New York three times in the 1957 World Series. In the greatest World Series pitching performance since 1905, Burdette did not allow a run in his final twenty-four innings.

And then there's Wayne Tolleson (born on this date in 1955), who played for the Yankees from 1986 to 1990:

- In 1987, Tolleson had five extra-base hits in 349 at bats. This futility set a league record.
- He hit .313 *cumulatively* in 1989 and 1990. During this period, he played in fifteen games as a designated hitter. Yankee managers Dallas Green, Bucky Dent, and Stump Merrill obviously forgot that they had the option of letting the pitcher bat.
- During his career, Tolleson went to bat over 1,900 consecutive times without receiving an intentional walk.

NOVEMBER 23, 1976

Doyle Alexander became the first significant Yankee loss to free agency. Alexander wound up spending the latter part of the 1987 season with the Tigers. His 9-0 record and 1.53 ERA helped Detroit beat the Yankees for the 1987 American League East championship.

Some free agents the Yankees coveted, but could not sign:

- Rod Carew
- Bobby Grich
- Mark Langston
- Greg Maddux
- Pete Rose

Born November 23, 1910
Hal Schumacher

He is one of thirteen pitchers to strike out five or more batters in an All-Star game. None of the thirteen was a Yankee.

Schumacher had an advantage that Yankee pitchers could not enjoy. He got to pitch to Yankee hitters.

NOVEMBER 24, 1949

Ted Williams beat out Yankees Phil Rizzuto and Joe Page for the American League's Most Valuable Player award. There was no repeat of the 1947 embarrassment. That year, Joe DiMaggio won. Triple Crown-winner Williams lost because a grudge-bearing Boston writer had refused to list Williams among his top ten choices.

Still, there was this media bias that helps make the Yankees so lovable. Rizzuto might have deserved to finish second, if the award had been limited to shortstops. Boston's Junior Stephens, whose fielding statistics were comparable to Rizzuto's, drove in 159 runs, ninety-four more than Rizzuto did.

Born November 24, 1911
Joe Medwick

The Cardinal outfielder is one of three players, none of them Yankees, to get four hits in the All-Star game.

Records for offensive performance in an All-Star game, none of which a Yankee holds or shares:

- most hits: four, shared by three players
- most runs: four, Ted Williams
- most home runs: two, shared by five players
- most RBI: five, shared by two players
- most stolen bases: two, shared by four players

NOVEMBER 25, 1990

ESPN's football programs, like *Game Day*, were on. People appreciated the numerous statistics that these shows presented. One bit of information that would have to wait for the baseball season: the Yankees lost all nine of their games on ESPN in 1990.

Born November 25, 1966
Mark Whiten

In his first at bat with the Mariners, Whiten hit a pinch-hit home run to tie the game. Seattle went on to beat the Yankees.

Whiten played for the Yankees in 1997. He hit five home runs in sixty-nine games. He had almost as many, four, in a single game with the Cardinals.

How players who wore number five for at least one season rank in career home runs hit:

- Hank Aaron is first, with 755. Aaron wore number five in his first season with the Braves.
- Johnny Bench ranks thirty-third, with 389.
- Tony Perez is thirty-ninth, with 379. Perez wore number five for the Red Sox.
- Joe DiMaggio (born on this date in 1914) ranks forty-fifth, with 361.

NOVEMBER 26, 1962

New York traded Bill Skowron, who would help the Dodgers beat the Yankees in the 1963 World Series. They received Stan Williams in return for their starting first baseman.

In a sense, the Yankees acquired a pitcher like Williams six decades too late. We have seen how New York was eliminated from the 1906 pennant race. Philadelphia's Harry Davis hit ball three, of what was intended to be an intentional walk, for the game-winning home run. (See September 25.)

As a Dodger, Williams had been told to issue an intentional walk. He hit the batter, reasoning it made no sense to throw extra pitches.

Baseball goats who spent part of their careers with the Yankees:

- Williams walked in the pennant-losing run in a 1962 Dodger-Giant playoff game.
- Fred Merkle failed to touch second base in a critical game. This failure wound up costing the Giants the 1908 National League pennant.
- Ralph Branca allowed Bobby Thomson's pennant-winning home run in 1951.
- Roger Peckinpaugh committed eight errors, as his Senators lost the 1925 World Series.

Born November 26, 1969
Sam Militello

In 1992, Yankee fans were optimistic, as Militello won his first two starts as a Yankee. By 1993, Militello was finished as a major-leaguer. He had a career record of 4-4, with a 6.75 ERA.

NOVEMBER 27, 1974

Baseball Commissioner Kuhn suspended Steinbrenner for two years, following the latter's conviction for making illegal campaign contributions.

These days, politicians seek votes by promising to be tough on crime. Often, they accuse their opponents of believing in the coddling of criminals. They point out this idea failed miserably in the 1970's.

These get-tough politicians could cite Kuhn's treatment of Steinbrenner. They could use it as a good example of why we should not return to the "soft-on-crime" policies of two decades ago.

Born November 27, 1892
Bullet Joe Bush

Yankee pitcher Bush twice blew eighth-inning leads in the 1922 World Series. By the end of that Series, Joe Bush's nickname referred to a Yankee fan's next purchase.

Worst career World Series winning percentages, by Yankee pitchers:

- George Frazier lost all three of his decisions, for a winning percentage of .000.
- Bush, Catfish Hunter, and Carl Mays all had 1-3 records and .250 winning percentages.
- Ralph Terry's winning percentage was .333. He had a 2-4 record.

(Minimum of three decisions. World Series records are those achieved as Yankee pitchers.)

NOVEMBER 28, 1974

It had been ten years since the Yankees had won a league or division title. In the 1974 season, only one Yankee had more than thirteen home runs. Pat Dobson, who would have a career winning percentage of .486, was the ace of the Yankee pitching staff. The Yankees were tenants at Shea Stadium. Bill Virdon was their manager. Steinbrenner was out of baseball.

On this Thanksgiving Day, there was reason to be grateful.

Born November 28, 1936
Gary Hart

Being caught with a "woman, not his wife" ended this U.S. Senator's presidential ambitions. Shortly thereafter, someone asked President Reagan's press secretary if he would like to be Steinbrenner's public relations man. Larry Speakes replied, "I'd rather be Gary Hart's."

United States Senators who have hurt the Yankees:

- Herman Welker was the Idaho senator who recommended that the Washington Senators sign future Hall of Famer Harmon Killebrew.
- Happy Chandler was a senator before he became commissioner of baseball. In that role, he fought with Yankee co-owner Del Webb.

NOVEMBER 29, 1966

New York traded third baseman Clete Boyer, who still had several good seasons left, for Bill Robinson and Chi Chi Olivo.

Olivo had been a thirty-five-year-old rookie in 1961. He was the second-best pitcher in the Olivo family. This is an accomplishment similar to being the second-best golfer in the Hatalsky family. (Morris was a journeyman golfer in the 1980's.) Following the trade, Olivo never pitched for the Yankees, or for any other major-league team.

Robinson would hit .206 as a Yankee. He eventually developed into a fine player. This was after New York traded him for Barry Moore, who never appeared in a game for the Yankees.

Born November 29, 1950
Otto Velez

Velez pinch hit three times for the Yankees in the 1976 World Series. He struck out each time.

Other useless Yankees with palindromic names:

- Truck Hannah appeared in 244 games as a catcher for the 1918-1920 Yankees. He hit .235 and committed thirty-four errors.
- Toby Harrah did not inspire Yankee fans to chant his last name. He had the range of a statue, while hitting .217, as the third baseman for the 1984 Yankees.
- Mark Salas hit .200 for the Yankees in 1987.
- Russ Van Atta* had ERA's of 4.18 and 6.34 in 1934 and 1935.
- Bob Oliver hit .132 in eighteen games for the 1975 Yankees.

* with apologies to palindromic purists

NOVEMBER 30, 1977

Dave Kingman left the Yankees and signed with the Chicago Cubs. He would hit another 266 home runs in the major leagues.

Born November 30, 1962
Bo Jackson

Jackson hit three home runs in a 1990 game against the Yankees. He left the game, in the sixth inning, with an injury.

Besides 1985 Heisman Trophy winner Jackson, other great college athletes who did damage to the Yankees:

- Dick Groat (All-America basketball player) played shortstop for the Pirates when they defeated the Yankees in the 1960 World Series.
- Alvin Dark (LSU football star) hit .417 against the Yankees in the 1951 World Series.
- Kenny Lofton (played on a Final Four basketball team at Arizona) led the American League in steals and hit over .300 for Cleveland from 1992 to 1996.
- Deion Sanders (All-America football player) hit .158 for the 1990 Yankees.

DECEMBER 1, 1979

The Sporting News announced the winners of Gold Gloves for fielding excellence. For the first of what would be three consecutive years, no Yankee received this award.

Died December 1, 1975
Nellie Fox

Fox, the American League's Most Valuable Player in 1959, led the White Sox to the pennant. Chicago finished fifteen games ahead of the Yankees.

Some low points of the Yankees' 1959 season:

- The Yankees were in last place in late May.
- In early summer, New York lost three, of four, games to the White Sox to drop out of the race.
- In July, Boston won five consecutive games over the Yankees.
- New York was mathematically eliminated from contention in early September.
- There were numerous injuries, which ranged from the costly (Mickey Mantle hurt his shoulder and his finger) to the unusual (Ryne Duren tripped and fell, breaking his wrist).
- None of the four players the Yankees acquired during the season was much help. Pitchers Ralph Terry and Gary Blaylock had a combined 3-8 record. Hector Lopez had the worst fielding average of any American League third baseman.
- Their fourth acquisition was outfielder Jim Pisoni. He had a name that looked like something a masochist with bad grammar would say. Yankee fans would have complied after Pisoni hit .176.

DECEMBER 2, 1971

New York acquired third baseman Rich McKinney from the White Sox. McKinney hit .215 in his only season with the Yankees. Yankee haters remember "McKinneeeey" for his four errors in a game, against the Red Sox.

Stan Bahnsen, whom the Yankees gave up for McKinney, appeared in forty-three games for the White Sox in 1972. This was only six more than McKinney played with the Yankees. Bahnsen, however, was a pitcher who won twenty-one games that season.

Players whom the Yankees traded, sold, or released, 1951-date, in transactions not mentioned elsewhere in this book:

- Hal Morris has a career batting average of over .300, in nine seasons with Cincinnati.
- Ron Davis averaged twenty-six saves a season, during his four years with the Minnesota Twins.
- Rick Reuschel won eighty-one major-league games after the Yankees thought he was through. A post-Yankee highlight for him was starting the 1989 All-Star game.
- John Wetteland has seventy-three saves in his first two seasons with the Texas Rangers.

Died December 2, 1976
Danny Murtaugh

Murtaugh managed the Pirates to a win in the 1960 World Series. This Series remains the most unbelievable ever. New York lost that Series, despite averaging eight runs and thirteen hits per game.

DECEMBER 3, 1992

Doug Drabek was in transition. Two days earlier, the winner of the 1990 Cy Young Award had left Pittsburgh and signed with the Astros. Drabek averaged fifteen wins a season, in his six seasons with the Pirates.

Drabek became a Pirate when the Yankees gave him away in a trade. He never fully lost the Yankee in him. In 1992, he became the only man to lose three games in a League Championship Series.

Born December 3, 1925
Harry Simpson

Simpson hit .083 for the Yankees, as they lost the 1957 World Series.

The worst batting averages by a Yankee, as the team lost the World Series:

- Carlos May had a batting average of .000 in the 1976 Series.
- With one hit in twenty-one at bats, Dave Winfield hit .045 in 1981.
- Irv Noren hit .063 in the 1955 Series.
- Willie Randolph's 1976 batting average was .071.
- Clete Boyer had a .077 average in the 1963 World Series. (Boyer had half of his at bats against Sandy Koufax. It would be less of a mismatch if you, the reader, played pool against a man whose first name is the name of a state.)
- Simpson hit .083 in 1957.

(Minimum of nine at bats, excluding pitchers)

DECEMBER 4, 1957

Chicago acquired Early Wynn. He earned the Cy Young Award, as the White Sox won the 1959 American League pennant.

Wynn, whose career lasted from 1939 to 1963, played in four decades. No player who spent a significant part of his career with the Yankees has ever achieved this distinction.

Born December 4, 1890
Bob Shawkey

Following the death of Miller Huggins in 1929, the Yankees needed a manager. Former Yankee pitcher Shawkey accepted the position, after interim manager Art Fletcher had turned it down. This appointment alienated Babe Ruth, who had expected the job. It also gave the Yankees a below-average manager. Shawkey never managed again in the major leagues after his Yankees finished third in 1930.

Some American League contemporaries of Ruth who, unlike the Babe, became player-managers late in their careers:

- Ty Cobb
- Tris Speaker
- George Sisler
- Eddie Collins
- Walter Johnson

DECEMBER 5, 1990

Following a major trade, Roberto Alomar and Joe Carter became Blue Jays. These players would play key roles, as Toronto won the American League East in 1991, 1992, and 1993. During these seasons, the Blue Jays finished an average of sixteen games ahead of the Yankees.

Born December 5, 1921
David "Boo" Ferriss

His 25-6 record led the Red Sox to the 1946 pennant. Boston finished seventeen games ahead of the Yankees, who heard Ferriss's nickname frequently that year at Yankee Stadium.

Some notes on the 1946 Yankees:

- Aaron Robinson led the Yankees in hitting. Something is wrong when your best batter is a career .260 hitter.
- Twelve American League players hit over .300 in 1946. None played for the Yankees.
- If the Indians had hit safely fifteen more times, the Yankees would have been the worst-hitting team in the American League.
- Randy Gumpert, whose career winning percentage is .464, was the Yankees' third-best pitcher.
- Forty-six players appeared in games for three Yankee managers that year.

DECEMBER 6, 1917

An explosion occurred when two munitions ships collided in Halifax harbor. This blast killed hundreds of people and caused extensive damage to this Canadian city. Given this tragedy, most people would acknowledge that Steinbrenner's becoming involved is no more than the second-worst thing to happen to the shipping industry.

Born December 6, 1953
Gary Ward

Ward signed with the Yankees as a free agent, following the 1986 season. He would hit twenty home runs and drive in 103 runs. Unfortunately for the Yankees, these were his combined totals for slightly more than two seasons.

Yankee hating by the numbers, part twenty-four:

- **92.** Total games the Yankees finished out of first place in the 1965 through 1968 seasons.
- **93.** Games the Yankees finished out of first place in the 1912 and 1913 seasons combined.
- **94.** Postseason games American League teams played between 1965 and 1975. None of these games involved the Yankees.
- **95.** Age at death of former Yankee Ray Fisher. He was banned from baseball for life at age thirty-three, making his sixty-two-year ban the longest served by any player.

DECEMBER 7, 1977

The Yankees paid the Braves one hundred thousand dollars for the privilege of picking up Andy Messersmith's expensive contract. Messersmith was injured and appeared in only six games in 1978. He had an 0-3 record, with a 5.64 ERA.

Born December 7, 1947
Johnny Bench

Cincinnati catcher Bench hit .533, as the Reds swept the Yankees in the 1976 World Series. His play inspired his manager, Sparky Anderson, to praise Bench. Anderson's praise was so effusive that he offended Thurman Munson, the Yankee catcher. Munson and the Yankees thought the catchers were comparable.

Debaters hone their skills by arguing difficult positions. A good debater could have argued persuasively that Walter Mondale would defeat Ronald Reagan in the 1984 presidential election. A better debater could have shown that disco music was here to stay. Only a world-class debater could have demonstrated that Thurman Munson was a better catcher than Johnny Bench.

Some comparisons of Bench and Munson, in their concurrent major-league seasons, 1970-1979:

- Bench hit more home runs in all ten seasons.
- He had more RBI in nine of these seasons.
- Bench had a better fielding average in eight of these seasons and won five more Gold Gloves than Munson did.
- Bench was named his league's Most Valuable Player twice; Munson won this award once.

DECEMBER 8, 1966

New York traded Roger Maris, who once hit sixty-one home runs in a season. They received Charley Smith, who hit sixty-nine home runs in his career. Years later, Johnny Blanchard commented on trades like this by the CBS-owned Yankees. Referring to the television star, the former Yankee catcher said, "Only Jackie Gleason could have made some of those trades."

Died December 8, 1909
Bill Hogg

Hogg lost nine straight decisions for the 1908 Yankees. He and teammate Joe Lake allowed more than three earned runs a game that season. Only three other major-league pitchers, with at least 150 innings pitched, did this.

The aces of the 1908 Yankee pitching staff:

- If you subtract Hogg's nine straight losses, he would still have had a mediocre 4-6 record.
- Lake's record was 9-22.
- Al Orth, who was nicknamed the "Curveless Wonder," was the winless wonder, with a 2-13 record.
- Jack Chesbro had a 14-20 record.

DECEMBER 9, 1982

We all make stupid decisions. Fortunately for most of us, the impact of these decisions is minor and not well-known. There are those, though, who thought Coca-Cola's formula needed changing, or that Gino Vannelli was a more promising talent than Bruce Springsteen.

On this date, the Yankees made their New Coke-Vannelli decision. They traded Fred McGriff, Dave Collins, and Mike Morgan for a washed-up Dale Murray. To make sure the trade was fair, the Yankees paid the Blue Jays four hundred thousand dollars.

Why the McGriff trade might be the Yankees' worst-ever:

- Murray had three wins, six losses, and one save during his three seasons with the Yankees.
- Through 1998, McGriff has hit 358 home runs.
- Collins played eight more seasons in the major leagues after the trade. He appeared in an average of 101 games a season. His best year was 1984. That year he hit .308, stole sixty bases, and led the American League in triples.
- Morgan has won over one hundred major-league games since the trade.

Died December 9, 1965
Branch Rickey

His integrating of baseball was one of the key factors contributing to the Yankees' demise. New York was slow to sign African-American players. On the date of Rickey's death, the Yankees had an aging Elston Howard, an ineffective Al Downing, a young Roy White, and a moderately talented Horace Clarke. Los Angeles had won the 1965 World Series with five African-Americans in their starting lineup.

THE McGRIFF TRADE (December 9)

DECEMBER 10, 1975

Yankee nemesis Bill Veeck (February 9) returned to baseball, as his purchase of the White Sox was approved.

Died December 10, 1980
Rosy Ryan

Ryan won the first-ever World Series game at Yankee Stadium, as the Giants beat the Yankees 5-4. This loss extended the Yankees' World Series winless streak to nine games.

Where the Yankees stand in World Series history:

- When the Yankees won their first World Series in 1923, five teams had won it twice.
- Nine different teams won the World Series before the Yankees did.
- Twelve of the sixteen major-league teams won a World Series game before the Yankees won one.
- Babe Ruth hit the first home run for the Yankees in the World Series. It was the thirty-second in Series play.

DECEMBER 11, 1951

Joe DiMaggio retired, despite the Yankees' efforts to convince him to play another season.

Born December 11, 1885
Art Wilson

This rather undistinguished backup catcher hit .289 for the 1912 New York Giants. None of the totally undistinguished Yankees, who appeared in more than fifty games that season, had a higher batting average.

Yankee hating by the numbers, part twenty-five:

- **96.** Games Jerry Narron and Brad Gulden played in 1979. These two shared the Yankee catching duties following Thurman Munson's tragic death during that season. They hit a combined .167 for the Yankees.
- **97.** Errors Bill Keister, the franchise's first shortstop, committed in 1901. His fielding average was .854.
- **98.** Games that Babe Ruth played in 1925. He missed fifty-six, due to injuries and suspensions.
- **99.** Best known role of actress Barbara Feldon, who also did a memorable ad for Top Brass. This company had a sign on the right field wall at Shea Stadium in 1964. Some 400,000 more people saw this sign than the corresponding sign at Yankee Stadium. The Yankees had become New York's least-popular baseball team.

DECEMBER 12, 1977

The Yankees signed Cincinnati closer Rawley Eastwick to a rich contract. Eastwick appeared in eight games for the Yankees and did not earn a save. Was he supposed to beat out Yankee relief aces Rich Gossage and Sparky Lyle?

Born December 12, 1902
Pee Wee Wanninger

Some athletes have truly intimidating nicknames. Jimmie Foxx was "the Beast." Hank Aaron answered to "the Hammer." "Dick Butkus" was an effective given name, as well as a nickname.

At the other extreme, there was Paul Wanninger. Neither his nickname, nor his one career home run, made pitchers tremble.

Pee Wee Wanninger's 1925 season, or why he was the worst shortstop in Yankee history to play a full season:

- Wanninger ranked last in batting average and in RBI among American League players with at least four hundred at bats. He ranked last among shortstops in chances per game, a measure of the ability to make plays.
- Wanninger had trouble with the balls he could reach. Six American League shortstops had better fielding averages than Wanninger's .944.
- He did not make up for his other shortcomings by being fast. His three stolen bases were well behind Johnny Mostil's league-leading forty-three.

DECEMBER 13, 1933

A's fans assessed the damage from the prior day's selling of Lefty Grove, Mickey Cochrane, and Max Bishop. Future spin doctors noted that A's owner Connie Mack had sold none of these players to the Yankees.

Teams strengthened by the selling of the Philadelphia A's stars:

- Boston acquired Grove and Bishop. Hall of Famer Jimmie Foxx would join his ex-teammates in Boston in 1935.
- Cochrane would lead the Tigers to American League pennants in 1934 and 1935.
- A year earlier, the White Sox had acquired Hall of Famer Al Simmons, as well as third baseman Jimmy Dykes, from the A's.

Born December 13, 1926
Carl Erskine

Erskine set a record by striking out fourteen Yankees, in the third game of the 1953 World Series.

In the 1952 Series, the Dodger right-hander pitched a complete game. He retired the last nineteen Yankee hitters and won 6-5.

DECEMBER 14, various years

Millions of holiday partyers chose a drink other than Ballantine beer. They opted not to have a "Ballantine Blast," as Yankee home runs were once called.

Born December 14, 1961
Jeff Robinson

In a key August 1987 game, this Tiger pitcher shut out New York 8-0. Robinson retired the last twenty-four Yankee batters.

Notes on some of the Robinsons who played for the Yankees:

- Bill twice hit below .200 as a Yankee outfielder in the 1960's.
- Aaron was a Yankee-trained catcher. He used this experience to cost Detroit a critical game in 1950. Robinson mistakenly assumed there was a force play at the plate and did not tag the winning run.
- Eddie hit .208 for the 1955 Yankees. Only four American Leaguers, with at least one hundred at bats, did worse.
- Bruce hit .118 in ten games as a Yankee catcher, in 1979 and 1980.

DECEMBER 15, 1900

Cincinnati traded Christy Mathewson to the New York Giants. In sixteen of Mathewson's seventeen seasons with the team, the Giants won more games than the Yankees did. Mathewson's 373 career wins were a major reason for this intracity dominance.

Born December 15, 1967
Mo Vaughn

Vaughn and Red Sox teammate John Valentin hit grand slams against the Yankees in successive innings. These accounted for all the runs in a 1995 game.

In the Christmas spirit, some nice things to say about the Yankees:

- They do not have a black, purple, and teal uniform that they wear on dates that are evenly divisible by eight.
- You can insult Steinbrenner at any gathering and immediately make at least two new friends.
- There has never been a ball hit at Yankee Stadium that bounced on the seam of the artificial turf and hit the ninety-seven-meter sign on the temporary fence.
- For all the fun we have had with players like Babe Ruth, Lou Gehrig, Joe DiMaggio, and Mickey Mantle, it is hard not to like them, or to appreciate their achievements.
- They have never had a mascot named Frankie the Yankee.

DECEMBER 16, 1954

Willie Mays was named the Most Valuable Player in the National League. He had led the Giants to a win in the World Series. Future lawyers were making the following argument in schoolyards: the Giants swept the Indians, who finished ahead of the Yankees. The Yankees, therefore, were not in the same league as the Giants, either literally or figuratively.

Born December 16, 1931
Barbra O'Neil ("Neil") Chrisley

This Tiger and Senator outfielder was not the only player with a feminine name to play against the Yankees. Jackie Mitchell, a seventeen-year-old girl, pitched against them in an exhibition game, in 1931. She struck out Babe Ruth and Lou Gehrig.

Christmas presents for Yankee haters:

- a team picture of the 1966 or 1990 Yankees, their two last-place teams in recent years,
- a tape of one of the episodes of the television series *Seinfeld,* depicting Steinbrenner as a buffoon who is tolerated because he has money,
- an unused ticket that the Yankees had printed, in anticipation of qualifying for the playoffs, or
- any product by a principal sponsor of a Yankee rival.

DECEMBER 17, 1951

Former Yankee player and coach Tommy Henrich began his career as a television broadcaster. Limited damage was done, as only a minority of Americans owned television sets.

Born December 17, 1880
Cy Falkenberg

Falkenberg had a 1.91 ERA for the 1908 Senators. This performance helped Washington finish seventh, ensuring the Yankees finished last. Not that the 1908 Yankees needed much help. They finished seventeen games behind the Senators.

I am part of a group of twenty that gets together annually. We meet at an inn in Lake Placid, New York. This inn has a selection of several dozen imported beers. All twenty of us believe a certain German beer is the worst of these beers. If we are correct, and if all Yankee teams were beers, the 1908 Yankees would be this beer.

More Christmas presents for Yankee haters:

- a video of *Damn Yankees*,
- any souvenir of the 1963, 1976, or 1981 World Series. New York lost four consecutive games in each of these series,
- a framed reproduction of the sports page describing any event mentioned in this book, or
- a copy of this book.

DECEMBER 18, 1918

The Yankees traded Ray Caldwell, who would subsequently pitch a no-hitter against them. His Yankee career was interesting, as Caldwell was not unfamiliar with the bottle. Caldwell disappeared for several weeks in 1916. He was ultimately found pitching in Panama.

Born December 18, 1886
Ty Cobb

Cobb tormented American League teams, including the Yankees, for twenty-four seasons. He set countless records, especially for highest career batting average, .367, and for most stolen bases, 892.

Greatest dominance by the league leader in RBI over the Yankee leader:

- Cobb had 108 RBI in 1908; Charlie Hemphill had forty-four.
- In 1912, Home Run Baker drove in 130 runs, while Hal Chase drove in fifty-eight.
- In 1914, Sam Crawford had 104 RBI. Roger Peckinpaugh had fifty-one.
- Carl Yastrzemski drove in 121 runs in 1967; Joe Pepitone drove in sixty-four.
- Sam Crawford and Bobby Veach each had 112 RBI in 1915, while two Yankees, Wally Pipp and Roy Hartzell, had sixty.

(Dominance is expressed in terms of percentage. For example, Cobb's 1908 total is 245% of Hemphill's total.)

YANKEE TEAMMATES (December 18, 23)

DECEMBER 19, 1983

Detroit signed Darrell Evans as a free agent. Evans would be a big part of the Tigers' 1984 and 1987 American League East winners. One of his better moments with Detroit occurred in 1987. Evans hit five home runs in an important three-game series with the Yankees.

Born December 19, 1934
Al Kaline

Kaline achieved what no Yankee has ever done. In twenty-three seasons with the Tigers, Kaline had more than three thousand hits, more than 350 home runs, and a postseason batting average of over .300.

Sports Illustrated's "Sportsman of the Year" selections of note:

- *SI* chose jockey Steve Cauthen, in the issue dated on this date in 1977. Cauthen beat out the Yankees' World Series hero, Reggie Jackson.
- Johnny Podres, the 1955 selection, was the Most Valuable Player, as the Dodgers defeated the Yankees in the World Series.
- Today, few would recognize the name of Bobby Morrow, the 1956 winner. *SI* chose this track star over Mickey Mantle, who had won the Triple Crown that season.
- Carl Yastrzemski, the 1967 selection, proved that winning the Triple Crown can help. From Southampton, N.Y., Yastrzemski had declined an offer to sign with the Yankees.
- Cal Ripken, Jr. had broken Lou Gehrig's consecutive-games-played streak in 1995, the year he was selected.

DECEMBER 20, 1946

By trading Gene Beardon to Cleveland, the Yankees took a major step towards dropping into third place in 1948. Beardon won twenty games for the pennant-winning Indians that year.

Born December 20, 1940
Thad Tillotson

Tillotson lost nine consecutive decisions in 1967 for the Yankees. That season, Red Sox pitcher Jim Lonborg threw at Tillotson. This led to a bench-clearing fight. Unfortunately for the Yankees, neither Lonborg nor Tillotson was seriously injured.

Yankee hating by the numbers, part twenty-six:

- **100.** Amount, in thousands of dollars, of the illegal contribution Steinbrenner made to the Nixon re-election campaign. It resulted in Steinbrenner's criminal conviction, and suspension from baseball.
- **200.** Career wins by George Uhle. These wins included a 9-0 shutout of the Yankees in 1921. This late-season win pulled the Indians to within one game of the Yankees.
- **300.** Exact number of wins by Lefty Grove, and by Early Wynn, who together pitched in the American League, never for the Yankees, from 1925-1963.
- **400.** Batting average by an extraordinary hitter. Eight players have achieved this. None played for the Yankees.
- **500.** Despite one of the league's higher payrolls, the Yankees failed to achieve this winning percentage four years in a row, 1989-1992.

DECEMBER 21, 1926

A potential scandal involving Ty Cobb and Tris Speaker became public. Former Detroit pitcher Dutch Leonard had accused these star players of conspiring to throw a game in 1919. According to Leonard, Speaker's Indians agreed to let Cobb's Tigers win a game between the teams. Detroit needed to win to finish ahead of the Yankees. Such a finish meant an extra five hundred dollars in league-paid bonus money for each Tiger player.

Commissioner Landis eventually cleared Cobb and Speaker. His official reason was that there was a lack of evidence. He could have noted that the goal of harming the Yankees justified the means.

Born December 21, 1911
Josh Gibson

The Negro League star is the only man to have hit a fair ball out of Yankee Stadium. This is something the Yankees, notably Mickey Mantle, have never been able to do.

Lions in winter: the oldest pitchers to win a postseason game against the Yankees:

- Grover Cleveland Alexander was thirty-nine years, seven months, and thirteen days old, when he won the second of two games in the 1926 World Series.
- Sal Maglie's victory, in the 1956 World Series, occurred when he was thirty-nine years, five months, and seven days old.
- Preacher Roe, aged thirty-seven years, seven months, and seven days, won for Brooklyn, in the 1952 World Series.
- Warren Spahn, was thirty-seven years, five months, and twelve days old, when he beat the Yankees for the second time in the 1958 Series.

DECEMBER 22, 1996

The New York Jets completed a 1-15 season. Numerous Yankee haters considered writing Steinbrenner, suggesting he hire Jets' coach Rich Kotite as a motivational speaker.

Born December 22, 1948
Steve Garvey

Garvey hit .333 in three World Series against the Yankees. His .417 average helped the Dodgers win the 1981 Series. So did having Tom Lasorda outmanage his Yankee counterparts, Bob Lemon and his ventriloquist, Steinbrenner.

Towards the end of each season, the NFL explains playoff possibilities. These are usually complicated. A hypothetical example would be, "Pittsburgh qualifies with a win, and a San Diego loss or tie, and a Cincinnati loss or tie. Pittsburgh also qualifies with a loss, provided Cincinnati loses, and New England wins by less than twenty-six points."

Lasorda would have been able to follow this. Steinbrenner would have consulted with his "football people." He then would have told Lemon what to think it meant. As a result, the Yankees would have had trouble with the part after "Pittsburgh qualifies with a win."

Some information on the Cy Young Award:

- Roger Clemens has won five Cy Young Awards. All Yankee pitchers combined have four. Steve Carlton (born on this date in 1944) and Greg Maddux have each won that many.
- Four teams, the Dodgers, Braves, Phillies, and Orioles, have had more winners than the Yankees have had.
- This is despite the pro-New York bias of the voters. Consider Sparky Lyle, the 1977 winner. Lyle was a relief pitcher who had five fewer saves than Boston's Bill Campbell. Lyle received the fewest votes of any winner of the past twenty-eight years. Jim Palmer (who had twenty wins, twenty-two complete games, and a 2.91 ERA) would have been a better choice.

DECEMBER 23, 1983

Steinbrenner was fined $250,000 for his comments about certain decisions on the Pine Tar Game. (See July 24, August 18.)

His comment on American League president Lee MacPhail was particularly odious. Perhaps hoping for a role in the next *Godfather* movie, Steinbrenner said of MacPhail, "He's anti-Yankee. If the Yankees lose the American League pennant (*sic,* division title) by one game, I wouldn't want to be Lee MacPhail living in New York."

Born December 23, 1889
Fritz Maisel

Among American League players with at least four hundred at bats in 1917, Yankee second baseman Maisel ranked last in batting average and in home runs. He was second-last in RBI. With one less RBI, Maisel would have won the "negative triple crown."

Some close postseason calls that went against the Yankees:

- Umpire Art Passerella (born on this date in 1909) called an obviously safe Yankee runner out at first base in the 1952 World Series. His call came in the tenth inning. Brooklyn went on to win the game and take a 3-2 lead in the Series.
- Brooklyn's Jackie Robinson stole home in the 1955 World Series. You cannot tell from photographs if Robinson really was safe.
- Lou Pinella was called out, even though he beat the throw to the plate in the 1978 American League Championship Series. According to the umpire, the Yankee outfielder's foot slid a couple of inches over the plate.
- Cleveland's Travis Fryman was safe on a controversial play in the 1998 American League Championship Series. Following his sacrifice bunt, Fryman ran, illegally, in fair territory all the way to first base. He appeared to have touched the base when the Yankee fielder's throw hit him. A former major-league umpire told the television audience that Fryman had interfered with the play and should have been called out.

DECEMBER 24, 1986

After five years with the California Angels, Reggie Jackson signed a one-year "farewell tour" contract with Oakland. New York made no serious effort to sign their former star, missing out on a profitable promotional opportunity.

Instead of Jackson, Dan Pasqua was the Yankees' left-handed designated hitter in 1987. His batting statistics were virtually identical to Jackson's with Oakland. With the exception of ill-advised people who had selected him in various baseball pools, nobody ever went to Yankee Stadium to see Dan Pasqua.

Died December 24, 1978
George McQuinn

McQuinn tied Babe Ruth's team record by striking out eight times in the 1947 World Series. These strikeouts were part of the forgettable .130 that McQuinn hit in this Series.

McQuinn had done better in the 1944 Series, when he hit .438 for the St. Louis Browns. His team was in that Series because of McQuinn's late-season heroics. He hit a two-run home run to clinch a 4-1 St. Louis win. This hit kept the Browns in the pennant race and eliminated the Yankees from contention.

Yankees who subsequently tied, then broke, the Ruth-McQuinn club record for strikeouts in a World Series:

- Like McQuinn, Snuffy Stirnweiss struck out eight times in the 1947 World Series.
- Joe Collins and Mickey Mantle fanned eight times, in 1953.
- Elston Howard equaled the team record in 1956.
- Mantle struck out nine times in the 1960 Series.

DECEMBER 25, 1960

Merry Christmas to Yankee fans who follow New York's NBA team. Their Knicks lost to Syracuse by sixty-two points, their worst losing margin ever.

Born December 25, 1899
Humphrey Bogart

Bogart played a gambler, Gloves Donovan, in *All Through the Night*. In this 1941 movie, Donovan had to leave Yankee Stadium with the bases loaded and two outs. Although the movie provides neither the inning, nor the score, it does tell us that Donovan had bet five thousand dollars on the Yankees. We, like Donovan, never learn the outcome of the game.

All Through the Night is primarily a warning against U.S. isolationism (Before Pearl Harbor, there was considerable American sentiment against becoming involved in World War II). On a smaller scale, it warns us that those who support the Yankees will not find satisfaction.

Two important Yankee losses in the movies:

- In *Major League*, the Yankees and the Cleveland Indians meet in a one-game playoff for the division title. In the bottom of the ninth, the Indians have the winning run on base. Cleveland's Jake Taylor (Tom Berenger) points to the upper deck, mimicking the Babe Ruth gesture of legend. He bunts, driving in the wonderfully named Willie Mays Hayes (Wesley Snipes).
- In *Damn Yankees* (January 24), the American League pennant race has come down to the last game of the season. Washington is playing the Yankees. With the Senators leading, Joe Hardy, the fictional hero, chases a fly ball. Washington's winning or losing depends on this play. Despite being transformed back into a middle-aged Senators fan as he chases the ball, he manages to catch it.

DECEMBER 26, various years

Bob Hope, an owner of the Cleveland Indians, was overseas entertaining the military. Dan Topping, an owner of the Yankees, was at a party, entertaining himself.

Born December 26, 1947
Carlton Fisk

Fisk was an intense rival of Yankee catcher Thurman Munson. During his major-league-record 2,226 games as a catcher for the Red Sox and White Sox, Fisk had numerous memorable plays. One came when he tagged two Yankee runners, who were running closely together, out at home.

Fisk broke the American League record for home runs by a catcher. Yogi Berra, a Yankee, had held this record.

Some scenes from the Fisk-Munson rivalry:

- They were involved in a 1973 fight at Yankee Stadium.
- One year Fisk received almost half a million more votes than Munson did for starting catcher in the All-Star game. Munson complained. Fisk replied, "He is jealous of me....He must think he's another Yogi Berra, which he isn't."

DECEMBER 27, 1984

Ed Whitson left the Padres to sign as a free agent with the Yankees. He became the first pitcher to parlay a 40.50 World Series ERA into a long-term contract. His career with the Yankees lasted forty-four games.

Low moments of Whitson's career with the Yankees:

- He scored a technical knockout over Yankee manager Billy Martin in a 1985 fight.
- Whitson became the target of so much abuse by the fans that the Yankees were unable to use him in games at Yankee Stadium.
- He was traded for Tim Stoddard, who had played for North Carolina State's 1974 NCAA championship team. This might have been a good trade if the Yankees had wanted to start a basketball team.

Born December 27, 1912
Jim Tobin

Pitching for Detroit in a 1945 game, Tobin beat the Yankees by hitting a three-run home run in the bottom of the eleventh inning.

DECEMBER 28, 1993

Yankee prospect Brien Taylor underwent reconstructive surgery on his left shoulder. He had injured this shoulder in a fight. Taylor, the first pick in the 1991 amateur draft, had received a record-setting bonus.

Taylor had two hopes: that this surgery could help him become a major-leaguer, or that he could learn to throw right-handed. So far, neither has occurred.

Born December 28, 1946
Bill Lee

Lee had a 12-5 career record against the Yankees. He played an important part in one of the Red Sox more memorable days of the 1970's. Lee and Roger Moret each beat the Yankees with complete game shutouts in a late-July 1975 doubleheader. These losses effectively eliminated the Yankees from that season's pennant race.

Some Bill Lee quotes about the Yankees:

- "I'm sure (Billy Martin) thinks Mussolini was just a nice guy whom Hitler led astray."
- "You take a team with twenty-five a____ and I'll show you a pennant. I'll show you the New York Yankees."
- "(The Yankees fight like) a bunch of hookers swinging their purses."
- "I had a vision of the ghost of Christmas past coming into my hotel room. It had the face of George Steinbrenner with Billy Martin's body."

DECEMBER 29, 1985

Newspapers featured summaries of the top sports events of 1985. One such event was the Toronto Blue Jays' winning the American League East Division championship. People got to read again about how Doyle Alexander, whom Steinbrenner had ridiculed, beat the Yankees 5-1, on the second-last day of the season. This loss eliminated New York from contention. Ernie Whitt, Lloyd Moseby, and Willie Upshaw supported Alexander with home runs.

Born December 29, 1975
Jaret Wright

Wright beat the Yankees in the second and fifth games of the five-game 1997 Division Series.

Youngest pitchers to beat the Yankees in the postseason:

- Fernando Valenzuela was twenty years, eleven months, and twenty-two days old when he beat the Yankees in the 1981 World Series.
- Ralph Branca beat New York in the 1947 World Series. He was twenty-one years, eight months, and twenty-nine days old.
- Wright won his first of two games in 1997 at the age of twenty-one years, nine months, and three days.
- Johnny Podres was exactly twenty-three years old when he won his first of two in the 1955 World Series.

DECEMBER 30, 1962

Green Bay beat the New York Giants in the National Football League's championship game. It is always a pleasure to see the home team lose a big game at Yankee Stadium.

Some other notable Giants' losses at Yankee Stadium:

- 52-20 to Cleveland, in 1964. This completed a 2-10-2 season.
- 23-17 to the Colts, in overtime, in the 1958 championship game,
- 48-21 to the Packers in 1967,
- 44-17 to the Steelers, in 1964, and
- 27-16 to the first-year Atlanta Falcons, in 1966.

(The Giants played at Yankee Stadium from 1956 to 1972.)

Born December 30, 1935
Sandy Koufax

Koufax set a record by striking out fifteen Yankees in the first game of the 1963 World Series. He also won the fourth game, as the Dodgers swept the Series.

Koufax never trailed in his two complete game outings. His ERA for the Series was 1.50. This was the worst ERA by a Dodger pitcher in the 1963 Series.

DECEMBER 31, 1999

Parties will mark the end of second millennium. (Some will point out the millennium actually will end a year later. They will be correct and lonely.) There will be listings of the most important achievements and of the most important people of the previous one thousand years. You will not find the Yankees or Steinbrenner on either list.

Born December 31, 1919
Tommy Byrne

In 1949, Byrne set a record for the most walks, 179, by a left-handed pitcher. He averaged nearly one walk per inning pitched.

Some other Tommy Byrne achievements with the Yankees:

- Byrne was the losing pitcher, as the Red Sox won the penultimate game of the 1948 season. This loss eliminated the Yankees from contention.
- In the fourth game of the 1957 World Series, Byrne hit Nippy Jones to start the Braves' winning rally.
- He lost the second game of a showdown doubleheader with Cleveland, late in the 1954 season.
- Byrne hit four batters in a game. In another game, he walked thirteen batters.

*** *** ***

With this note on Tommy Byrne, we end our review of 366 dismal days in Yankee history. I hope you found the preceding 1,098 items enjoyable. I also hope that inept play by the Yankees in the next couple of seasons makes a major rewriting of this book necessary.

Bibliography

Alexander, Charles. *Rogers Hornsby*. New York: Henry Holt and Company, 1995.

Allen, Maury. *Where Have You Gone Joe DiMaggio?*. New York: E.P. Dutton & Co., Inc., 1975.

Allen, Maury. *You Could Look It Up*. New York: Time Books, 1979.

Anderson, Dave. *Pennant Races: Baseball at its Best*. New York: Doubleday, 1994.

Anderson, Dave; Chass, Murray; Creamer, Robert; and Rosenthal, Harold. *The Yankees*. New York: Random House, 1981.

Angell, Roger. *The Summer Game*. New York: Ballantine Books, 1984.

Asinof, Eliot. *Eight Men Out*. New York: Holt Rinehart and Winston, 1963.

Barber, Red. *1947-When All Hell Broke Loose in Baseball*. Garden City: Doubleday and Company, 1982.

Berra, Yogi. *The Yogi Book*. New York: Workman Publishing, 1998.

Boswell, Thomas. *How Life Imitates the World Series*. Garden City: Doubleday and Company, Inc., 1982.

Bouton, Jim with Shecter, Leonard. *Ball Four*. New York: Macmillan, 1970.

Boyd, Brendan C. and Harris, Fred C. *The Great American Baseball Card Flipping, Trading and Bubble Gum Book*. New York: Warner Paperback Library, 1975.

Caray, Harry with Verdi, Bob. *Holy Cow*. New York: Berkley Books, 1990.

Carmichael, John, editor. *My Greatest Day in Baseball*. New York: A.S. Barnes and Company, 1945.

Carter, Craig, editor. *The Complete Baseball Record Book*. St. Louis: The Sporting News Publishing Company, 1992.

Charlton, James, editor. *The Baseball Anthology*. New York: Macmillan Publishing Co., 1991.

Cobb, Ty with Stump, Al. *My Life in Baseball, The True Record*. Garden City: Doubleday and Company, Inc, 1961.

Creamer, Robert. *Babe: The Legend Comes to Life*. New York: Simon & Schuster, Inc., 1974.

Devaney, John and Goldblatt, Burt. *The World Series, a Complete Pictorial History*. Chicago: Rand McNally and Company, 1981.

Dickson, Paul. *Baseball's Greatest Quotations*. New York: Edward Burhingame Books, 1991.

Durocher, Leo and Linn, Ed. *Nice Guys Finish Last*. New York: Simon & Schuster, 1975.

Einstein, Charles, editor. *The Fireside Book of Baseball*. New York: Simon and Schuster, 1956.

Einstein, Charles, editor. *The Second Fireside Book of Baseball*. New York: Simon and Schuster, 1958.

Eskenazi, Gerald. *The Lip*. New York: William Morrow and Company, 1993.

Gammons, Peter. *Beyond the Sixth Game*. Boston: Houghton Mifflin, 1985.

Goldstein, Richard. *Spartan Seasons*. New York: Macmillan Publishing Co., Inc, 1980.

Golenback, Peter. *High, Wide and Tight: The Life and Death of Billy Martin*. New York: St. Martin's Press, 1994.

Greenspan, Bud. *Play It Again, Bud*. New York: Peter H. Wyden, Inc., 1973.

Gutman, Dan. *Baseball Babylon*. New York: Penguin Books, 1992.

Halberstam, David. *October, 1964*. New York: Villard Books, 1994.

Halberstam, David. *Summer of '49*. New York: Avon Books, 1989.

Hemingway, Ernest. *The Old Man and the Sea*. New York: Simon and Schuster, 1995.

Lee, Bill and Lally, Dick. *The Wrong Stuff*. New York: Penguin Books, 1984.

Levine, Peter, editor. *Baseball History*. New York: Stadium Books, 1990.

Libby, Bill. *Thurman Munson, Pressure Player*. New York: G.P. Putnam's Sons, 1978.

Lieb, Fred. *Baseball as I Have Known It*. New York: Grosset and Dunlap, 1977.

Light, Jonathan Fraser. *The Cultural Encyclopedia of Baseball*. Jefferson, N.C.: McFarland & Company Inc., 1997.

Linn, Ed. *The Great Rivalry. The Yankees and the Red Sox 1901-1990*. New York: Ticknor and Fields, 1991.

Lowry, Philip. *Green Cathedrals*. Reading, Mass.: Addison-Wesley Publishing Company, 1992.

Luciano, Ron and Fisher, David. *Strike Two*. New York: Bantam Books, 1984.

Luciano, Ron and Fisher, David. *The Umpire Strikes Back*. New York: Bantam Books, Inc., 1982.

Lyle, Sparky and Golenback, Peter. *The Bronx Zoo*. New York: Dell Publishing Co. Inc., 1979.

Macmillan. *The Baseball Encyclopedia*. New York: Macmillan, 1996.

Mann, Jack. *The Decline and Fall of the New York Yankees*. New York: Simon and Schuster, 1967.

Mantle, Mickey and Herskowitz, Mickey. *All My Octobers*. New York: Harper Collins, 1994.

Mantle, Mickey and Pepe, Phil. *My Favorite Summer: 1956*. New York: Dell Publishing, 1991.

Maris, Roger and Ogle, Jim. *Roger Maris at Bat*. New York: Duell, Sloan & Pearce, 1962.

Mazer, Bill with Fischler, Shirley and Fischler, Stan. *Bill Mazer's Amazin' Baseball Book*. New York: Kensington Publishing Corp., 1990.

Meany, Tom. *Baseball's Greatest Players*. New York: Grosset and Dunlap, 1953.

Mitchell, Jerry. *The Amazing Mets*. New York: Grosset and Dunlap, Inc., 1964.

Mitchell, Jerry. *Sandy Koufax*. New York: Grosset and Dunlap, Inc., 1964.

National Football League. *The Official National Football League 1994 Record & Fact Book*. New York: Workman Publishing Co., 1994.

Neft, David; Cohen, Richard and Neft, Michael. *The Sports Encyclopedia: Baseball.* 1998 edition. New York: St. Martin's Griffin, 1998.

Nelson, Kevin. *Baseball's Even Greater Insults.* New York: Simon & Schuster, 1993.

Nemec, David. *Great Baseball Feats, Facts & Firsts.* New York: Penguin Books U.S.A. Inc., 1989.

Nemec, David. *The Absolutely Most Challenging Baseball Quiz Book Ever.* New York: Macmillan Publishing Co., Inc., 1977.

Nemec, David. *The Even More Challenging Baseball Quiz Book.* New York: Macmillan Publishing Co., Inc., 1978.

The New York Times Book of Baseball History. New York: Arno Press, 1975.

Okrent, Daniel and Wulf, Steve. *Baseball Anecdotes.* New York: Harper Perennial, 1989.

Peary, Danny, editor. *We Played the Game.* New York: Hyperion Press, 1994.

Pepitone, Joe with Stainback, Barry. *Joe, You Coulda Made Us Proud.* Chicago: Playboy Press, 1975.

Porter, David. *Biographical Dictionary of American Sports: Baseball.* New York: Greenwood Press, 1987.

Ritter, Lawrence. *The Glory of Their Times (New edition).* New York: William Morrow, 1966, 1984.

Robinson, George and Salzberg, Charles. *On a Clear Day They Could See Seventh Place- Baseball's Worst Teams.* New York: Dell Publishing, 1991.

Robinson, Ray, editor. *Baseball Stars of 1965.* New York: Pyramid Publications, Inc., 1965.

Robinson, Ray, editor. *Baseball Stars of 1966.* New York: Pyramid Publications, Inc., 1966.

Ruth, Babe and Consodine, Bob. *The Babe Ruth Story.* Scholastic Book Services, by arrangement with E.P. Dutton & Co. Inc., 1967.

Scheinen, Richard. *Field of Screams.* New York: W.W. Norton and Company, Inc., 1994.

Shaughnessy, Dan. *The Curse of the Bambino.* New York: Penguin Books, 1990.

Smith, Red. *The Red Smith Reader.* New York: Vintage Books, 1983.

Smith, Red. *To Absent Friends.* New York: Athenium Publishers, 1982.

Smith, Ron, editor. *The Official Major League Fact Book.* 1998 edition. St. Louis: The Sporting News, 1998.

The Sporting News. *Official N.B.A. Guide, 1997-98 edition.* St. Louis: The Sporting News Publishing Co., 1997.

The Sporting News. *Baseball Trivia Book.* St. Louis: The Sporting News Publishing Co., 1983.

The Sporting News. *Baseball Trivia 2.* St. Louis: The Sporting News Publishing Co., 1987.

The Sporting News. *Baseball's 25 Greatest Pennant Races.* St. Louis: The Sporting News, 1987.

Stark, Benton. *The Year They Called Off the World Series*. Garden City Park: Avery Publishing Group Inc., 1991.

Steinberg, Cobbett S. *TV Facts*. New York: Facts on File Inc., 1980.

Sugar, Bert Randolph. *Who Was Harry Steinfeldt*? Chicago: Playboy Press, 1991.

Sullivan, George and Powers, John. *Yankees: An Illustrated History*. Englewood Cliffs: Prentice-Hall, Inc., 1982.

Terrace, Vincent. *The Complete Encyclopedia of Television Programs, 1947-1976*. Cranbury, N.J.: A.S. Barnes and Co., Inc., 1976.

Thorn, John and Palmer, Pete with Reuther, David. *Total Baseball (Second edition)*. New York: Warner Brothers, 1989.

Turkin, Hy and Thompson, S.C. *The Official Encyclopedia of Baseball*. New York: A.S. Barnes and Company, Inc., 1963.

Uecker, Bob and Herskowitz, Mickey. *Catcher in the Wry*. New York: G.P. Putnam & Sons, 1982.

Veeck, Bill and Linn, Ed. *Veeck- As in Wreck*. New York: Ballantine Books, 1976.

Whitson, Joel. *Billboard Book of Top 40 Hits*. New York: Billboard, 1996.

Wiley, Mason and Bona, Damien. *Inside Oscar*. New York: Ballantine Books, 1986.

The author used, as additional reference sources, *Sports Illustrated* (1966 to date) and the *New York Times* (microfiche editions, 1900 to date) as well as numerous programs, yearbooks, and magazines in his personal collection.

Additional copies of *This Date in New York Yankee Hating* are available through:

William D. Maharg Publishing
P. O. Box 25908
Greenville, S.C., 29616

Please contact us at this address or visit our Web site at:
http://www.yankeehater.com